WHEATON PUBLIC LIBRARY
574.52643 MAD
Madson, John.
Where the sky began :land

S0-AZP-912

3 5143 00100624 8

WHERE THE
SKY BEGAN

WHERE THE SKY BEGAN

LAND OF THE TALLGRASS PRAIRIE

JOHN MADSON

Illustrations by Dycie Madson

HOUGHTON MIFFLIN COMPANY BOSTON

1982

Copyright © 1982 by John Madson
Illustration copyright © 1982 by Dycie Madson

All rights reserved. No part of this work may be reproduced
or transmitted in any form or by any means, electronic or
mechanical, including photocopying and recording, or by
any information storage or retrieval system, except as may
be expressly permitted by the 1976 Copyright Act or in
writing from the publisher. Requests for permission should
be addressed in writing to Houghton Mifflin Company,
2 Park Street, Boston, Massachusetts 02108.

Library of Congress Cataloging in Publication Data

Madson, John
Where the sky began.

Bibliography: p.
Includes index.
1. Prairie ecology—United States.   2. Prairies—
United States.   3. Prairies—United States—History.
I. Title.   II. Title: Tallgrass prairie.
QH104.M3   574.5′2643′0973   81-6937
ISBN 0-395-25718-2   AACR2

Printed in the United States of America

V 10 9 8 7 6 5 4 3 2 1

Early versions of some of this material appeared in
"The Running Country" published in *Audubon* in July 1972
and "Grandfather Country," *Audubon*, May 1982.

TO LAWRENCE R. WAGNER

10/6/8

13.95

Bx T

To make a prairie it takes a clover
and one bee, —
One clover, and a bee,
And revery.
The revery alone will do
If bees are few.

— EMILY DICKINSON

Contents

PROLOGUE   xi

PART I. THE PLACE

1. Beyond the Wooden Country   3
2. Fire, Ice, and Mountain   29
3. The Lawns of God   51
4. The Far Gardens   81
5. Prairyerths   107
6. A Prairie Bestiary   125
7. The Great Weathers   166

PART II. THE PEOPLE

8. Grandfather Country   197
9. After the Plow   236
10. People Pastures   257

APPENDIX   287
SELECTED REFERENCES   303
INDEX   311

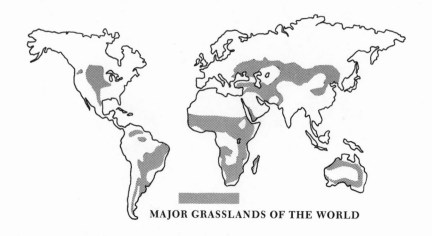

MAJOR GRASSLANDS OF THE WORLD

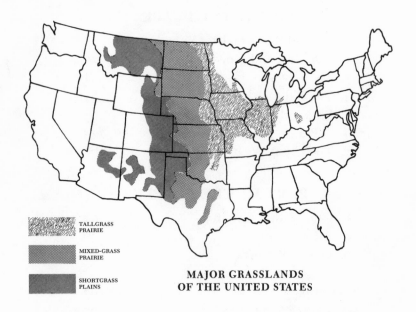

TALLGRASS
PRAIRIE

MIXED-GRASS
PRAIRIE

SHORTGRASS
PLAINS

**MAJOR GRASSLANDS
OF THE UNITED STATES**

Prologue

THEY WERE BLIND MEN describing an elephant, those first Europeans, sending back word of the New World in terms of the forests or swamps that lay a few leagues beyond the tidelines.

They had no clues to the heartland itself. There was no hint of the freshwater seas that lay farther west, of mighty rivers draining watersheds the size of central Europe, of mountain ranges that ran from subarctic to subtropics. Least of all was any consciousness of the great interior grasslands that lay far from any ocean. They knew nothing of that country and could not have understood it had they known it was there — for grassland of such magnitude was wholly alien to the western European mind.

The newcomers brought no real knowledge of grasslands; it is doubtful that any had seen the open steppes of Eurasia, and few had even heard of that region. They surely knew nothing of African veldt, South American pampas, or Australian lowlands. To those first European explorers and colonists, grassland probably meant snug meadows, deer parks, and pastures safe behind fence and wall. They had no basis for even imagining wild fields through which a horseman might ride westward for a month or more, sometimes traveling for days without sight of trees.

And even when the grasslands were finally met and shakily framed in some sort of geographical context, they were not really comprehended. Most arrivals ventured timidly into the edges of the grass and clung to the outriders of forest like mice hugging a wall. For this was alien land, not only in physical appearance but in its harsh rejection of familiar custom; it diminished men's works and revealed them to a vast and critical sky, and forced people into new ways of looking at the land and themselves, and changed them forever. The world had opened into a light-filled wilderness of sky and grass that would open its people as well, freeing them of certain dogma, breaking old institutions, and shaping new ones to fit the land. Each wave of American settlement from east to west had progressively deepened New World naturalization, and no settlers were altered more deeply than those who drew away from the treelands and became true grasslanders at last.

Most easterly of the interior grasslands, and first to be entered by settlers, was the vast domain of tallgrasses that lay against the wall of deciduous eastern forest. It was a belt of grassland that hooked down out of southern Canada, broadened to six hundred miles through the Midwest, and ran for more than a thousand miles toward the Gulf of Mexico. It was a temperate savannah of unbelievable fertility, as those who put roots into the deep black soils would learn. It was flowing emerald in spring and summer when the boundless winds ran across it, a tawny ocean under the winds of autumn, and a stark and painful emptiness in winter when the great long winds drove in from the northwest. It was Beulahland for many; Gehenna for some.

It was the tall prairie.

THE TALLGRASS PRAIRIE
OF THE CENTRAL UNITED STATES

PART I
THE PLACE

1

Beyond the Wooden Country

ONE OF THE FIRST THINGS that the new colonists must have known, as anchor chains rumbled down through hawseholes, was that they had never really seen trees before. Wherever they had begun — in the snug shires of England, the meadows of Brittany, or the diked fields of Holland — they had seen nothing to compare with this wall of forest that rose behind the coast of America.

It loomed abruptly from rocky shores, or stood farther off beyond the salt marshes and open savannahs of pine, or behind coastal grasslands. But it was always there, a limitless wilderness of trees, the infinite and forbidding sweep of forest that extended from the portals of the New World as far west as any man knew, and beyond, the greatest forest that western man had seen during the Christian era.

It was a vast crazy quilt of trees in which forests of broadleaved hardwoods alternated with pure stands of white pine growing from old burns and storm-torn parts of the deciduous forests; there were communities of oaks and maples, and other communities of hemlock, beech, and basswood that drove deep into the unknown heart of the continent for a thousand miles, bordered on the north by the spruce-fir wilderness of Canada and on the south by southern hardwoods that opened into the savannahs of the Gulf Coast.

This infinity of trees reached from the Spanish Sea to the

barrens of Hudson Bay, and westward into lands scarcely imagined, with some trees towering nearly two hundred feet above open forest floors that were too shaded for under-growth. Many years later, Francis Parkman would call it "vast, continuous, dim, and silent as a cavern." It was said that a gray squirrel could travel inland from the Atlantic coast for nearly a thousand miles and never touch the ground. Old novels tell of the "pale woodsmen" of the eastern for-ests — not a reflection of race, but of lives spent under trees. An old Wyeth illustration for *Last of the Mohicans* has Leather-Stocking coming into a small glade in such forest and looking up at the sky, cap in hand, his face lit with sun and wonder.

But about six hundred miles inland, something began hap-pening to the thick fabric of deciduous forest. It began to show rents and gaps, with occasional openings. There were fewer tulip-trees, chestnuts, magnolias, and evergreen hem-locks. More and more, the forest consisted of oaks and hick-ories on the uplands, and maple and basswood on lower ground. There were places where the trees thinned and were undergrown with coarse grasses and strange shrubs. And here and there the trees ceased entirely, and the land opened up into meadows of tall grasses.

The earliest land-lookers moving west from New England pushed through great forests of oak, chestnut, and white pine. South of Lake Erie they began entering forests of hard maples and beeches. In what is now Ohio, they skirted great swamps and found small grassy openings in the forests be-yond. Something was happening — no one was sure what. But out there back of beyond, far past the coastal ranges and the leagues of forest, the land changed and began opening to the sky. The Dutch and English colonists did not know just where this happened, or what it looked like, and they made little effort to learn more. It was a confused rumor, a vague impression of new lands lying out there beyond the familiar, of strange deserts and mountains in the Spanish country.

And north of the English settlements, certain churchmen and soldiers were growing restless in Montreal, looking westward and wondering about a water passage to the Pacific.

❧

The French were first to break free from the eastern settlements, voyaging west and southwest of Montreal and Quebec in a quest for new lands, new routes, and heathen souls.

Late in the seventeenth century they plunged into the wilderness up the St. Lawrence and Ottawa, and west across the chain of Great Lakes. Past walls of fir, spruce, and pine they drove their canoes up dark rivers, across vast new lakes, through Lake Huron, and across Lake Michigan to Green Bay and the mouth of the Fox River, or down to the headwaters of the Illinois and south into the Mississippi. Staying with the water routes, traveling steadily on lake and river, they left the brooding conifer forests of the north and began to break out into a strange new world of sun and endless meadow.

From the first, the French reports effused over the fertility and beauty of the opening landscape.

Roughly written by the light of smudge fires, or scrawled in secret because writing might be regarded as sorcery, these journals were kept by leaders with no time to waste — men constantly concerned with supplies, illness, repair of canoes, discipline, the uncertainty of their goals, and with Indians who had never seen a white face. Yet, in spite of all that, many of the early reports are almost boyish in their wonder and delight with the new country.

Louis Joliet, after his epic 1673 exploration down the Illinois and Mississippi, reported to his superiors:

At first, when we were told of these treeless lands, I imagined that it was a country ravaged by fire, where the soil was so poor that it could produce nothing. But we have certainly observed the contrary; and no better soil can be found, either for corn, or for vines, or for any other fruit whatever . . . There are prairies

three, six, ten, and twenty leagues in length and three in width,
surrounded by forests of the same extent; beyond these, the prairies begin again, so that there is as much of one sort of land as of
the other. Sometimes we saw grass very short, and, at other
times, five or six feet high; hemp, which grows naturally here,
reaches a height of eight feet. A settler would not there spend
ten years in cutting down and burning the trees; on the very day
of his arrival, he could put his plough into the ground.

Père Louis Hennepin, in his 1683 *Description de la Louisiane,* gave a loving account of the new country. A boastful
man, he neglected self-praise for a time to praise the new
country:

> There are boundless prairies interspersed with forests of tall
> trees, where there are all sorts of building timber, and among the
> rest excellent oak like that in France and very different from that
> in Canada. The trees are of prodigious girth and height, and you
> could find the finest pieces in the world for shipbuilding . . . the
> fertility of the soil is extraordinary.

When Allouez set off down the Illinois River to continue
the work of Père Marquette, he wrote:

> We proceeded, always continuing to coast along the great prai-
> ries, which extend farther than the eye can reach. Trees are met
> with from time to time, but they are so placed that they seem to
> have been planted with design, in order to make the avenues
> more pleasing to the eye than those of orchards. The bases of
> these trees are often watered by little streamlets, at which are
> seen large herds of stags and hinds refreshing themselves, and
> peacefully feeding on the short grass.

Similar praise was lavished by many French explorers:
Marquette, Membré, Hennepin, Joutel, Lahontan. And in
spite of his incredible hardships in the Mississippi Valley, the
great La Salle never wavered in his admiration of the smiling

meadows that he and his countrymen called "prairies" from the first.

The word is in common use in France and Quebec in reference to grassland; in Belgium and parts of France, "prairie" may generally mean a grassy orchard or park with scattered trees. In one of the earliest French church reports, Père Hennepin referred to the *"belles préries"* of the Illinois River valley. The word has lasted, not just as a label for a particular kind of landscape, but as a prefix for place names. The rivers of La Salle and Joliet are still dotted with such towns as Prairie du Chien, Prairie du Rocher, Prairie du Sac, and Prairie du Pont. There's only one departure from this: in Algonquian the word for prairie was *"mouscatine,"* and that name was chosen for a city on the Iowa bank of the Mississippi.

Today, reading through the early French journals and reports, it can be seen that "prairie" meant far more than mere parkland to the adventurers of New France. The *coureurs de bois,* suddenly become *coureurs des préries,* showed the joy of men emerging from darkness into light. Behind them were the ambush-threatened portages of the north, and the foaming rivers where hard-traveling men might lose supplies and be forced to live on stews of rock tripe and tree bark. Now they were on broad placid rivers, provided by *le bon Dieu* for a swift and direct passage. Though still beset by sickness, clouds of biting flies, and the danger of unknown savages, they were in the sun again, with larks above and flowers at their feet, as proper Frenchmen should be. Nameless danger in the dim alder hells of a long portage is one thing; facing it in full sunlight, under open sky and birdsong, is another. No wonder they wrote of "this fruitful champayne countrie" and spoke adoringly of the sunny fields south of Lake Michigan.

Assuredly, there was a vein of French ebullience in all this. But it must be considered that those early reports were not meant as literary offerings to the public; they were official documents intended for tough, no-nonsense bishops, gover-

nors, and military commanders. Such men would not take
kindly to fabrication and reckless adornment. They required
facts, and if the lily of New France wanted any gilding, they
would gild it themselves. It follows, then, that the field journals from *Louisiane* were eminently sincere and responsible.
And if certain explorers, such as young Père Marquette,
showed the excitement of schoolboys on holiday, it was surely
because they had really found something to be excited about.

The early French reports and their glowing descriptions of
the new country were apparently not circulated widely at
the time nor for many years after. An Englishman named
Croghan, in 1765, wrote of his journey through western Indiana: "It is surprising what false information we had respect-
ing this country; some mention these spacious and beautiful
meadows as large and barren savannahs. I apprehend it has
been the artifice of the French to keep us ignorant of the
country."

But if Croghan was "ignorant of the country," it is doubtful that he had been misled by the French. The French
chronicles rarely, if ever, dismissed the prairies as "barren savannahs." If the English knew so little of the new country,
they really had no one to blame but themselves.

❦

Long before La Salle's canoes ever floated on the Mississippi,
and for nearly a century thereafter, the English were absorbed in their affairs along the eastern seaboard, chopping
trees and hanging a few witches and leaving the vast interior
lands to the Spanish and French. They established their ports
and snug colonies, and began to pour naval stores, tobacco,
and furs across the Atlantic, making little real effort to penetrate much farther inland. At the time, they had little reason
to do otherwise; the task of colonial development was a demanding one, and there was no lack of good land where they
were.

But the colonies were filling. Between 1700 and 1776 the British colonists swelled from 350,000 to 3,000,000, and the pangs of land-hunger began to sharpen. So did frontier resentment against the Crown's reluctance to permit westward expansion, and there was a new stir among Anglo-Americans east of the Appalachians when a surveyor named Thomas Walker found the Cumberland Gap in 1750. The barrier ranges had been breached just at a time when the colonials were beginning to chafe at any barriers to western settlement, physical or political.

In an attempt to keep the colonists at home and under the thumbs of royal governors and tax assessors, Parliament issued a stern proclamation in 1763 that officially set the crest of the Appalachians as the limit of western expansion. It was a waste of good English ink; the American colonists had caught the heady scent of new lands blowing through the Cumberland Gap. Through this new passage a Pennsylvanian named D. Boone blazed a Wilderness Trail over to the rich promise of Kentucky, and a whangleather breed of Americans began to diffuse westward over the mountains. The first pack train of Kentucky settlers arrived at the site of Boonesborough on April 20, 1775 — the day after a group of angry farmers had fired on British troops at Concord.

Six years of revolution and bloody border war expunged the royal edicts, created a vast new public domain, and threw open the back doors of the old colonies. Agents of the new republican government journeyed west to the Mississippi for an official look at the United States' back yard, and at the great river that marked our property line. In 1791 Captain Thomas Morris, an emissary to the Illinois country, reported:

> Soon after we came into extensive meadows; and I was assured that those meadows continue for a hundred and fifty miles, being in winter drowned lands and marshes. By the dryness of the season they were now beautiful pastures, and here presented itself one of the most delightful prospects I have ever beheld; all the

low grounds being meadow, and without wood, and all of the high grounds being covered with trees and appearing like islands; the whole scene seemed an elysium.

Settlers westering through Kentucky saw something similar when they came into an almost treeless, crescent-shaped meadow that opened nearly 6000 square miles in the heart of the virgin forest. Since it lacked trees and was therefore of questionable fertility, it was promptly dubbed "The Big Barrens." West of this strange grassland the forest closed in again — but it had given some early settlers a taste of things to come, a glimpse of lands ahead.

The heartland of the continent became American property in 1803 when political turmoil in France enabled Thomas Jefferson to buy "Louisiana" — an area as large as western Europe — for three cents an acre.

The President lost no time in dispatching Lewis and Clark to the far Northwest to find a suitable route to the Pacific and explore the immense new holdings of the United States. Other land-lookers were at work, as well, and some of their reports confirmed suspicions that the Louisiana Purchase was something less than a bargain. At about the time Lewis and Clark were returning down the Missouri, Zebulon Pike was ranging through the grasslands of what would be Nebraska and Kansas, which he later described as "a desert — a barrier — placed by Providence to keep the American people from a thin diffusion and ruin." The tone of that comment was echoed by Monroe's personal report to Jefferson that the lands south of Lake Michigan were a rather hopeless piece of property.

Such sour attitudes, however, were not shared by certain geologists, surveyors, and soldiers being sent into the new lands. The reports of *those* early travelers often shone with admiration for the new country and, like the earlier French journals, carried the ring of sincerity. Many were written by matter-of-fact men for official purposes — they were not literary flights calculated to impress eastern editors, but were objective statements by tough-minded surveyors and explorers. One of these reports, made by a geologist named Owen at about the time the trans-Mississippi prairies were opening to settlement, was apparently meant for a congressional committe. Owen was objective enough, but when he got around to describing the Upper Mississippi, he took wing:

> At the Mississippi, the prairie for the most part extends to the water's edge, and renders the scenery truly beautiful. Imagine a stream a mile in width, whose waters are as transparent as those of a mountain spring, flowing over beds of rock and gravel — fancy the prairie commencing at the water's edge, a natural meadow of deep green grass and beautiful flowers, rising with a gentle slope for miles so that, in the vast panorama, thousands of acres are exposed to the eye. Sometimes the woodland extends along this river for miles continuously, again, it stretches in a wide belt off into the country, marking the course of some tributary streams, and sometimes in vast groves of several miles in extent, standing alone, like islands in this wilderness of grass and flowers.

ꙮ

It was what the people were waiting to hear. An observer in New York State wrote:

> Nothing so strongly indicates the superiority of the western country as the vast emigration to it from the eastern and southern states . . . I was informed by an inhabitant of Cayuga in April, 1816, that more than 15,000 wagons had passed over the bridge at that place within the last eighteen months, containing emigrants to the western country.

There were eastern families that had been ruined by the War of 1812, newly arrived English farmers escaping the cruelly unjust Corn Laws of their homeland, settlers who had never really succeeded in the Old States, and restless adventurers with an itch for new country. There was a Manifest Destiny to pursue, and a welling tide of emigrants hungrily pursued it.

Pittsburgh and Wheeling were two great jumping-off places for this emigration. Many of the settlers headed down the Ohio to eventually stop in southern parts of Ohio, Indiana, Illinois, western Kentucky, or over in Missouri. But some bore straight west across the old trade routes and buffalo roads, pressing overland across northern Ohio and Indiana into what would be Illinois — and it was there that they met tall prairie.

Overwhelming as it must have been to the French *voyageurs*, it may have been doubly impressive to the land-hunters of the East. They had been born in forest, with the forest frontier never far beyond. They had left there and traveled slowly through hundreds of miles of the familiar tree-scape they had always known. And while they had a vague notion of larger grasslands somewhere to the west, nothing they had seen in the "barrens" of Ohio and eastern Indiana had prepared them for what they found beyond the Wabash. For they came to it abruptly, with little preparation, as if emerging from headland forest to find an unexpected ocean spread before them.

George Flower, in his *History of the English Settlement*, told of seeing eastern Illinois prairies in 1817:

> Bruised by the brushwood and exhausted by the extreme heat we almost despaired, when a small cabin and a low fence greeted our eyes. A few steps more, and a beautiful prairie suddenly opened to view.
>
> At first, we only received the impression of its general beauty. With longer gaze, all its distinctive features were revealed, lying in profound repose under the warm light of an afternoon's summer sun. Its indented and irregular outline of wood, its varied surface interspersed with clumps of oaks of centuries' growth,

its tall grass, with seed stalks from six to ten feet high, like tall and slender reeds waving in a gentle breeze, the whole presenting a magnificence of park scenery, complete from the hand of Nature, and unrivalled by the same sort of scenery by European art.

For once, the reality came up to the picture of imagination. Our station was in the wood, on rising ground; from it, a descent of about a hundred yards to the valley of the prairie, about a quarter of a mile wide, extending to the base of a majestic slope, rising upward for a full half-mile, crowned by groves of noble oaks. A little to the left the eye wandered up a long stretch of prairie for three miles, into which projected hills and slopes, covered with rich grass and half-grown trees, from four to eight in a clump.

After traveling from the Atlantic shore to the Wabash River, a thousand miles of gloomy forest, or running the length of the Ohio and Mississippi rivers, with a prospect ever bounded by impenetrable foliage, the entrance into one of these beautiful and light expanses of verdure is most enchanting, the beautifully indented outlines of woods and the undulating surface of the prairie affording innumerable sites for tasteful dwellings, the ornamental clumps of full-grown oaks scattered by the hand of nature so that they defy imitation by art, the bright verdure, rich herbage, affording food for innumerable flocks and herds, the beautiful flowers, the transparent atmosphere, the soft zephyrs wafted from the South in bland and rich volume, all combine to impress the enchanted beholder with pleasing feelings, even to delusion.

The prairie had brought George Flower into full bloom. And however purple that blooming may have been, the color has stayed fresh and still shows the relief and wonder that so many prairie-finders felt.

They marveled at the opening country with its strange broad meadows and lush grasses. Small never-to-be-forgotten incidents stuck in their minds, such as the three land-lookers from Ohio who had joined a band of Potawatomi in 1824 to

cross the prairies of northwestern Indiana. When one of the
men reined his horse off the trail a few steps into a patch of
big bluestem grass, the rest of the party passed him unseen.
People remembered such things, for they conveyed the character of the new land.

From 1815 on, a swelling stream of enthusiasm flowed
back to the East. There were two frequent analogies in these
prairie descriptions: one to the sea, the other to English
parks. Another Illinois traveler wrote: "We rode slowly over
Boltinghouse's Prairie and viewed several beautiful sites for
communities. Indeed, we all agreed that Duke Hamilton
Park was not at all degraded by being compared to it."

Judge James Hall, describing early Iowa in *Plumbe's
Sketches* in 1839, noted:

> These plains, although preserving a general level in respect to
> the whole country, are yet in themselves not flat, but exhibit a
> gracefully waving surface, swelling and sinking with an easy
> slope, and full, rounded outline, equally avoiding the unmeaning
> horizontal surface, and the interruptions of abrupt angular ele-
> vation. It is that surface, which, in the expressive language of the
> country, is called *rolling*, and which has been said to resemble
> the long, heavy swell of the ocean when its waves are subsiding
> to rest after the agitation of a storm.

A typical gazetteer of the period sang:

> The attraction of the prairie consists of its extent, its carpet of
> verdure and flowers, its undulating surface, its groves, and the
> fringe of timber by which it is surrounded. Of all these, the latter
> is the most expressive feature — it is that which gives character
> to the landscape, which imparts the shape, and marks the bound-
> ary of the plain. If the prairie be small, its greatest beauty con-
> sists in the vicinity of the surrounding margin of woodland,
> which resembles the shore of a lake indented with deep vistas,
> like bays and inlets, and throwing out long points, like capes and
> headlands.

Another cause for wonder was the brightness of the opening land, its qualities of light and space. Some of the early settlers were lyrical about this, as if they were really seeing the sun for the first time. And perhaps they were.

> The gaiety of the prairie, its embellishments and the absence of gloom and savage wildness of the forest, all contribute to dispel the feeling of loneliness which usually creeps over the mind of the solitary traveler in the wilderness. Though he may not see a house or a human being, and is conscious that he is far from the habitations of man, the traveler upon the prairie can scarcely divest himself of the idea that he is traveling through scenes embellished by the hand of art. The flowers, so fragile, so delicate, and so ornamented seem to have been tastefully disposed to adorn the scene.

Again, Judge Hall:

> The scenery of the prairie is striking and never fails to cause an exclamation of surprise. The extent of the prospect is exhilarating. The outline of the landscape is sloping and graceful. The verdure and the flowers are beautiful; the absence of shade, and consequent appearance of profusion of light, produce a gaiety which animates the beholder.

Taking literally, as they often were, such reports celebrated a rolling meadowland as tastefully designed as an English park, carpeted with blooms and judiciously landscaped with fine trees, all under a perpetual flood of soft sunlight that made the emigrant want to kick up the heels of his bullhide boots. There were places, during certain seasons, when prairies might have just that effect.

But there were other reports, of the times when any gaiety faded with the sun and was shut off by interminable weeks of winter overcast, when gloom settled down on the prairie in somber shades of monotony and dread. One early visitor wrote of the winter prairie: "A prospect more bleak and

lonely, when night is closing in, and you press toward some
distant grove whose treetops cannot yet be discovered above
the monotonous plains, is inconceivable."

And so monotony, gloom, and loneliness were added to the
prairie lexicon. In 1818, C. Atwater said of the western Ohio
prairies:

> To the traveller, who for several days traverses these prairies and
> barrens, their appearance is quite uninviting, and even disagree-
> able. He may travel from morning to night, and make good
> speed, but on looking around him, he fancies himself at the very
> spot whence he started. No pleasant variety of hill and dale, no
> rapidly running brook delights the eye, and no sound of wood-
> land music strikes the ear; but in their stead, a dull uniformity of
> prospect, spread out immense.

Years later, a naturalist named Allen would add:

> With all the beauty and novelty of the primal flora of the prai-
> ries, the traveller, after a few weeks of constant wandering amid
> their wilds, is apt soon to experience a monotony that becomes
> wearisome, the full degree of which he scarcely realizes till the
> soft green sward and varied vegetation of cultivated districts
> again meet the eye.

The response of an early traveler to the prairie country
must have varied broadly with his attitudes toward the forest
lands that he had left (for whatever reasons), his own imagination, how and where he first saw prairie, the season in
which he saw it, and whether or not he found what he was
looking for.

There were men who sent glowing reports back to "The
Wooden Country" to recruit more emigrants — with mo-
tives more economic than esthetic. Some of the sugary prose
came from practitioners of fine writing; the new country
gave them a chance to stretch their literary wings in the
manner of the day, heaping hyperbole upon hyperbole in

plain, step through a screen of sumac and wild plum, and stand blinking in a land that blazed with light and space. He was at the eastern edge of the Grand Prairie of Illinois; from there, north to Lake Michigan and west to the Mississippi, the prairies opened and broadened, sometimes spanning fifty miles without a tree to break the fabric of grassland.

This was the real beginning, from which the world opened into tallgrass prairie that covered northwestern Indiana, the northern two thirds of Illinois, almost all of Iowa, reaching up into southern and western Minnesota to the broad grasslands of Manitoba, and over into the eastern portions of the Dakotas and Nebraska, with a long tongue extending down through western Missouri, eastern Kansas, into eastern Oklahoma, and on into the Cross Timbers Country of Texas. An incredibly rich region of deep, fat soils, it had analogs in other parts of the world: the pampas of South America and some western parts of the Russian steppes. But these true prairies of North America stood apart from all other grasslands — unique in form and mood, and in their impact on a people.

❦

It was largely a world of grass and sun, but there were trees. The vast eastern forest did not surrender completely to the conditions that favored grass, but continued to struggle out into the tall prairie — often in a rich mosaic of trees and grass.

In what are now southern Michigan and Wisconsin, large areas of grassland wore scattered groves of bur oaks in buffer zones between the pure grasslands farther west and the unbroken forests to the east. Some of these "oak openings" covered a hundred square miles or more — sunny woodlands of striking beauty. The broad-canopied oaks were widely and evenly spaced so that their branches rarely interlocked. There was little or no underbrush on the grassy floors of these open woods, and one settler said that "a two-horse wagon could easily be driven among the trees." These natural parks lacked the intensity of the pure prairies and the somber depths of the eastern forests. A winter traveler in Calhoun County, Michigan, wrote in the mid-1800s:

> Lost as I was, I could not help pausing frequently when I struck the first bur-oak opening I had ever seen, to admire its novel beauty. It looked more like a pear orchard than anything else to which I assimilate it — the trees being somewhat of the shape and size of full-grown pear trees, and standing at regular intervals apart from each other on the firm, level soil . . . Here, too, I first saw deer in herds; and half-frozen and weary as I was, the sight of the spirited creatures, sweeping in troops through interminable groves, where any eye could follow them for miles over the smooth snowy plain, actually warmed and invigorated me, and I could hardly refrain from putting the rowls to my tired horse, and launching after the noble game.

Occupied wholly by neither trees nor grass, such transition zones extended up into Manitoba, where an aspen savannah up to 150 miles wide separated the great conifer forests from the western grasslands, which were dotted with aspen groves for miles. The western edge of the Big Woods in Minnesota was not sharply limited — the oaks and hickories there simply grew thinner and smaller and more restricted to stream valleys until the country finally became treeless grass. Farther southwest, in eastern Oklahoma and Texas, forest advanced into the tallgrass prairie in wide oak-hickory savannahs. Certain clay ridges in prairie Iowa had open groves of oaks and maples, huge-boled and ancient, that really did look like royal deer parks. The ground beneath such trees was free of undergrowth and carpeted with shade-tolerant grasses and flowers. Those old upland groves are mostly gone today, but now and then you may see a sentinel oak at the edge of a high pasture. After a hard rain, the closely grazed ground at such a place may glitter with flint flakes — the red men knew prime summer camps when they saw them.

But in many tallgrass prairies, the break between forest and grassland was shockingly abrupt. There was no gradual thinning of trees, no transition in which prairie grasses mingled with open groves. A man would walk through forest among many of the same flowers and trees that he had known in Pennsylvania, and then suddenly enter a border of wild plum, redhaw, and crabapple several yards wide, with an outer edge of hazel, dogwood, and coralberry that was canopied with wild grape. He would break through a narrow belt of sunflowers, and then out into an open world of limitless sky and distance. At his back were the familiar trees and flowers of the Old States; out front were prairie coneflowers and compass-plants, and a vast sea of grasses in an entirely new plant association. In ten strides he had passed from one world to another, across what was probably the sharpest, clearest boundary between any of the major floristic provinces of the New World.

A few isolated groves did survive precariously as islands far out into this prairie. These were trees whose seeds were distributed by birds or wind — wild cherry, ash, hackberry, and maple. Such stands rarely held any nut trees, such as oak or hickory, whose seed dissemination depended on certain woodland birds and tree squirrels. In real prairie, those isolated trees were often trees in trouble — scrubby, wind-racked, and scarred by fires. The uplands belonged to the grasses, and to storm, fire, and wind. In deep prairie it was only in sheltered stream bottoms that trees grew well. They advanced westward largely along the corridors of stream valleys, shrinking from the harsh and alien uplands that were claimed by grass.

Along the wet margins of some streams there might be peachleaf willows up to sixty feet high, towering over the shrub willows and beds of smartweed. Along older creeks

there might be wild plum, wild cherry, box-elder, and soft maple. If the flood plain was broad, it grew walnut, hackberry, and elm, with American elm in the moister sites. Scattered through the bottomlands as part of the elm association were sycamores and cottonwoods — the former being found only in easterly parts of the tall prairie.

In all of this, certain eastern trees became increasingly scarce. An early eastern traveler might see beeches all the way to northeastern Illinois, but there they virtually ceased and were largely replaced by basswood. Growing up in central Iowa, I never saw a beech tree until I was twenty years old and took a trip to Ohio.

long flights of cloying description. Such stuff, by the way, was often written in the East to which the writers had returned — and which they never left again.

There were also bitter critics who simply found the new country too much for them, or who were too loyal to the forests of home ever to admit the qualities of prairie. Some writers disliked the prairie world before they ever saw it. Charles Dickens, in his *American Notes,* makes it rather clear that he didn't care much for America in general and for the West in particular. He didn't like the countryside, the traveling conditions, his traveling companions, frontier settlements, or frontier settlers. By the time he had reached the Mississippi, he was prepared to draw a bead on the first prairie that he saw:

> Looking toward the setting sun, there lay stretched before my view a vast expanse of level ground; unbroken, save by one thin line of trees, which scarcely amounted to a scratch upon the great blank . . . There it lay, a tranquil sea or lake without water, if such a simile be admissible, with the day going down before it: a few birds wheeling here and there, with solitude and silence reigning paramount around. But the grass was not yet high; there were black patches on the ground; and the few wild flowers that the eye could see were poor and scanty. Great as the picture was, its very flatness and extent, which left nothing to the imagination, tamed it down and cramped its interest. I felt little of that sense of freedom and exhilaration which the Scottish heath inspires, or even our English downs awaken. It was lonely and wild, but oppressive in its barren monotony. I felt that, in traversing the Prairies, I could never abandon myself to the scene, forgetful of all else . . .

Another literary traveler on the prairie frontier was Washington Irving, who made an extensive trip through western Missouri and eastern Kansas and Oklahoma in the late 1830s when that region was traveled only by a few traders, hunters, and soldiers. He was a forest man to the bone, and it didn't

take long for the novelty of the prairie to pall on him. Like
other early sightseers, it was hard for him to accept the open
country for its own unique values, and he could not resist
comparing it to forest:

> To one unaccustomed to it, there is something inexpressibly
> lonely in the solitude of the prairie. The loneliness of a forest
> seems nothing to it. There the view is shut in by trees, and the
> imagination is left free to picture some livelier scene beyond. But
> here we have an immense extent of landscape without a sign of
> human existence. We have the consciousness of being far, far be-
> yond the bounds of human habitation; we feel as if moving in the
> midst of a desert world.

It seemed to resolve to this: that there were some men for
whom the prairies held answers they had never found in the
forests of the East, men who were never again drawn back
into trees once they had known prairie. Perhaps they were
genetic sports that had leaped several generations of cultural
evolution, and were born plainsmen who instinctively sensed
that they had come home. Or maybe they just liked all that
sky.

To other men, transition from eastern forest to western
prairie was deeply disturbing; they shrank from the prairie
and its jarring qualities of light and space, alarmed by its
vastness. They were likely normal men of their day, or any
other day, reluctant to pull up their roots and reverse the
lifestyle of generations — men who preferred landscapes
with tangible limits, and assurance of the proximity of others.
The true prairie, in the early days, offered little of either.

Some were from families who for eight generations had
never really seen sunset on a treeless horizon; they were accustomed to a sun that rose through trees and set through
trees, traveling across a narrow sky above the home valley.
Now they stood under an infinite vault of sky in a world reduced to three immensities: the grass below, the sky above,

and the single horizon beyond. It was a land of excesses — of blazing light and great weathers where a man stood exposed, fully revealed. Some men reveled in this — in being the tallest solid figure in a landscape, regarding horizons at eye level and casting a shadow fifty yards long. Others felt shrunken by it, diminished spiritually and physically, and crept back into the sheltering forest from which they had come.

Politicians arrived, looked around, and went back home to report. Dickens returned to England; Irving to upstate New York. William Cullen Bryant saw a prairie and hurried back to New England to write some poems about it. But most men came and stayed, unable to return East or never wanting to. And through the flights of purple prose, the commercial blandishments of speculators, the sour journals of the disenchanted, the labored scrawls to the folks back home in York State, and the technical reports of early surveyors and far-ranging dragoons, the dimensions and character of the tall prairie began to take form.

❦

It was becoming apparent that the grasslands of interior America were ranged in three vast belts that ran generally north and south.

The first real grassland seen by travelers from the East was tallgrass prairie, the region found and named by the French, with giant grasses up to twelve feet high in some places. Farther west, this merged into "mixed prairie," which still wore tallgrasses on lower, well-watered elevations but which was composed of shorter midgrasses in greater frequency. As big bluestem grass was a character of the tall prairie, so little bluestem was characteristic of the mixed prairie. In turn, that mixed prairie melted off into shortgrass country — the Great Plains, with their short wheat grasses and buffalo grasses.

These were the great central grass zones of the new land. There were also coastal prairies along the Gulf of Mexico, the palouse prairies of Washington and Oregon, dry grasslands of the far Southwest, the rich pastures of California, and many others. But the main contiguous expanse of American grassland was the one that sprawled for a thousand miles from the western limits of the deciduous forest to the front ranges of the Rockies.

The factors that shaped tall prairie, mixed prairie, and the shortgrass plains are still at work; the original grassland types are today marked by the crops that have replaced them. Across the center of the United States at the midlatitudes, corn and soft winter wheat occupy the region of the old tallgrass prairie. West of there, into the mixed-grass ranges, fields of hard winter wheats and dry land grain sorghums extend out to about the 97° meridian. The line of the 100th meridian, which generally marks what we regard as the boundary of the real West, is the general eastern edge of the Great Plains — a region today of hard winter wheat, some grain sorghums, and livestock. The species have changed but the essential prairie forms have not. Iowa's prairie country still produces tallgrasses in the form of corn; central Kansas grows mid-height grasses in the form of wheat; and the Great Plains is still a major producer of bovids — but in terms of cattle instead of bison.

The eastern beginnings of the tall prairie occurred as far back as northwestern Pennsylvania, where grassy openings appeared in heavy forest, increasing in size and frequency through Ohio and Indiana and down into parts of Kentucky. Travelers westering through the Cumberland Gap would not enter these strange meadows until they struck the Big Barrens of Kentucky, and land-hunters heading down the Ohio River from Pittsburgh would not meet real grasslands until after they had reached the Mississippi. But an overland traveler heading straight west from Pennsylvania would strike prairies of increasing magnitude until, twenty miles beyond the Wabash River, he might walk up out of the forested flood vanced into eastern forest. Trees existed at the sufferance of grass in a world swelling in height and distance toward the far mountains, and the grass seemed jealous of its great spaces.

Yet, even without trees, those spaces were not featureless monotony to the people who really learned them. Within the prairies were many landscapes. There was tallgrass country about as flat as land could be, expanses of grassland that had been planed and gouged by the last glacial advances in landscape so young that it had not yet cut deep drainage patterns — a wilderness of potholes, marshes, and open lakes. But much of the prairie had a fine roll and break to it, with the land billowing off to the skyline and some timber hiding in the deep folds — older prairie, with enough geological age to have developed distinct watercourses and drainage systems. There were hanging bogs with strange calcareous flora, "walled" lakes with cobble beaches and orderly shorelines of glacial boulders, waves of flowers advancing with each stage of the growing season, and myriad patterns and textures of grasses that varied moment by moment with sun and wind and the cloud shadows that drove across the land. There were a thousand worlds within this one world of grass. Some men sensed that at once; others never did.

And from those first black-frocked Jesuits to the Norwegian settlers who drained and broke the last of the wet northern prairie, there was the same nagging question. Why grass? Why had the land suddenly run out of trees?

2

Fire, Ice, and Mountain

THE TWO OF US were driving through northern Iowa on story assignment, staying on back roads, and taking a long detour around work.

I was pontificating on natural history, partly to pass the time and partly to needle Jim — a born agnostic who delighted in puncturing outdoor dogma. And with the ink barely dry on my diploma, I kept him well supplied with dogma.

There was a neglected fenceline, shaggy with big bluestem grass. I gestured grandly at the fields and stated: "All was once grass. Nary tree."

Jim opened one eye.

"Why?"

"Come again?"

"Why no tree?"

"Because it was all grass." Lamely.

"I shouldn't have asked. Now, with no more of your adroit fencing, say why it was all grass."

I dipped into my formal botany, scraped bottom, and came up empty. In five years at a land grant school in a prairie state, no one had told me why prairie. Jim closed his eye again. End of prairie lecture.

After twenty-five years of wondering, I still come up

empty. Or almost. It's not a lonely feeling; there's plenty of company. Many men have wondered about prairie, are still wondering about prairie and the forces that created and maintained it. As far back as 1870, a midwestern scientist observed that the treelessness of prairie was "one of the most hackneyed questions" in natural history. By the turn of the century at least ten different reasons for prairie existence were listed in the scientific journals. Most of these were pat answers, but since then the new science of plant ecology has revealed a profound equation that makes particle physics look like *McGuffey's Reader.*

The pattest of all answers was simply that prairie soil was too infertile to grow trees. And so, having nothing better to do, it grew grasses. To men born and reared in eastern forests, it seemed inconceivable that any land unable to grow trees could possibly be fertile ground. This was expressed in the report from James Monroe to Thomas Jefferson, describing northern Illinois:

> A great part of the territory is miserably poor, especially that near Lake Michigan, and that upon the Illinois consists of plains which have not had, by appearance, and will not have a single bush on them for ages.

An early Illinois pioneer named Fortesque Cuming apparently agreed:

> The land is here the worst I had seen since I had left the banks of the Ohio; it had been gradually worse . . . and for the last two miles before we came to Marshons it had degenerated into natural prairies or savannahs, with very little wood, and none deserving the name of timber . . .

Although journals and reports of the early pioneer period rarely expressed this idea that treelessness of prairies was a result of poor soils, reminiscences made much later by some early settlers indicate that it was widely believed at the time — an odd impression in view of the fact that many of the natural grassy clearings of the East had long since been occupied by productive farms. In any event, that misconception quickly vanished once settlers had really begun to break prairie sod and put in crops.

There was another theory that grassland had developed in the absence of coarse soil materials. And while it is true that many prairie soils and their parent materials are fine-textured, that theory overlooked the point that many grasslands thrive on rough, rocky ground. The prairie condition was also attributed to bison trampling and grazing, and Kansas railroad promoters wooed eastern farmers with assurances that the grasslands would become Elysian groves once the Indians were gone and the prairie fires were stopped.

Not bad guesstimates, all in all, considering the skimpy fund of information on which they were based. But there was no pat answer. Native grasslands were rooted in some incredibly old reasons, caused and sustained by elemental forces that lifted some lands to the sky and tore others to their foundations.

❧

Our northern grasslands took shape during the most recent ticks of the geological clock, under the great glacial advances of the Pleistocene.

Mile-thick rivers of ice flowed down from their northern foci to grind, tear, and pile in a prodigious back-and-fill operation. There were four major ice sheets: the Nebraskan, Kansan, Illinoisan, and Wisconsin, beginning less than a million years ago and moving in a series of great advances and retreats. The glaciations drew their names from the modern Midwest, for it was there that they made their mightiest invasions, grinding down over Minnesota, Michigan, Wisconsin, parts of the Dakotas and Nebraska, most of Illinois and Iowa, and halfway into Missouri.

For 100,000 years the valley of the Upper Mississippi was

an arctic waste. The vast ice sheets, planing and scraping millions of square miles, ground incalculable tonnages of rock into fine fragments — delivering much of the load as a glacial till of sands, gravels, clays, rocks, and huge boulders that had been torn from the land surface hundreds of miles away to be dumped elsewhere. As the glaciers retreated, meltwater flowed in myriad rivers and streams gray with glacial debris that was finally dropped in outwash deposits. Ceaseless winds swept over these extinct glacial rivers, lifting clouds of rock flour and carrying them eastward in prehistoric dust storms — eventually depositing the powdery aeolian soil called "loess."

Such aeolian loess is ideal for the growth of grasses and is probably the most common parent material of the world's grassland soils. If climate permits, trees will grow readily on it — but it is highly permeable stuff that quickly loses water, and also loses trees if the general climate turns warmer and drier. Some of the deepest deposits of loess in the United States are in the Upper Midwest in regions that were glaciated and later grew to tallgrass prairie. Something like 70 percent of our original American grasslands were formed on deposits created by glacial ice, lakes, streams, or winds.

The Ice Age alone did not create modern prairie, for there are prairielands that were never glaciated. But it did refine soil bases that were laden with mineral wealth and ideally suited to nurture the beginnings of our richest grassland formations. The ice carved and shaped, prefacing the northern prairie and setting the stage for the first North Americans, profoundly influencing all life in the upper reaches of our northern hemisphere. However, the real parent of the grasslands was climate, and the prairie climate had been formed eons before the glaciers by a vast geological revolution.

※

There was a time, perhaps 65 million years ago during the Cretaceous Period, when North America was a relatively even landscape with a bland climate to match. Marked temperature variations occurred from north to south, even as now, but through most of North America the average temperatures and rainfall were higher than today. In such a climate, trees clothed much of the continent in forests similar to those now covering the East — beech, maple, hackberry, and associated species.

But incredible forces were stirring deep in the earth and ramifying up into the thin terrestrial crusts. For ages the lands warped and buckled in a series of immense upheavals and sinkings. In what is known as the Laramide Revolution, great mountain chains rose along the western edge of North America to become the Rocky Mountains, the Sierra Nevada, and Mexico's Sierra Madre.

Then, as now, North American weather patterns were dominated by westerly winds. The Pacific air mass, freighted with water vapor, moved inland to drop its moisture over great distances. But with the irruptions of lofty new mountain chains, a rain shadow was formed. The masses of water-laden air reaching these mountains were forced to great heights and rapidly chilled, condensing and dropping their water content. The Pacific Mountain air mass must travel over three mountain ranges before it reaches the midcontinental plain; three times its winds are cooled and emptied of moisture, watering the western slopes of the mountains more heavily than those facing east. By the time the main westerlies pass the crest of the Continental Divide, they are virtually wrung dry. It was there, east of the Rockies 25 million years ago, that North American grasslands began to flourish in the rain shadow of the new mountains.

Even before the rising of those mountains, a general warming and drying trend had begun to shift the midcontinental forests from such conifers as pine and sequoia to the hardwood forests of later times. The rain shadow cast by the western ranges tipped the balance even further, creating a central climate that strongly favored grasses. A vast region was opened to the sun, with temperature extremes it had never known before. A huge grassland developed from the arctic to the subtropics, varying from desert to arid, and from semiarid to humid to wet grasslands, depending on the vagaries of local climate patterns. Old types of animals changed or died. Early horses in the forests of the semitropical Oligocene had teeth adapted to leaf-eating, but the horses evolving through the drying, opening Miocene show steady progressions of folding tooth enamel as they adjusted to a diet of tough, abrasive grasses.

Lands lying at the eastern feet of the Rockies were most strongly affected, for they were under the deepest part of the rain shadow. Several hundred miles east, the drying effect of the mountains began to be alleviated by masses of moist air sucked northward from the Gulf of Mexico. It was this progressive wave of developing precipitation that defined the three great types of North American grasslands. In eastern Colorado, with its 16 inches of annual rainfall, the natural grass associations are from six inches to one and a half feet tall. In central Kansas, rainfall increases to about 24 inches annually — which is reflected in midgrasses from two to four feet tall. And in the St. Louis area, with as much as 30 inches of rain each year, the tallgrasses may be twice as high as a man.

Since the Laramide Revolution, when the heartland of a continent was denied old sources of moisture, there have been countless climatic shifts of cooling and warming, with the continental scale tipping to forest and back to grassland. Some of these shifts were strong enough to expand polar caps into the recurring ice sheets of the Pleistocene, with warming trends driving the glaciers northward in long interglacial periods.

This age-long whipsawing of climates has been most evident in the central United States, far removed from the tempering influence of large water bodies and with abrupt extremes of temperature and weather. It is an area whose upper parts were occupied by glacial ice while its southerly regions were laved by the air masses of a subtropical sea. It is a great cleavage zone lying at the eastern limit of the mountains' rain shadow and the western limits of humid forest. As a meeting ground of North American weathers, it is also a battleground of two great floristic groups — the trees and the grasses — whose respective advances and retreats, like those of the glaciers, are ordered by the high command of climate.

Only yesterday, in geologic terms, one of these climatic shifts began to repel the Wisconsin glaciation. It wasn't long ago; glacial ice still hung in the upper reaches of Lake Superior and Lake Michigan only nine thousand years ago. The influence of the Wisconsin's huge ice masses lingered briefly as a relatively cool, moist climate, and the newly revealed glacial plains were occupied by a great forest of spruce and fir.

Here and there, fragments of that forest persist as Pleistocene relics within the tallgrass prairie. In parts of northeastern Iowa, where the land stands on its hind legs and shows its limestone muscles, survivors of that cool boreal forest still exist as stands of a white pine–white birch association. There are places, on north-facing slopes where the subsoils are cooled by spring seeps and deep galleries in the underlying limestone, where Canada balsam grows. Years ago, while prowling around an ice cave in northeastern Iowa — a strange little place where air currents reverse the seasons and there is ice in summer and water in winter — we found a single plant of Labrador Tea. No one knew how it came to be there; maybe it was brought by some northern bird and managed to survive in the cool, moist draft at the cave entrance. Or perhaps it and its relatives have always been around there — little Ice Age remnants that are as out of joint with the times as mastodons in a cornfield.

But the boreal forests that thrived in the cool, wet breath of the retreating glaciers were short-lived. There followed a long period of drying and warming, possibly with severe, prolonged droughts. The balance had tipped in favor of plants more tolerant to heat and drought — first to hardwood forests and ultimately to grass. The tall grasslands at the continent's center pushed eastward south of the Great Lakes in a long peninsula of prairie that extended to Ohio and beyond, taking many of its animals with it. In forest Pennsylvania, fossil remains have been found of a typical prairie mammal, the thirteen-lined ground squirrel, and a typical grasslands bird, the sharp-tailed grouse.

This grass-favoring shift of climate began at least 8000 years ago and continued for another 4000 years. It saw the rise and fall of the eastern prairie peninsula — one of the enduring riddles of plant ecology.

There are several theories about the ways in which the prairies extended themselves eastward. One is that ground cover under open hardwood forests developing after the glacial retreat contained certain prairie plants that spread eastward on land bared by melting ice. Or that the eastward march of prairie occurred somewhat later, between the time when conifers were retreating northward and hardwood forests were migrating up from southerly regions where they had been in *refugia* during glaciation, with some kind of prairie association driving a long eastward wedge into the transition zone between retreating conifers and the advancing hardwoods. Perhaps the eastern grasslands simply developed in place under thinning forest cover — growing dominant as even the hardwood forests faded under warmer, drier conditions.

This eastward advance of prairie probably climaxed at about the beginning of the Christian era. The great postglacial period of dry warmness was ending, and the phytopendulum began swinging the other way. It has been swinging ever since, in a long trend of moister, cooler climate that tends to favor tree growth.

The effects of this first appeared in the easterly extensions of the prairie peninsula — regions where the tallgrasses had been pushing their environmental limits. The hardwood forests of the East counterattacked and advanced westward, reinvading the tall prairies and sending out long fingers of advance troops. Enclaves of grass were surrounded, cut off, and by-passed — to survive as prairie outriders in unbroken forest. Whenever a particular floristic group is forced to retreat with any degree of speed, certain colonies are often isolated — surviving for a time as outposts before they are eventually overwhelmed and replaced by the dominant floristic group that surrounds them.

There have been contentions that a strong eastern invasion by prairie never did occur, and that those "prairie relicts" are simply freak scars in original forest — places where grasses took over because local conditions did not favor tree growth. However, there are good reasons to believe that a postglacial prairie advance had happened, and that forest was retaking grasslands long before white men arrived.

How far the pendulum might have swung, if it had not been checked by white farmers who created vast disruption in the tall prairie, can only be guessed at. Maybe, if discovery of the New World had been delayed until 3000 A.D., some future Marquette might have found Illinois to be solid oak-hickory forest, and Iowa might have been as timbered as pioneer Ohio. Nebraska might have had bur-oak openings far into the state, billing itself as "The Parkland of the Midwest." But we'll never know.

In this seesawing conflict between trees and grass, many groves may have persisted after prairie had begun its eastern advance, with relicts of postglacial forest surviving far out into the grassland. Here again, a question: Had the first white men seen prairie trees that were relicts of an earlier defeated forest, or were those trees invaders that were marching westward into a losing prairie? Probably the latter. Climate was trending in favor of trees, and it is more likely that the prairie

groves and woodlands seen by the first white men were part
of a recent advance rather than survivors of an older retreat.

In any case, it was an incredibly hard-fought war. Ground
claimed by established climax prairie is not easily retaken by
trees, nor can prairie easily invade mature forest. This silent
struggle between trees and grass is the grimmest conflict ever
joined by two major plant groups in North America. It has
been going on in some form for perhaps 25 million years
across a broad battlefront that has seen countless victories
and defeats on both sides — and the intrusions of glacial
epochs and corn farmers are only interludes, and of little
consequence.

❧

One of the strongest barriers to a forest advance into tall
prairie is the tough, dense prairie sod.

For one thing, prairie plants often use all of the available
water in the top six inches of soil — which calls two strikes
on any tree seedling trying to root itself there. Besides, most
of the rain falling on mature tallgrass prairie in late summer
simply never reaches the ground; it clings as droplets and
water film on the leaves and stems of grasses. In a light
shower, 97 percent of the water falling on a dense stand of
big bluestem will remain on the grass. Even in a heavy rain,
only a third of the water ever gets to the soil surface — and
walking through tall prairie grass after a summer shower will
drench a man as thoroughly as if he had plunged into a creek.
On horseback, he will be wet to the waist.

In drought years this lack of available soil moisture is even
more acute — and in wet years a tree seedling on prairie will
be engulfed by a tide of growing grasses. On upland prairies
under midgrasses, a tree seedling may receive less than one
third of the light intensity on a bright summer day. A little
farther downslope, where grasses are ranker and higher, a
tree seedling may get only one percent of the available sun-

light. The same fierce contest for living space extends down, as well, out of the light. One may dig a trowel into a lowland forest floor and come up with soil that is not wholly occupied with plant parts, but in tallgrass prairie every cubic inch of soil surface is a mass of rootlets. Half a square meter of big bluestem sod may contain nearly thirteen miles of fine hairs and rootlets; even if a tree seedling does manage to survive lack of light and moisture, it must put root into a dense mat of established competition.

The jealous resistance of tall prairie sod dooms most tree seeds shortly after they sprout — and may ultimately doom even those trees that manage to establish themselves. In tallgrass prairie, even though it is trending into a forest climate, invading trees are on dangerous and alien ground.

The oldest known tree in Iowa was a gnarled, 369-year-old red cedar near Spirit Lake in the northwestern corner of the state. By prairie standards it was an incredible patriarch, for in central Iowa the largest bur oaks may be less than 200 years old. This evokes two possibilities: that such trees had arrived in prairie Iowa only within the past few hundred years, or that their lives are simply much shorter than that. The second idea is the more acceptable.

It's true that certain native trees, and such introduced upland prairie trees as the American elm, can make extremely rapid growth in the rich prairie soil once they are established. An upland elm may add an inch in diameter in only one year; an English oak planted in central Iowa reached a girth of nearly eight feet in only forty-seven years. But in spite of their swift growth, the trees in prairie were relatively short-lived and often died before reaching their known age potential. Botanist Henry Conard believed that this occurred because these large, flourishing trees reached the point where available water supplies couldn't keep up with the growth of their crowns. A tree might die of disease or other causes, but Conard cited inadequate water as the predisposing cause.

Although tall prairie now lies within a marginal forest climate, the limited success of prairie trees may occur because that climate has been in effect only a relatively short time — possibly no more than 1000 years in some regions. This could account for the fact that prairie persists in a forest climate — and for the fact that some prairie groves were on prairie soils that trees hadn't occupied long enough to convert to typical forest soils. It may require 2000 years or more to produce any major changes in prairie soil profiles that have been invaded by trees.

The lay of the land had little to do with the occurrence of prairie. Tall prairie is found in a great array of situations: glaciated and unglaciated, well-drained and wet, level and hilly, and over a variety of parent soil materials — loess, glacial till, clay, sand, and rock. The one factor that dictates the presence of prairie and a relative absence of trees is a critical degree of evaporation.

A botanist named Edgar Transeau refined this idea in some classic studies of the 1930s. He obtained certain numerical ratios by dividing the annual rainfall of a region by the annual rate of evaporation. This "depth of evaporation" depends on several things: the temperature of the evaporation surface, relative humidity of the air, and wind velocity. These are also the basic factors that influence transpiration of plants — the transmission of moisture from plant to air.

Transeau plotted his ratio values on a map of the eastern and central United States, noting that the Great Plains are marked by a rainfall equal to 20 to 60 percent of the evaporation. In a prairie region where forests are confined to low ground, the ratios varied from 60 to 80 percent. When he plotted this range of ratios on a map, he found a remarkable agreement with the actual distribution of prairie. The region indicated by ratios between 80 and 100 percent was coincident with the occurrence of oak openings and open forests, with groves on the uplands and dense forests down below. And in areas where rainfall is from 100 to 110 percent of evaporation, the ratios corresponded with the region of the eastern deciduous forest center.

Professor Transeau's brilliant work defined the limits of plains and prairies in numerical values that expressed decreasing precipitation and increasing evaporation. Where inches of annual evaporation exceeded inches of precipitation, the conditions favored grass over trees. Warmer, drier, windier regions tended to be grasslands; the moister regions were largely forest. Much of the tall prairie lies in a general transition zone in which evaporation and precipitation are almost equal. In wet cycles the balance tips in favor of trees; in drought cycles, the balance favors tallgrasses.

But even though tall prairie may have about the same annual rainfall as woodlands not much farther east, exposure to prairie sun and wind tended to minimize the advantage to trees.

Wind is a prime component of the grassland climate, and the pioneer Iowa botanist, Dr. Bohumil Shimek, considered its effects. Prairies and plains offer little surface friction to wind, which sweeps almost unchecked over great distances. Wind breaks the twigs and leaves of trees and drives sand and dust against delicate leaf tissues. The shaking of a plant also increases its rate of transpiration — a process of water loss that the plant may control by closing the stomata, or tiny pores, of its leaves. But this means that the processes of respiration and nutrient assimilation are also checked. And if the mechanical shaking of a tree is prolonged — as it can be on most upland prairies — the tree may be seriously weakened.

In full tallgrass prairie, where trees often thrive in certain low drainages, the crowns of such trees may never extend above the headlands. Valleys offer reasonably good protection to trees — especially when they lie at right angles to the prevailing spring and summer winds. Shimek noted the effects of this where western Iowa streams tend to flow directly into the prevailing summer winds, while eastern Iowa streams draining to the Mississippi flow at right angles to these hot, desiccating air currents. The relatively sheltered, southeasterly flowing Iowa streams have (or had) more timber than those flowing southwest.

Near my home in southwestern Illinois, towering bluffs rise above the eastern shore of the Mississippi. Some of these are great limestone walls capped with mounds of loess; others are steep hills of pure loess rising out of the river's flood plain as the "coast" of Illinois. Some trees crown these loessian highlands, but the full western exposures usually are treeless and wear relicts of tallgrass prairie.

On such locations, the west-facing hillsides take the full force of prevailing summer winds as well as the sun's maximum intensity — the solar bludgeon that falls most heavily, say, at 2:00 P.M. on an August day. The precipitation–evaporation ratio at such exposed highland edges is far lower than that of the east-facing, forested hillsides only a few hundred yards behind, inducing a prairie-plains climate at the edge of eastern woodland. Most tallgrass prairie species grow there, as well as some plains types. There is even native prickly pear cactus — not the lustiest cactus in the world, maybe, but cactus sure enough. In a similar situation on the loess bluffs of western Iowa above the Missouri River, not only cactus is found but yucca and buffalo grass as well. In such places the land does not face sun and wind obliquely, but has confronted the full intensity of the prevailing elements — and has been claimed by plains and desert plants that are hundreds of miles east of their main range.

In spite of such barriers — which were often by-passed — the broad-leaved trees of the east marched westward into the grasslands. The advance might be spearheaded by lowland trees with winged seeds — soft maple, cottonwood, green ash, and elm — following the line of least resistance up the alluvial courses of streams and creeks. These pioneers might be followed by certain trees with edible fruits — buckeye, wild cherry, hackberry, and Kentucky coffee-tree. When conditions were right, the advance of the trees along moist valley floors might proceed at a rate of about a hundred feet per year. There are places along streams where trees have advanced a mile beyond their limits of fifty years before.

From the floor of a stream valley, the attack might also proceed up the shoulders of the flood plain, with a vanguard of oaks and hickories advancing into the relatively dry soils at the upland's edge. There the trees would begin meeting the first fierce resistance of the upper grassland, and the front ranks of the assault were composed of species that were specially equipped to establish a beachhead. At the outer edges of the oak-hickory advance would be tangles of wild plum, sumac, and other shrubs that overhung the prairie grasses, weakening them and providing something of a seed bed for oak and hickory fruits. The shrub line marched slowly outward, often led by sumacs that extended themselves with underground stolons rather than seed, dying from behind as the shade of the following trees deepened and advancing forward as their own thin shade weakened the prairie grasses. The first prairie farmers found that native sod was much easier to break near the forest edges, for it was in that battle zone that the grasses were weakening.

It was a painfully slow process; at best, the shrub zone might average less than thirteen feet per year out into the upper prairies. And even in that weakened edge, only certain trees were equipped to succeed. The bur oak is one; if there is a tree designed to invade prairie sod, it's this tough oak with its deeply lobed leaves and huge-capped acorns. It succeeds by growing deep and fast before it ever puts on much growth above-ground where tiny tree leaves must struggle for light in the lush ranks of native grasses. In southeastern Nebraska, a bur-oak seedling may drive down a nine-inch taproot before its first leaves ever unfold. That taproot may reach five feet during the first summer of growth; at the same time, the leafy shoot above the ground may be less than twelve inches tall. By the third summer, the roots of the little oak may occupy a column in the prairie soil that is four feet in diameter and six feet deep, and the tree itself is a three-foot sapling.

Still, the woodland advance was not steady. Although the long pull of climate might favor a general spread of woodland into grassland, there were abrupt setbacks.

In plant ecology, it is held that environmental extremes are more important than the means — and such extremes as a prolonged drought or a series of raging prairie fires on a particular front may change vegetation more in a few years than a century of relatively stable weather conditions. During severe droughts, such as the seven-year parching that began in 1934, oaks and other trees bordering grasslands died back. Their lost ground was quickly seized by grasses. An analogous effect occurred farther out in the open country, where tall prairie was invaded by short plains species. In only a few years of severe drought, the work of decades of forest climate was undone.

Trees are technically *phanerophytes*, or "exposed plants." Their twigs, branches, and leaves are bared to the elements all or part of the year. Trees also need adequate moisture that must be distributed throughout the year. And if there's one thing to be expected in grasslands, it is drought of greater frequency, duration, and severity than any of the dry periods occurring in easterly forests.

In contrast to most trees, prairie grasses are children of sun and wind. Their linear, erect leaves offer far less resistance to wind than do a tree's broad leaves, and when grouped in a mass, the grasses as a whole receive the greatest possible amount of sunlight. In midsummer, one acre of grass may present as much as ten acres of leaf surface to the sun. Grasses can adjust, adapt, and spread by various degrees of tillering, reproducing through their root systems as well as by seeding. Unlike trees, a grass's growth and vigor is not impaired when leaf tips are broken or bitten off, for grass grows from the base, not from its tips. The life processes of grasses retrench each autumn and go underground, lying dormant in a deep, dense root system that keeps its own mechanisms of reproduction. In general, grasslands can thrive under greater extremes of heat and cold, wetness and dryness, than can trees.

Under the best of general conditions, eastern woodlands would have difficulty in reinvading landscapes that had been dominated by a prairie climate for thousands of years. Wet cycles encouraging a westerly advance of trees would often be offset by drought cycles that enabled grasses to regain some of their lost ground. Yet, in spite of all this, the long struggle was tending in favor of the invading eastern woodlands as climatic cycles in the Midwest averaged out as an increasingly woodland climate. There were countless halts and surges, and even temporary retreats, but the woodlands proceeded westward. Forest engulfed the prairies of Ohio and Michigan, occupying 90 percent of Indiana and about half of Illinois, and was apparently making progress on all fronts when man appeared.

But the grasslands had a powerful ally — a ravaging force against which most trees could not hold their prairie gains. Some of the plains Indians called it "Red Buffalo." The white man called it many things. It was wildfire.

❧

Fires in tall prairie could be terrible, spanning the horizons with walls of flame forty feet high and roaring across the grasslands as fast as the wind. That wind was often a prevailing westerly that drove the flames against the most vulnerable front of tree growth — that tentative, insecure, west-facing beachhead where the trees were directly confronted by sweeps of upland grass.

These fires had two causes, and many effects. The original tall prairie lay in a collision zone of three major air masses:

one from the northwest, another from the Gulf of Mexico, and the westerlies pouring eastward over the Rockies. It is a wild, violent joining of weathers that vary greatly in moisture and temperature, producing savage storms with tornadic winds and salvos of electrical fire. The lightning fires that ignited sun-cured grasslands — often with no accompanying rain — were common enough. And they were augmented and intensified by early men.

When the first copper-skinned hunters crossed the Bering land bridge, they brought their own fire and an already ancient tradition of using it to burn land. They kindled the open country to drive game herds, or to make the grasslands more attractive to grazing game, and as a weapon in warfare. They started accidental prairie fires during their signaling, and

when they left fires burning in abandoned camps. For one reason or another, American Indians set fires almost anywhere they would burn — in forest, jungle, savannah, and plain.

The role of Indian-fire in maintaining and perpetuating natural prairie has been assigned great importance ever since the white man first entered the great grasslands. Joliet was one of the first to mention it, and few prairie writers passed up the chance of commenting on it. Lewis and Clark, in the March 6, 1805, entry in their *Journal,* noted: "a cloudy morning & smoky all Day from the burning of the plains which was set on fire by the Minetarries for an early crop of grass, as an inducement for the Buffalow to feed on . . ." In the first issue of the *American Journal of Science* in 1819, it was reported that Indians fired grassland to improve pasturage for game as well as to hunt. So there is an old and persistent image of the red man as a Neolithic arsonist, putting the torch to his prairie landscape. There is no doubt that this did occur — but there's reason to doubt the magnitude of its effect. There was an awful lot of grassland out there for a few thousand men to keep burning, and the main job was probably always accomplished by lightning. Still, the Indian had a hand in it, and may have been effective in burning prairies that had not been swept for some time by natural fires.

Another question: Did prairie lands have well-established forests and upland groves that were pushed back by the arrival of fire-using Indians? Or had natural fires merely retarded the forest advance on certain fronts, slowing it but not stopping it? Some competent scientists suggest that forests were formerly deep into prairie, and were pushed back to the limits found by white men as a result of more than 5000 years of Indian firing. It's been postulated that relatively recent woodlands occupied as much as half of Illinois, but that half of those woodlands were destroyed by fire until, at the time of the white man's arrival, Illinois prairies occupied over 70 percent of the land. This has been attributed almost solely to Indian-caused prairie fires.

Some of the Indians living in the oak openings of southern Michigan called fire *sce-tay* — which also happened to be their word for "prairie." The synonym implies that fire was a frequent and familiar component of prairie life and that there was a recognized cause-and-effect kinship between grasslands and the fires that regularly fed on them. Men living as closely to the land as the Indians would certainly observe that fire was inimical to most prairie trees and shrubs — but that prairie arose like a phoenix from the charred meadows.

A grassland holocaust, by and large, is easily endured by native prairie. Grasses are highly fire-tolerant. Like their associate forbs, the herbaceous prairie plants, grasses are pre-adapted to fire. Their life processes are largely underground, out of reach of flames, and the fiercest blazes of early spring and autumn were fed by dead, dry plant parts during times when the vital processes of the prairie were safely dormant in roots, rhizomes, and underground parts that are shielded by a heavy sod. Temperatures in a prairie fire may reach 400° F three feet above the ground, but an inch or two beneath the soil's surface the temperature may rise only a few degrees.

Grasses and prairie forbs carry their winter buds safely underground. But woody shrubs and seedling trees, which bear their buds for next year's growth above the ground, are easily killed by fire. And even though a tough, thick-barked old bur oak may resist a "cool" fire on thinly grassed uplands, the oak's seedlings are highly vulnerable. As shrubs of the woodland edge are charred and withered by flames, which might continue to lick through dry leaf litter to kill tree seedlings within the woodland itself, another niche of environment was strengthened in favor of grass. The efficiency of fire in maintaining grasslands could be seen along many prairie waterways. Because the fires were most often driven by westerly winds, the western borders of lakes and streams usually had much less timber than did the eastern sides, and some lakes in treeless prairie had islands that were densely wooded.

Not only are encroaching shrubs and trees killed by a well-fed, wind-whipped prairie fire, but the fire-tolerant grasses may draw benefits from the apparent chaos.

The black ash surface resulting from burning increases the rate of spring warming on burned prairie. So does the removal of thick grass mulch, permitting more light, warmth, and moisture to touch the soil itself, stimulating grasses and forbs. Growth and vigor of prairie may suffer in thick, unburned mats of dead grass parts that have built up for several years. This dense mat locks up certain nutrients as well as densely shading and insulating the prairie soil — preserving winter chill into the beginning of the normal growing season. Fire helps set the stage, unlocking nutrients and returning them to the earth, exposing seed beds to sun and rain, and enhancing the flowering of dominant grasses. To climax prairie, fire tends to be a releaser. To invading woodland, it is a suppresser.

Yet, fire itself is not the cause of prairie. Lacking a prairie climate, there is no way that fire can generate climax grassland. Prairie fires result from prairie, not the opposite. In a prairie climate, where fire is essentially an acute and ultimate form of drought, it can help maintain prairie and even, rarely, extend it. In a strong forest climate, repeated fires may result in open scrub, but not in climax prairie. Fire was only one of many factors that influenced original tallgrass prairie, and like those other factors it was caused and controlled by the master force of climate.

❧

For a while, after the white man had begun settling on the prairies, there were more fires than ever. Some were firebreaks burning out of control, or pasture-burnings suddenly whipped by wind. There were sparks from chimneys, and the burning wadding of muzzle-loading shotguns fired at prairie game. Injuns were often blamed, even if there wasn't a red man within fifty miles. But with a little time, the great prairie fires waned and ceased. Native grasslands were being put to the plow, not only removing fuel but creating cultivated lands that were effective firebreaks. F. Gerhard, in 1857, wrote of the Illinois prairie: ". . . three furrows were plowed all around the settlement to stop the burning of the prairies, whereupon the timber quickly grows up . . ."

The trees came on. They were coaxed and nurtured in upland groves and windbreaks, consolidating their old gains and making new ones. Areas in Illinois that had once held small stands of prairie or open savannahs were converted to closed forests within a few years after the annual fires had ceased. In some broad flood plains, such as the Missouri River's, the strongest belts of trees had been along the banks beside the main river bed, and trees farther back had shared the alluvial bottoms with great bands of combustible grasses. After settlement, and the control of wildfire, unplowed lowlands were quickly covered with trees, and the flood-plain prairies vanished.

The white man had checked the age-long battle between prairie and woodland. He was partisan to neither, and destroyed many woodlands as swiftly as he created others. But the net gain was in favor of trees; the net loss was the prairie's. The sodbuster killed most of the tall prairie directly, with his breaking plow — and just as surely, he destroyed much of the rest by killing the Red Buffalo.

3

The Lawns of God

LONG AGO, the prairie grasses taught me that I have more in common with Rip Van Winkle than with Leather-Stocking.

Oh, I'll rush around through the boondocks if the occasion demands. But even then I keep an eye peeled for prime loafing areas — especially through midday when most of the action is slow, anyway. Maybe I'll shut down beside a sandbar log by a creek riffle, dozing to water music and the rattle of kingfishers. And there's a favored place under a bur oak at the edge of a clay bluff where I can stretch out and look past the toes of my boots and down over the bends of my home river.

But the best loafing place of all, come high summer, is in the deep grasses of a certain quarter-section of original prairie.

It is just below a swell of ground between the tallgrasses of the low flats and the midgrasses at the crest of the rise, a place where bunch-forming prairie dropseed grows in solid clumps a few feet apart. The intervals between these little hassocks are heavily matted with dried grasses in a resilient bed, slightly curved and conforming perfectly to a horizontal man. The mat of last summer's grasses is springy and firm; beneath it is the deep bed of fluffy prairie loam that is wholly

unlike the solid black soils of adjacent croplands. There are
no clods, stones, sticks, or roots in this bed. With one of those
firm sods of prairie dropseed as a pillow, it makes for as fine
an afternooning as any loafer could want.

I lie there just under the wind, the grasses harping and
singing faintly, their tones rising and falling, the prairie
world washing over me. There is no point in moving; with a
little time, the wind will bring the world to me in a steady
and varied traffic. Watching under the brim of my hat I see a
dragonfly, alias devil's darning needle, darting downwind to
the slough off below. Next comes a squadron of monarch butterflies on their way to some crimson patch of butterfly milkweed. A male bobolink arrives twenty feet above me, hanging on the wind and stating his territorial claims with a flow
of bubbling song, and then slides off to the east. His departure
reveals the red-tailed hawk that he had eclipsed — a mote
that swings and drifts, too high to be hunting and too late to
be migrating, and plainly soaring just for the sheer exuberant
hell of it, exulting in the prairie thermals that cushion his
pinions from below and the prairie sun that beats on them
from above. The hawk appears to be busily occupied, but he
doesn't fool me. He's just another loafer. It takes one to know
one.

Thoughts while loafing:

Not even Rip Van Winkle could have slept for twenty
years on a prairie. The place for that is a deep glen that en-
closes a man in a snug vessel of trees and hills, insulating him
from the sky and wind. A grassland crackles and flows with
stimuli, charging a man to get on with something. A prairie
never rests for long, nor does it permit anything else to rest.
It has barriers to neither men nor wind and encourages them
to run together, which may be why grasslands men are notorious travelers and hard-goers, driven by wind and running
with it, fierce and free.

Forests have surely housed many free and fierce people,

but I somehow imagine them as being preoccupied with laying ambushes in thickets, worshiping oak trees, and painting their bellies blue. I could never take Druids seriously. They're not in the same class as Cossacks, Zulus, Masai, Mongols, Comanches, Sioux, the highland clans of treeless moors, and trail drovers tearing up Front Street. Grasslanders, all.

There was a vein of wild exultation in such men. It wasn't just the high-protein diet, nor even that some of those men were mounted — although the horse people were among the wildest of all. I have a hunch that it was the mood of the land, stimulating its people with openness, hyperventilating them with freedom in a world of open skylines and few secrets. Such grasslanders never seemed to harbor the nasty little superstitions that flourish in fetid jungles and dank forests. Their superstitions were taller, their sagas and legends more airy and broad, and running through their cultures was a level conviction that they were the elite. While some forest people retreated into the shadowlands, men of the open had no choice but to breast the fuller world — and often came to do so with pride and even arrogance. It was a sense that was transferred almost intact when men left the land and took to the open seas, or learned to fly. They were all part of the same — wanderers beyond horizons, children of the wind who belonged more to sky than to earth, conscious of being under the Great Eye . . .

High above the red-tailed hawk are the steady ranks of cloud, coasting down the westerlies. When I first lay down here they were dragging their shadows across me; now they are driving their shadows ahead of them, telling me that the afternoon is wearing on. Which is as much clock as anyone needs. The hawk, not occupied with loafing thoughts, has already heeded his clock. He is losing altitude and returning to work. It's time that I did the same.

❦

INDIAN GRASS

BIG BLUESTEM

Loafing done, I stand up in the wind.

I see each oncoming gust before I feel it — advancing swiftly across the prairie in a long wave of motion, sometimes escorted by patches of cloud shadow that change the tone and color of the grassland as the wind changes the shape. More than in forest, and even more than on sea or lake, it is here that the wind is most visible. The ripening grasses bend and winnow, the waves of our air ocean rolling over the wild meadows until, as Willa Cather put it: "The whole country seems to be running."

The wind will enter the distant grove of trees with a roar, for it resents the oaken strength of trees and shouts and growls as it wrestles them, tossing their crowns furiously. But out here on the open prairie that wind only sighs and whispers, passing over the grasses with little resistance. The grasses bow to the wind's force, acquiescing to its passage and letting it go unchallenged and undiminished.

Tallgrasses are adjusted to their lives with wind; their tough stems are resilient and slender, strong without weight or broad dimension, and slipping easily out of the wind's grasp. Much of this sinewy strength is provided by the outer rind of the grass stem, which is reinforced by an oxide of silicon — a sort of primitive fiberglass. This is the stuff that gives a glossy, polished appearance to maturing grasses and may comprise 70 percent of a grass's ash content. Certain bamboos contain so much silica that a knife can be whetted on their stems, and the hollow interiors of those stems may contain white residues of hydrous silica called *tabishir* — almost identical with the hydropane variety of mineral opal. Traces of biogenic opal in old soils may remain for thousands of years — fossil evidence that grasslands once existed in regions that have long been forested

Silicon apparently serves grass as lignin serves trees; both reinforce the cellulose of cell walls and allow those plants to attain heights that they could never reach if they relied solely on the turgor pressure of their cells and were tightly inflated with their own juices. My favorite belt knife testifies to the mineral toughness of ripe grass stems. It is good steel, and kept very sharp, but cutting a few armfuls of ripe Indian grass will dull the knife almost as much as dressing a bull elk.

A lot of creative engineering has been lavished on grasses. The stems, or "culms," have joints called "nodes," which are solid partitions that reinforce the tubular stems at regular intervals and provide rigid anchor points for the base of each leaf. The internodes between these joints are usually hollow, although they may be filled with pith, as in corn. In all cases, the internodes of the culms are thin-walled, light, flexible, and remarkably strong.

At each joint of the grass stem is a leaf whose lower part is a split sheath wrapped tightly around the stem. At the summit of this sheath the grass leaf flattens, departing from culm in a long, narrow blade. The junction of leaf sheath and blade may have a small "ligule" — a stiff little membrane in some grasses — that reduces the amount of water that might flow down the leaf blade and into the sheath, promoting the growth of fungi. Some grasses have semicircular auricles at the juncture of blade and sheath, tightly grasping the stem with pincers that reinforce the grip of the sheath and resist tearing by wind.

The leaves of many prairie grasses have special structures for adjusting to drought. Canada wild rye, the bluestems, and Indian grass have leaves of nearly uniform thickness, with groups of large "hinge-line" cells in the upper epidermis of the leaf tissue. These hinge cells lose water rapidly, contract, and cause the leaf to roll up in a long tube. The pores through which water vapor is normally transpired are on the inside of this tube, and the exposed lower surface of the leaf is highly impervious to water and allows no loss of precious water vapor during drought periods.

Grass leaves are also neatly adapted to withstand grazing

by animals. These leaves grow from their bases on the stems, and not from the tips. If a grass blade is eaten, it continues to grow; if the stem itself is eaten, new shoots are produced by old stem bases near the surface of the ground. When such stem bases are numerous, the grass forms a characteristic tuft or bunch.

The flowers of grasses are insignificant little structures, lacking fragrance, nectar, and bright colors. There's no spectacular floral envelope, or corolla, but only two or three delicate scales. Grass flowers are wind-pollinated, with no need to attract insects. The grass fruits themselves are usually small — but are amazing little packages of superbly balanced nutrition that are infinitely important to man. All of our tame cereals, of course, have been bred from wild grasses. Yet the wild grasses continue to be of immense value in their original form — anchoring and building soils, and producing meat and wool. And there may always be outdoor purists who insist that wild rice is the only acceptable stuffing for roast wild turkey and Canada goose, and that the split-bamboo flyrod and citronella mosquito lotion are hallmarks of the ultimate trout fisherman.

As grasses depend on wind for pollination and fertile seed production, most also depend on wind for the spread of those seeds. Some tiny grass seeds float for great distances on wind; the little spikelets of Vasseygrass, *Vaseyochloa multinervosa,* have been recovered by research planes at 4000 feet. This grass, introduced into Louisiana from South America a century ago, has been wind-spread from Virginia to Southern California.

Other grass seeds are transported by animals. I have discarded wool socks (that I foolishly wore with low moccasins in late summer) rather than pick out the barbed spears of some needlegrasses and wild barleys that turned the socks into bristling masses that were torture to wear. Such seeds can be maddening to sheep and other heavy-coated animals.

Equipped with long bristles or "awns" that twist and untwist with changes in humidity and temperature, they can literally screw their barbed points through fur and into flesh to cause painful sores and infection. And during those barefoot summers of boyhood, we learned to dread the spiked fruits of another grass, *Cenchrus pauciflorus,* the sandbur.

For spreading out of place, the grasses depend on transport of seed by wind or animal. For spreading in place, they rely on special stems that creep underground or just above the surface. The underground stems, or rhizomes, are jointed culms that extend laterally below the earth's surface and produce new stems and rootlets from the tip of the rhizome or from its nodes. A stolon is a reproductive stem that grows along the surface of the ground, putting down rootlets from its growing tip. A perennial grass may form a dense sod, a mass of individual stems, by either rhizomes or stolons. All of which are anchored and nourished by a dense crowd of fibrous roots and rootlets that extend deep into the prairie loam and may support a clump of tallgrass for half a century.

Each stem of prairie grass stands straight, a slender antenna between the flood of solar energy and the deep banks of stored energy within the soil. Unlike the miserly trees, a grass does not hoard that energy by tying it up in woody structure. The grass spends itself freely and annually, deepening and fattening the black soils below and pouring strength into the animal biomass above. Climax prairie is the product bought with all this spending, an investment of energy that compounds itself. Each creature of the prairie community, from bison to corn farmer, has shared the dividends of the grass. Each, in its own way, has proclaimed that "all flesh is grass."

❧

My loafing prairie has most of the main components of any tallgrass prairie, allowing for the fact that it's rather flat and

poorly drained country of the type most recently glaciated — a sort of child land whose face hasn't really jelled
into mature features.

Still, the lay of the land is modestly varied — with little
swells and swales and enough physical relief to encourage
some plants that like their feet moist and others that like
their feet comparatively dry.

Off below me is a rank belt of sloughgrass, marking a wet
swale of the kind that early wagoners learned to avoid by
watching for "black grass." Although sloughgrass is a rather
serious green, it can hardly be regarded as "black." But the
sedges just beyond it are a somber conifer-green that shows
dark against the vivid tones of the upslope grasses.

Sloughgrass is the most hydric of the tallgrasses, loving
deep, moist, poorly aerated soils that other prairie grasses
would never tolerate. It marks the last low advance of the
prairie grasses to the edge of marsh and slough. Just beyond it
begin the sedges, grading into cattails and bulrush. With
time, sloughgrass will fill a swale of low land, raising it above
its former cattail and sedge vegetations and converting the
place to rich prairie soil that will be occupied by tall grasses
that require slightly drier conditions. Almost transcontinen-
tal in its range, sloughgrass is a common land-builder at the
edges of water — from the brackish marshes of the Atlantic
coast to wet swales in the Far West.

Also called "prairie cord grass" (presumably because of its
tough leaves and stems), its Sunday name is *Spartina pectinata*. Some call it "ripgut," and you need only run your hand
along the edge of a leaf to see why. The leaf-edge is finely
serrate, with a stiff wire edge like a good butcher knife. Before I learned to wear gloves while cutting mature sloughgrass for dog bedding, I used to wonder who was harvesting
whom.

That's a prosperous stand of ripgut down there; it's doing
well, and by late summer the wiry floral stalks may rise nine
feet above the boggy soil. It comes on rather late, often in

mid-April, but then grows faster than any other prairie grass. The root system is tough and dense — a tangled mass of coarse, gnarled, woody rhizomes and rootlets that form a sod as solid as a floor. In a woodless country, such a plant was put to special uses. Twisted faggots of tough sloughgrass leaves and stems made pretty good fuel, and sloughgrass sod was probably the best of any for building sod houses. The Mandans and other prairie Indians used the leaves to thatch their permanent lodges, covering that thatching with several inches of soil. Prairie settlers adopted this, and often used sloughgrass to thatch haystacks and outbuildings. If cut early in the summer, before it toughened, sloughgrass made good hay — but the leaves had a way of tangling so badly that it took a good man to pitch a great forkful up onto a hayrack. Even when loaded, the hay was still a problem. Old-timers have told me that entire loads of fresh-cut cord grass hay had an enraging habit of slipping off a wagon — and then the heavy work of pitching the hay began all over again.

In spring and early summer, sloughgrass is one of the preferred grasses for grazing, but by late summer it is much too coarse and tough for forage. When cured, however, it's useful for livestock bedding because it doesn't break down easily. I've never found anything better for a dog kennel. All in all, useful stuff.

The prairie around me appears to be a rather uniform, sunswept grassfield that varies somewhat in tone and texture. At a closer look, these grass patterns begin to resolve into rather distinct communities that are graded according to elevation and drainage. The lushest, tallest grasses occur lower down, through the poorly drained swales and flats. These are the hydric grasses such as ripgut, requiring plenty of moisture. Just beyond them are more mesic grasses, still in well-watered soils but farther from the slough edge and extending up the gentle slopes. Even farther up are the shorter xeric, or "dry-loving," grasses on the relatively exposed, well-drained crests of the prairie swells. Height classes of these wild grasses express water supply, just as trees do. The early settlers confused the picture by referring to "low prairie" and "high prairie" — an allusion to elevations of the land and not to the height of the grasses. Generally, low prairie has high grasses and high prairie has low grasses.

Downslope from where I stand, just this side of the dark swale of sloughgrass, is a lighter-colored, less dense grass with strong glossy leaves and upper parts with a rather lacy, open look. This is switch grass, *Panicum virgatum*, another excellent hay and livestock food. It lacks the dense, jungly appearance of the sloughgrass; the ground beneath it appears to be more open, and its midsummer seed heads are opening into broad spangles up to two feet wide. The plants are not as tall as the cord grass, nor even as tall as some grasses farther up the slope, but some of the panicled seed heads may stand six feet high. Here and there among the patches of switch grass are the heavy, bearded heads of a wild grain — the Canada wild rye, *Elymus canadensis*, its green, heavy seed heads already nodding on the slender four-foot stems. Greenish-blue, and up to nine inches long, the heavy spikes of wild rye were used as food by some Indians.

Closer toward me — stretching up the lower and middle contours of the long gentle slope where I am standing — is an old friend. The symbolic grass of tall prairie, an official stamp of prairie authenticity, the big bluestem or *Andropogon gerardi.*

This is one of the great dominants of true prairie, the most universal of the prairie's tallgrasses and a marvel to the early settlers who plunged into it and left accounts of big bluestem so tall that it could be tied in knots across the pommel of a saddle. That, and the stories of bluestem pastures so dense and deep that cattle vanished in them and could be found only if a herdsman went to high ground or stood in his saddle to watch for telltale movement in the sea of towering grasses. Such anecdotes are so common that they are trite; yet there's

no reason to doubt them. In my home county in central Iowa, early settlers carved routes through the big bluestem prairie by dragging heavy logs chained to teams of oxen. Big bluestem sod, with its coarse rootstocks and rhizomes, was a favorite for building sod houses. Almost as good as sloughgrass sod, it was far easier to cut.

The big bluestem association — the singular community of grasses and flowers commanded by big bluestem — has been called "the true prairie, *the* prairie." Big bluestem covered the secondary flood plains of broad stream valleys, advancing upslope along gentle hillsides and benches. In old Illinois, it was the climax grass of uplands as well as lowlands, and in Wisconsin and Iowa entire townships were covered with big bluestem — a reflection of the generous rainfall and gentle drainage of those regions. On some Kansas prairies, big bluestem apparently hid cattle even on some of the uplands, and the Flint Hills of eastern Kansas are still called "The Bluestem Hills" by some ranchers. Farther out in the drier prairies, this lofty grass retreated down into protected swales and ravines. But it reigned wherever good moisture levels prevailed — from the low valleys of Lake Winnipeg south, down through the alluvial flats of prairie rivers and well-watered uplands with gentle drainage gradients, all the way to the Gulf Coast of Texas.

It is a mighty grass. The leaf growth may stand three feet above the ground, and the strong seed stems often rise over six feet high. In my little patch of backyard prairie, well-watered and fertile, the culms of big bluestem extend higher than I can reach — at least nine feet tall.

It has other names, such as "bluejoint," which confuses it with similar grasses. One of the common names is "turkey foot," or "bluejoint turkey foot," because of the distinctive three-branched seed head that is unmistakable. It takes its most common name from the bluish-purple bloom of the main stem.

Although it is generally a lowland grass, big bluestem avoids the moist, heavy, poorly aerated soils in which cord grass thrives. Big bluestem wants plenty of moisture, but occupies a middle ground between the wet and dry, between the hydric and xeric. It is *mesic* in its moisture needs — an ecological analog of domestic corn. The finest corn habitat today is that in which big bluestem reigned yesterday.

For some obscure reasons, big bluestem tended to move up the slopes following settlement — giving rise to the old saying that "bluestem followed the settler." The well-drained prairie uplands were usually the ones first broken and planted to crops, and the typical midgrasses of those uplands were the first of the wild prairie grasses to be wiped out by cultivation. If those plowed fields were left fallow, big bluestem and other tallgrasses often moved in and the growth of midgrasses was not renewed. Today, big bluestem is likely to occur in prairie relicts that were originally occupied by midgrasses, which is not to say that big bluestem was immune to the ravages of cultivation. Like other tallgrasses, it was a magnificent hay and pasture grass — although it had to be mowed for hay early in the season before it became tough and sinewy. But the upper parts of the prairie were usually the first to be broken and cultivated, giving the lower stands of big bluestem a slight reprieve — and a limited opportunity to replace midgrasses that the pioneers had found somewhat easier to plow.

The stands of big bluestem below and around me are an almost closed community as far as other grasses are concerned. Forming dense sod and thick foliage, turkey foot greatly reduces light penetration to the soil and discourages most shorter species. This apparently doesn't deter its own shaded seedlings; the leaves of big bluestem seedlings can synthesize food under light values that may be only five percent that of full sunlight. It is a tall, strong, vigorous "dominant" — in the sense that its influence largely dictates the conditions under which other plants in its community must develop. Even where there may be some open ground between the sods of big bluestem, the overwhelming influence of this mighty grass prevents occupation of that soil by lesser types. In the lushest parts of the tall prairie region, the *Andropogon gerardi* community is a terminal association that has maintained its integrity for thousands of years.

But there is something that I miss on this northern Iowa prairie — or know that I'll miss when the tall grasses are fully mature.

There is little Indian grass here, the *Sorghastrum nutans* so familiar farther south in my section of southwestern Illinois and more southerly parts of the tallgrass prairie country. It is almost identical with big bluestem in size and requirements, but isn't as happy on the northern prairies. There's quite a bit of it in the Flint Hills and points south, but even in its best range it isn't as abundant as big bluestem. It has a relatively weak spot in its life history — an inability to tiller and form underground rhizomes under tough competition, and it is unable to spread as strongly as big bluestem.

Yet it's a spectacular grass — every bit as tall and showy as turkey foot, with leaves that branch off the stem at a 45° angle instead of drooping and spreading as widely as big bluestem's. Ripe Indian grass is a golden lance that is usually a bit more erect than bluestem and is somewhat more likely to be found at all levels of the prairie — on certain uplands as well as slopes and bottom ground. The leaves are usually broader and a bit lighter in color than big bluestem's, and long before its plumelike seed head appears, Indian grass can be identified by a distinct little clawlike ligule on the upper surface of the leaf blade where it joins the sheath. (In their early stages of growth, before any floral parts appear, several features identify the tallgrasses. Sloughgrass has its finely serrated leaf edges; Indian grass has that special ligule. Big bluestem has a slightly flattened lower stem and usually has hairy lower leaves, and switch grass has a dense nest of fine, silvery hairs where the leaf blade joins the sheath. Of these wild grasses, Canada wild rye is the only one that has strong, pincerlike auricles tightly clasping the stem at the base of the leaf blade.)

Although Indian grass is less likely than big bluestem to be found in broad, dense stands, there is a four-acre patch of pure Indian grass on an open hillside in the woods near my home. This lies along the route of my Saturday morning excursions with Cub Scouts and Girl Scouts — which still mix like oil and water in spite of the unisex trend. I've often led these yelling emulsions of boys and girls to that stand of *Sorghastrum* — priming them with a couple of suitable Indian yarns and then sending some of them into the tallgrass as ambushers, to be followed by the main wad of ambushees while I lounge on the hilltop. The rich yellow depths of the Indian grass — it's called "goldstem" by some — undergo a wracking convulsion. It seems a rather modest adventure, I know, but being an Indian four feet tall who's lost in a fastness of eight-foot grass is about as much as you could ask of a September morning. And there's always a kid or two who gets lost in there. A search party is organized, solemnly charged with a sense of mission, and sent to the rescue — giving me another half-hour of idleness.

A big patch of tall *Sorghastrum* is the ultimate playground. The kids are safely lost in deep grass that soaks up their noise and energy, finally spewing them out tired, quieter, and almost human. Another plus for prairie.

❧

Upslope from the big bluestem and Indian grass, the midgrasses begin — less rank, more finely foliaged, and standing little more than waist-high at maturity.

Of all these (and there are more midgrasses than tallgrasses), the little bluestem *Andropogon scoparius* is the

greatest dominant — as much the master of its upland realm as its tall cousin is of the lower ground. Together, the two bluestems constituted nearly three fourths of the cover on original tallgrass prairie. In some transition zones, as in the western parts of the Flint Hills and lower reaches of Nebraska's Sand Hills, big and little bluestem may grow in mixed stands of almost equal proportions. But farther west, in the mixed prairies lying between the tallgrass country and the Great Plains, little bluestem may represent 90 percent of the grassy vegetation.

It is a shorter, finer, more delicate grass than big bluestem, without the characteristic turkey-foot seed head. The flower stalks of little bluestem rarely grow more than three feet tall — the ripening seeds equipped with fluffy plumes that named the plant "prairie beardgrass." Like big bluestem, it is superb forage for tame and wild grazers, and the weight gains of cattle on well-managed bluestem pastures can be phenomenal. For over a century the vast bluestem pastures in the Flint Hills of eastern Kansas have been prized for their spring and summer forage, and are historic finishing range for Texas cattle.

Little bluestem leaves are more slender and wiry than those of big bluestem, and until they mature the leaves are light green. Then they begin developing a distinctive reddish cast that deepens in autumn into rich russet, bronze, and maroons. An autumn ridge of little bluestem is unmistakable — the prairie's reply to the hard maples and sumacs of the forest. Big bluestem also develops a winey shade in late fall, but never matches that of its little cousin.

To see both bluestems in late summer is to see prairie. Especially under what Wallace Stegner called "the grassy, green, exciting wind, with the smell of distance in it." As you stand on a long prairie swell in summer fields of little bluestem, wind is apparent not only in waves of motion but in shades of varying green. Pressed downwind away from you,

the little bluestem prairie is the light green of upper leaf surfaces. Turn and look behind you — there, upwind, the prairie
is darkened with deeper underleaf tones and shadow. A puff
of wind runs past not just as visible shape and motion, but
as a shifting wave of color distinct from the whole, something like the undercurl of a tall ocean comber just before it
topples.

By comparison to little bluestem, other midgrasses are
rather minor characters in most portions of the prairie. However, my loafing prairie — a rather flat, poorly drained place
with no uplands worth mentioning — has no little bluestem
that I know of. The dominant "upland" grass here is prairie
dropseed, a midgrass that is apparently tolerant of poor
drainage because I can see it growing on some of the flats
below. All around me are the distinctive sods of prairie dropseed. Early this spring, when part of the prairie was burned,
these dropseed bunches emerged as firm little hassocks on the
prairie soil — straight-sided and rather cylindrical, up to six
inches high and a foot across. At such times, my khaki-clad
posterior has a chronically charred appearance, for a dropseed sod is a perfect place to sit and take notes. Each of these
sods becomes a dense clump of yellow-green, gracefully
drooping leaves that may be as much as eighteen inches high.
By late summer the seed stems will be three feet tall, each
terminating in a broad, spreading panicle that bears the
rather large seed heads.

Farther north, little bluestem is increasingly mingled with
needlegrass, June grass, porcupine grass (*Stipa spartea*) and
the wheatgrasses. Yet, even in southwestern Manitoba, two of
the commonest prairie species are big and little bluestem.
And farther south and west, in warmer and drier regions, it's
no contest. Little bluestem is king.

Needlegrass, one of the midgrass dominants of the northern prairies, once reigned over thousands of square miles of
uplands. It is a grass of the sandy prairie rises, with long ta-

June grass are familiar parts of the homeland; to the Oklahoma farmer, Indian grass and broomsedge are just as familiar. Both farmers know big bluestem, for turkey foot is a universal component of tallgrass prairie.

There are about 150 kinds of grasses in tallgrass prairie, but probably no more than ten of these ever achieve any real dominance in their own special parts of the prairie. Most of the grasses are of minor importance, also-rans in terms of total prairie cover but genuine prairie components nonetheless. In terms of total range, and density within that range, nothing can compare with the two bluestems. They are succeeded in rank by Indian grass, sloughgrass, switch grass, prairie dropseed, and sideoats grama — followed by dwindling proportions of Canada wild rye, June grass, porcupine grass, the wheatgrasses, needle-and-thread, the needlegrasses, and others.

❧

In the smooth, undulating sweep of my loafing prairie there are no angular interruptions, no sharp gradients. Any breaks in the land are masked and smoothed by the summer waves of high grasses. But a few yards away from me, crowned by a mass of blue milk-vetch, is an odd mound about twelve feet in diameter and two feet higher than the surrounding level. Forty yards away there is another. All in all, there are over a hundred of these strange mounds on the Kalsow Prairie.

Called "Mima mounds," they take their name from the Mima Prairie south of Olympia, Washington — a place that's studded with the little hillocks. They resemble burial mounds as much as anything, and were once thought to be Indian gravesites — although digging always fails to produce any bones or artifacts. Here at Kalsow these mounds range in diameter from six to seventy-two feet, and some rise several feet above the prairie. They are most obvious in late winter when the prairie vegetation is flattened and the slightest relief in the landscape is revealed, but even in midsummer the strange, alien mounds are distinct because they support different plants than the prairie around them.

No one is sure how these Mima mounds are formed. The most common theory is that they were begun by animal digging — certain ants or perhaps pocket gophers — and enlarged by frost heaves and differential contraction and expansion of the soil, growing larger as they caught dust blown in from adjacent farmlands. There is no doubt that they attract animals; they often show signs of digging, and the mounds often are soft and friable, with the consistency of a new gopher mound, although gophers alone would never raise mounds as large as these.

The mound itself is a loose column of earth that may be six feet deep. It lacks any sort of soil profile, and is obviously created by a digging, heaving, and mixing action of some sort. Back in the late 1950s, a young graduate student named John Tester grew interested in Mima mounds in Minnesota's Waubun Prairie. He dug into the subject in late autumn and winter, and found large numbers of toads hibernating in the loose soil of the mounds, evidently moving up or down in relation to temperature and staying just under the frost line. One mound less than thirty feet in diameter held 3276 toads that had burrowed an average of three feet deep — moving nearly four tons of soil in one year. Toads may not have caused those Mima mounds, but they certainly helped maintain them. Other diggers did their part, too, and so did frost and soil expansion.

Whatever their cause, the Mima mounds are a broken thread in the native fabric of the prairie. They are intense, isolated foci of disturbance that are exploited by plants that otherwise would not invade the unbroken prairie. Some of the Mima mounds here are crowned with thick little stands of Kentucky bluegrass — a foreign invader that may occur nowhere else in the heart of this native prairie. The mounds often host weed species whose seeds were blown in or carried in from the surrounding farmlands: lamb's quarters, bedstraw, bitter-weed, and bindweed. At the same time, the mounds seem to repel such prairie natives as rattlesnake-master, leadplant, blazing-star, and wild indigo. Each Mima mound is a microenvironment occupied by nonprairie — a beachhead of invasion, a sort of Ellis Island of the prairie world that accommodates foreigners. There may be a few prairie species that tolerate such disturbance: wild rose, sloughgrass, Canada wild rye, and a couple of native sunflowers may be found on or beside the mounds. But most of the originals seem to shun the mounds, and refuse to occupy them.

With some tactical support by man, those foreign invaders on their Mima mound beachheads could end up dominating a prairieland.

Original prairie plants are classed as "decreasers" or "increasers," according to their response to human land use. Most are decreasers, fading swiftly and vanishing in the course of heavy grazing, mowing, and plowing. Rugged and successful as they are in their climax habitat, they are often pathetically vulnerable to land-use pressures — especially those wild legumes and grasses that are eagerly sought by livestock and are sensitive to the overgrazing and trampling that occurs in most modern pastures.

As the prime native plants are weakened by such intensive use, their dominant grip on the prairie is also weakened, and the increasers are released by this lessening of dominance. In most of the tall prairie, such forage grasses as big and little bluestem were simply unable to support the relentless pressures of cattle, horses, sheep, and mowing, and native grasses were replaced by Kentucky bluegrass — a type that can withstand almost unlimited grazing.

It isn't just a matter of livestock grazing on the grass leaves, for a grass leaf grows from the base and if the leaf tip is bitten off or cut, the leaf continues to grow. The critical factor is whether or not the growing point of the leaves is repeatedly removed.

A bluestem grass shoot is a succulent cylinder of leaf sheaths — the older ones outside, the younger leaves within. The first new leaves develop from the growing point of the individual grass plant, which remains in the surface soil. When the foliage of big bluestem is about two feet high, the growing point that produces the leaves may be several inches above the soil. If that growing point is far enough out of the soil so that it can be grazed by livestock, no new leaves will be produced. Switchgrass, one of the most sensitive "decreasers," extends its growing point far out of the soil as early as May, and is readily "grazed out" early in the growing season. And although a grass plant may survive without developing seed, it cannot survive long without foliage and root development. By contrast, such "increaser" grasses as Kentucky bluegrass maintain their growing points at a level with the soil surface, where they are protected from grazing and continue to produce leaves indefinitely.

Prairie grasses are rugged individuals that have adapted through millennia of heat, drought, fire, and competition. But as "decreasers," their growing points must be conserved and allowed to replace any leaf growth that has been lost. Light grazing that is limited to leaves has no serious effect. But heavy grazing and close, frequent mowing can tip the balance in favor of bluegrass, which is highly tolerant of close cropping — as every suburban lawnkeeper knows.

Under normal prairie conditions, Kentucky bluegrass has hardly a chance. For one thing, prairie is most combustible in early spring and fall when a maximum dry plant debris is present — periods when bluegrass is green and growing but when the native warm-season grasses have either not begun their annual growth or have completed it. Bluegrass will be killed by fires that have no effect on big or little bluestem, and during the summer heyday of the native grasses shading is so intense that bluegrass could not thrive even if that was the bluegrass's strong growing season — which it is not.

But let the ancient continuum be repeatedly broken so that the native sod is weakened — decreasing plant detritus and fire, and increasing light intensity under the thinning native grasses — and bluegrass quickly gains mastery. Continually aided by its allies of overgrazing and trampling, it triumphs over the disadvantaged native species. Now the tables are turned, and even if the bluegrass pasture is left fallow indefinitely, a successful retaking of that lost ground by the full community of prairie plants is a painfully slow process that may require two hundred years.

Kentucky bluegrass, let it be said, isn't a "bad" grass. It is usually a highly valued grass. Generally regarded as a native of Europe that was introduced with other seeds by the early colonists, it can't even be condemned as an alien invader — for there is evidence that it is native in southern Canada. But as a strong increaser, it is bad in the sense that it almost irreversibly replaces native grasses when the latter are weakened. Welcome or not, bluegrass takes over.

Today, tall prairie in its vast original form has vanished. All the components are still there, but they have been fragmented and scattered, surviving in little outposts that are beleaguered and besieged by the trained armies of domestic plants. The original prairie plants no longer are joined in the great climax association in which they thrived for thousands of years. So it goes — for now.

And we drive along interstate highways through what was once tall prairie, past roadsides of brome, through landscapes of bluegrass pastures and neat fields of pampered grains, with woodlots and groves thriving where trees scarcely existed for fifteen thousand years. But up there in a neglected fence corner are a few towering culms of big bluestem. The wild grasses are waiting. The originals, bred and conditioned by a

particular climate in special ways. Let those fields be abandoned by man — as they will all be, someday — and the
tame grasses and interloper weeds will lose their strongest
ally. The ancient war of selection and adjustment will be renewed more furiously than ever. For years, perhaps centuries, a riot of strong exotics may dominate the land. But
sooner or later the old stocks will reassert themselves, and
native prairie will reclaim its ancient holdings — with man
beyond any point of rejoicing or interference.

❧

I am asked, now and then, how one can know native prairie
when he sees it. How does genuine prairie emerge from the
landscape — what sets it apart from fallow pasture, or from
cultivated land gone wild and weedy?

Most prairie relicts are small, lingering as scraps and edges
in a tame landscape, and it takes a practiced eye to spot such
little remnants. But there should be no question if the surviving prairie has enough size to retain something of its old character and integrity, for it is strikingly different from the fields
and pastures around it.

Several years ago I was hunting for a small prairie preserve
in Iowa that I'd never seen, and I was having a devil of a time
finding it. The place had an area of only twenty acres, had
just been bought by the state, and hadn't exactly been
heralded as the newest thrill center of the Cornbelt. No one
seemed to know much about it, or care, although one old
farmer voiced the unsolicited opinion that it must be a waste
of good corn ground. So I just moseyed around through that
March countryside of spring plowing, brushy creek bottoms, and
overgrazed bluegrass pastures, looking. Some of the pastures
were greening up, and there were a few fields of vivid winter
wheat; otherwise, the farmscape was a drab pattern of deep
black and dull grays that lay in geometric blocks and strips.

Then I turned a corner and saw it, a half-mile east of me,

spread across two low hillsides that sloped down to a little creek lined with ash and box-elder.

My first impression of Sheeder Prairie was of badly worn and weathered canvas, somewhat ragged and patched, and bleached into soft grays, off-whites, and faded duns. It was entirely different in tone and texture from anything else in that landscape, with an indefinable shaggy, fierce look that drew one's eyes from the tame lands around it. From any angle it occupied stage center, fixing attention with that strange magnetic quality that can always be felt but never explained, that sure quality of wildness. The surrounding fields lay about like stolid domestic animals, passive and bland, awaiting the pleasure of their masters. The little prairie crouched on its hillsides, still its own master in a wholly mastered land, aloof and brooding and ordered by no commands save those of sun and rain. Once, long ago, I saw a buffalo bull in a small herd of domestic cows. This was the same. There was the same effect of surprise, and then the sharp sense of contrast between a wild original and its spiritless descendants.

As a game biologist and hunter, my second impression of Sheeder Prairie was that of a place worth going to and being in — a feeling that I found to be shared by a coyote, several pheasants, a couple of quail coveys, and the first upland plovers of the year.

At any season, there is *variety* in the prairie aspect. This is most apparent in original prairie with marked changes in elevation and varied communities of grasses — each different from all others at any time of year, and each lending its distinctive shade, pattern, and texture to the whole. In mid-spring and early summer, the varying greens and height classes all respond differently to wind and light. In late summer a prairie's tallgrasses are like nothing else, and there's no mistaking a stand of nine-foot big bluestem that gives way to the midgrasses of the upper slopes, the whole scene shot with

vivid flashes of color that vanish and reappear as the wind
shifts the grassy screens before myriad flowers.

In winter, there is a differential weathering and bleaching
that never occurs in monocultured fields and pastures. A
prairie's cool-season grasses tend to cure in tones of gray,
white, and pale yellows, while the warm-season grasses turn
golden, tan, russet, and bronze. You'll see this in fall and winter, driving west of Topeka on Interstate 70 approaching the
Flint Hills. It isn't just that the sky opens up, or that the land
suddenly rises in tall ranks toward the West, but the hills are
a winey russet with a richer tone than the croplands behind — and you know that you're looking into leagues of
treeless bluestem pasture.

Those are the long looks. A closer look at a patch of native
prairie will reveal a number of plants that you may seem to
know from somewhere, with a sense of having seen them
from the corner of your eye in some field edge long ago. Here
in prairie they are all brought together, and reassembled in
original community. But there are likely to be strange, spectacular plants that are new to you. In all my ramblings
through the Midwest, I can't recall ever seeing wild indigo or
rattlesnake-master that wasn't growing in a prairie relict of
some kind. That's the only place you'll find them — they just
aren't the sort to volunteer in a lawn or at the edge of a garden, and once you see them you'll never forget them.

Some tracts regarded as "prairies" are simply old pastures
that have been neglected for a long time, and now contain a
few native flowers and grasses and a number of foreign invaders. They invariably have a long record of plowing, mowing,
or heavy grazing; and the marks of such practices may linger
indefinitely. Such a history will usually disqualify a particular
area as "native" prairie, although some light grazing and
mowing won't seriously affect a prairie's pedigree.

There are certain prairie indicators that are quite accu-
rate, for such plants do not occur in concert if the land has

been intensively used. Well-drained uplands of original prairie will invariably be occupied by stands of little bluestem, prairie dropseed, sideoats grama, and other native midgrasses. Farther downhill, of course, there will be vigorous stands of the tall stuff: big bluestem, Indian grass, sloughgrass, and airy patches of tall *panicum*. Depending on the season, there will be such forbs (any nonwoody plant that is not a grass) as compass-plant, rattlesnake-master, blazingstar, yellow star-grass, blue-eyed grass, black samson (also called purple coneflower), yellow coneflower, bottle gentian, wood betony, penstemon, and many others. Wild legumes such as leadplant, purple prairie clover, and wild indigo are usually sure signs of genuine prairie, for they are among the first to vanish from tamed land and are often the last to return. Conversely, a closed community of old-stand prairie isn't likely to include such familiar invaders as purple vervain, Canada thistle, dandelion, ragweed, Kentucky bluegrass, red clover, or brome.

There are only a few tall prairies left today, but they are worth seeking — worth going to and being in. They are the last lingering scraps of the old time, fragments of original wealth and beauty, cloaked with plants that you may never have seen before and may never see again. If you are a man, stand in such a place and imagine that you hold your land warrant as a veteran of the War with Mexico, looking out over fields of lofty grasses on your own place at last, your own free-and-clear quarter-section share of the richest loam in the world. If you are a woman, watch your children at play in wild gardens of strange flowers, and imagine your nearest neighbor twenty miles away.

If you are a child, lie in a patch of blazing-star and dream of Indians.

NEW JERSEY TEA

LUPINE

TURK'S-CAP

LOBELIA

WOOD BETONY

CANADA WINDFLOWER

YELLOW STAR-GRASS   ALUMROOT   SHOOTING STAR   MEADOW ROSE   HOARY PUCCOON

4

The Far Gardens

GRASS AND SKY WOULD BE ENOUGH. With only those, the summer prairie would be a smiling, running spread of cloud shadow and wind pattern.

But the tall prairie goes beyond that.

From the first greening of spring to the full ripening of autumn, it is spangled by a vivid progression of flowers — a rainbow host that first enamels the burned slopes of early spring and ends months later with great nodding blooms that rise above a man's head. Sometimes as secret and solitary as jewels, but often in broad painted fields, the prairie flowers come on — lavender, indigo, creamy white, pink, coral, gold, magenta, crimson, orange, and palest yellow and blue, their flowers tending from ice to flame.

Unlike those woodlands that do much of their blooming in spring, tall prairie blossoms through all the green months and into autumn. There are also likely to be more species of flowers in a tall prairie than in woodland of the same latitude. And while woodland flowers carpet galleries among the trees and can rarely be seen beyond the middle distance, prairie flowers reach out in a long perspective — their vistas often limited only by horizons and acuity of vision. In early summer I like to sit on a prairie rise with a pair of strong binoculars, glassing a foreshortened landscape in which flowers and birds are closely compressed — a half-mile of color and motion distilled into a few hundred yards. You can't do that in most woods.

The prairie flowers come on in waves, each in its own time, some blooming briefly and others persisting for weeks. Except for a short period early in the growing season, the flowers must compete with a rising tide of grasses. The smallest and most delicate appear during spring, while those of late summer and early fall are usually taller and coarser — although there are a few stalwarts in spring and some delicate blossoms hidden in the deep grasses of late summer. All may begin growing at about the same time; some just mature much later than others, needing months of growth if they are to compete with the towering August bluestem. Spring or fall, prairie flowers are as tall as they need to be.

The first are prevernal, "before spring," and like their cousins in the woods they finish their blooming and fruiting cycle before heavy canopies begin to close over them. Most of these earliest prairie flowers appear before mid-May and are never much more than six inches tall. The best-known is the pasqueflower, with tulip-like blooms ranging from white to pale lavender, its stem and leaves wearing a dense covering of fine silken hairs. It gives the impression of a small flower trying to keep warm and having a tough time doing so, for pasqueflowers may bloom on bare, exposed crests of old glacial moraines while there are still patches of snow on the sheltered slopes behind them. Brave little flowers, often braver than I. More than once, the lowering skies and sharp gray winds of late March have hustled me off the prairie before I'd finished photographing the first pasqueflowers. But no matter — at such times their blooms are usually closed, anyway.

Another of the prevernal flowers is prairie cat's-foot, *Antennaria neglecta*. The scientific name is useful here, for this plant belongs to the "pussytoes" genus *Antennaria* and not to the "catfoot" genus *Gnaphalium.* Confusing? Keep going. One of the names for pasqueflower is "prairiesmoke," which is also a common name for purple avens. And a common name for purple avens is "old-man's whiskers," although there's a type of tree lichen in the West that's called "old-man's beard," which also happens to be a Missouri name for the fringe tree. It's all part of a wild game of semantic Ping-Pong in which the referees speak Latin and Greek.

Anyway, out there along the bleak swells of early spring prairie the white, woolly mats of cat's-foot are returning, and that's what counts. Some of the leaves may have remained alive all winter, and now, in early April, they are putting up short stems and the pale, furry, clublike blooms that reminded some forgotten plant-namer of the curled paws of a white kitten. Spreading by stolons, these odd little flowers often form large patches in the open places between sod-forming grasses.

There may also be the first of the prairie anemones, cousins to the pasqueflower, standing a foot tall on slender stems that tremble in the slightest puff of spring breeze — a characteristic that named them "windflowers." Usually white but sometime violet with clusters of golden stamens, they bloom on some northern prairies in late April and are the tallest of the prevernal prairie flowers.

Then, one bright morning in early May, sun-washed prairie slopes may look as if patches of spring sky had fallen on them, and you know that the bird's-foot violets have arrived. This is the most magnificent of our violets, with each leaf trebly lobed and resembling a bird's foot. It's a large flower as wild violets go, spanning an inch or more with the two upper petals of rich lavender and a floral heart of deep orange.

When the bluestem grasses begin to appear in mid-April it is a signal for the spring flowers to get on with it, for they are small plants that are easily overtaken by the rising grasses.

The hilltops now are splashed with false dandelion, Indian paintbrush, and mats of groundplum. The new grass is spangled with tiny purple, white, and blue grass flowers and yellow upland buttercups. Prairie and meadow violets are coming on, with vetch and the first of the false indigo. Along the creeks and at the edges of low swales are marsh marigold, yellow star-grass, and heart-leaved violets. The prairie pinks come into bloom, enameling the slopes of young grasses with pink, white, and purple. With them come the puccoons, rich orange splashes among the greens and pinks.

In the flood tide of spring, wild indigo begins to appear, sometimes four feet tall and strangely treelike, the terminal branches laden with clusters of creamy blossoms that will produce the black, inflated seed pods. Wild indigoes are usually found along the midslopes and lower benches of the prairie elevations. The sap of some species becomes purplish when exposed to air, and some old, dried plants may be boiled to produce a poor grade of indigo dye — which accounts for the generic name *Baptisia,* taken from the Greek term "to dip."

If I had to choose favorites from the spring prairie flowers, I suppose that two of them would be yellow star-grass and blue-eyed grass. Neither are grasses, but are delicate, grasslike little things with blooms less than an inch across. They don't amount to a whole lot, but I knew their names before I ever knew the plants themselves, and I liked them from the beginning. Blue-eyed grass is one of the irises — a most modest iris, to be sure, but one standing high in favor if not in size. At the very tips of the wiry, flattened stems are yellow-centered blue flowers an inch across. Yellow star-grass is a member of the daffodil family, its slender floral stems growing from a tuft of narrow, grasslike leaves. Each little flower is a six-pointed star of bright yellow.

Wild strawberry flowers may show as early as mid-April with their five white petals and yellow centers that later become scarlet berries. Most of the prairie varieties are only about six inches high or less, and their berries may be only a half-inch in diameter. But small as they are, they are supreme in flavor. No tame strawberry can match them. Rising above one of my favorite fishing ponds is an open hillside that may be carpeted with these little, half-hidden berry plants. And although it's less than a hundred yards from the pond edge to where I park my car on the ridge, I have taken over an hour to cover that distance — grazing my way up the slope on hands and knees. Late in a June afternoon, with an appetite whetted by eight hours of fishing and no lunch, it's the only way to travel.

One of the May prairie flowers that gave me trouble years ago was a lush cone of beaked yellow blossoms with a cluster of rather fernlike basal leaves. It seemed common enough, but I just couldn't find anyone who could give me a fix on it. It finally turned out to be wood betony, a member of the snapdragon family. It's also called "lousewort" because European members of this genus were believed to cause cattle to become infested with lice. From the standpoint of either fact or aesthetics, it's a name worth ignoring.

Late spring sees spiderwort, with its three-petaled flowers of rich blue and gold-tipped stamens that rise from a fluffy blue fringe. This is one of the dayflowers, family *Commelina-ceae*, named because the flowers are open for only one morning. The narrow arching leaves are folded lengthwise and tightly clasp the stem. On northern Iowa prairies we usually see these in June, although they may bloom in May in Missouri and points south. In sandy parts of the May prairie there are clumps of hoary puccoon with their yellow-orange, five-petaled flowers a half-inch across — rich warm blossoms in a community of flowers that are predominately blue, lavender, and white. As the seasons warm, so will the prevailing colors of prairie flowers — and the grandmother's quilt of native prairie will glow with patches of crimson, gold, and brilliant yellows.

The last week of May, more or less, marks the end of the

BUCKEYE

PAINTED LADY

SNEEZEWEED

PURPLE AVENS

BUSHY VETCH

PURPLE MILKWORT   SIDEOATS GRAMA   DROPSEED

vernal aspect of prairie flowering. Spring has passed into summer, and the flowers are taller now. Daisies begin to appear, with larkspur and purple coneflower. There are fiery prairie lilies and clouds of wild roses that mark the official opening of summer.

About the only thing that "them politicians down in Des Moines" ever did that pleased our Grandma Posegate was to make the prairie rose Iowa's state flower. Her wild roses range from white to coral to the deepest rose tones, the color of a flower often changing with age and exposure, centered with a mass of yellow stamens and freighting the summer wind with a fragrance like no other. Entomologists have always marveled at the speed with which the introduced honey bee spread into the western wilderness. Well, it's not surprising. The first bees probably got a whiff of a June prairie and flew nonstop all the way from Plymouth Rock.

Through June and into mid-July there may be flaming Turk's-cap lilies as tall as a man, with rich recurved petals of vivid red-orange. These are natives, similar to the tiger lilies that have escaped from gardens to grow in dense beds along some roadsides near farmhouses, but the Turk's-caps are often much larger. This great prairie lily may reach a height of eight feet, a single stem bearing forty of the brilliant blooms. They are never abundant, but aren't so rare that you're not likely to see one in a scrap of unharmed prairie — if its bulbs have escaped the spades of the flower hunters.

Early summer also brings on many members of the mint family, with their square stems and opposite leaves. One of the commonest of the prairie mints is American germander (also called "wood-sage"), bearing a pyramid of lavender flowers. Another is wild bergamot, or "horse mint" — a big plant, often over three feet tall, with round clusters of fringed flowers at the tops of its branches.

The rarest floral displays of the old prairie were the exquisite wild orchids of broad low flats, prairie swales, and marsh edges. The *Spiranthes,* or ladies'-tresses, are delicate little plants not usually taken for orchids, with small white or yellow flowers that spiral up their stems in fragile spikes. The little white flags of this orchid may dot some Nebraska hayfields in late September a month or so after the last mowing, and it is the only prairie orchid that may be more abundant today than it was in original tallgrass prairie. Those original prairies may also have held *Cypripedium,* the lady's slipper or moccasin-flower. Although orchid authorities generally relate these to rich woodlands or woodland bogs, they may once have occurred deep in the prairies as well. Pioneer prairie writer Herbert Quick recalled a large yellow orchid — possibly the yellow lady's slipper — that grew in prairie swales, and wrote that the "largest and finest" of the wild orchids in frontier Iowa were found far back in the marshes. These, he said, grew "two to three feet tall with great white and purple blooms and floral pouches big enough to hide a hummingbird." This seems to fit *Cypripedium reginae,* the stunning showy lady's slipper, with snowy lateral petals and sepals and a great white floral pouch suffused with pink and mottled with rose-purple. Although I've never seen a record of this orchid in tall prairie, I like to think that it may have been there.

The most typical prairie orchid was, and is, the prairie white fringed orchis *Habenaria leucophaea.* It's a stout plant, often four feet tall, with a cluster of fringed white blooms that bear floral spurs over two inches long. At twilight these flowers breathe a delicate fragrance that attracts a certain crepuscular sphinx moth — the only insect that can pollinate this plant.

High summer also brings the rich red-orange masses of butterfly milkweed, *Asclepias tuberosa.* It is the only one of the milkweeds without milky sap, usually growing in rich, heavy soil on wind-protected slopes and producing masses of brilliant blossoms that may be over thirty inches in diameter. It had to be named "butterfly-weed"; it has an irresistible attraction for butterflies in general and monarchs in particular, and squadrons of monarchs may be found at a big clump of butterfly-weed at one time.

By the Fourth of July the butterfly milkweed and a host of other showy prairie flowers are coming on strong. Each week now brings a new wave of change. Almost all the flowers are bigger and bolder than ever; they must be, to keep pace with the rising prairie grasses. Black samson, or purple coneflower, is in bloom, with prairie larkspur, prairie phlox, ox-eye daisy, prairie cinquefoil, wild indigo, and leadplant. If you can make but one annual visit to a patch of tallgrass prairie, the Fourth of July is a good time to do it.

Early one July, as photographer Carl Kurtz and I stood by a fence looking out over an Iowa prairie, a small bird lit about seventy yards away. The binoculars revealed a brilliant male goldfinch perched on a lone stalk of rattlesnake-master, flanked on one side by a stand of white larkspur and on the other by crimson banks of butterfly milkweed, the entire foreground covered by beds of white and blue prairie phlox. Carl handed me the binoculars and groaned; he had only his big view camera that day and no telephoto lens. It was just as well; it would have been a hokey shot. Much too garish and obvious. No one would have believed it.

In terms of families, genera, and species, the tall prairie carries an incredible roster of native flowers. All the great families are there: *Iridaceae, Orchidaceae, Leguminosae, Euphorbiaceae, Labiatae, Scrophulariaceae, Rosaceae, Umbelliferae,* and many others. But all of these pale in terms of frequency and number of individuals when compared to the great family *Compositae* — the daisy family. Someone has said that tall prairie should not be called "grassland" but "daisyland," for the summer prairie is a flaming riot of goldenrods, ironweeds, bonesets, fleabanes, daisies, coneflowers, sunflowers, asters, blazing-stars, rosinweeds, compass-plants.

INDIAN GRASS

BLAZING-STAR

RATTLESNAKE-MASTER

BLACK SAMSON

PRAIRIE
CLOVER

PRAIRIE CONEFLOWER   BUTTERFLY MILKWEED   LEAD PLANT

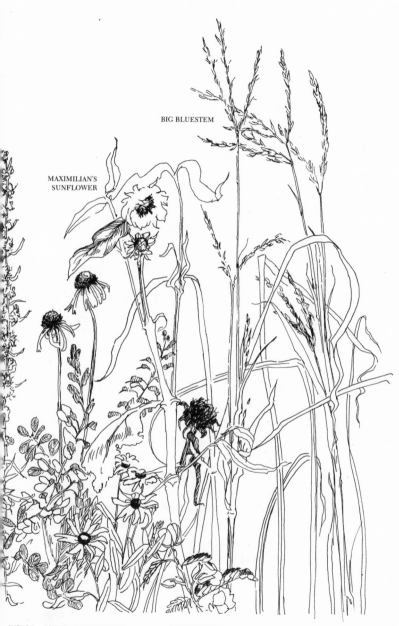

BIG BLUESTEM

MAXIMILIAN'S
SUNFLOWER

INDIGO   BUTTER CONEFLOWER   PARTRIDGE PEA

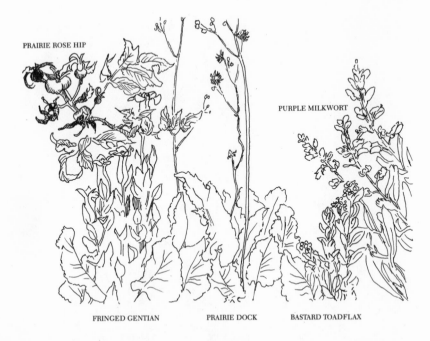

PRAIRIE ROSE HIP

PURPLE MILKWORT

FRINGED GENTIAN   PRAIRIE DOCK   BASTARD TOADFLAX

The daisy, in some form or other, is as characteristic of tall prairie as are grass and grasshoppers.

A prime member of this great family reunion is the compass-plant, named because the set of its great leaves marks the prairie meridians. The edges of those leaves, especially in younger plants, are inclined to be directed north and south with the flats of the leaves facing the rising and setting sun. Compass-plant leaves look something like oak leaves afflicted with gigantism — they may be over two feet long and half as wide, deeply lobed, with the largest leaves near the ground and the strong, coarse floral stalks rising as high as ten feet. The all-yellow blooms are several inches in diameter, and the whole plant has a sunflowerish look.

Pioneers sometimes used compass-plant stalks to mark the

edges of wagon routes over the wild prairies — tying scraps of cloth to the tall stems to indicate safe passage around boggy swales and sloughs. They also found that the plant produced a pretty good brand of native chewing gum. Drops of clear sap exude from the upper third of the stem and solidify with exposure. It has an odd, pine-resin taste that's pleasant enough, but it must be firmed up before it's chewed. A couple of summers ago I tried some of this sap while it was still liquid. It's surely the stickiest stuff in all creation, and I literally had to clean it from my teeth with lighter fluid.

Another prairie classic is the purple coneflower, or black samson. This composite may be almost four feet tall, a strong stem with its terminal flower of purple, straplike rays and a brownish center disk. The entire flower may be five inches across, and unlike other coneflowers its disk is dome-shaped rather than cone-shaped. Even after the "petals" are shed, black samson is still distinct with its straight or gracefully twisted stem that is slightly swollen near the seed head.

The prairie coneflowers *Ratibida* are much the same size, but with bright yellow rays instead of purple. The central disk of some flowers is a brown, elongated cone or cylinder that may be two inches tall and only a half-inch thick. Actually, the "flower" of such a composite consists of two types of flowers. The smallest and most numerous are contained in the center of the flower and called "disk flowers." The others are the strap-shaped "petals" of the flower, called "ray flowers." Daisies, coneflowers, and sunflowers are of this type. But a composite's head may consist entirely of disk flowers, as with ironweed or thistle, or of ray flowers as in chicory and dandelion.

Our most familiar coneflower is the black-eyed Susan, of the genus *Rudbeckia*. Sometimes more than three feet tall, with rough and hairy leaves and stems, it flowers with a rich butter-yellow bloom with a dark brown center, often growing in dense beds. Nearby is the spectacular ox-eye daisy, with its golden disk and white rays.

One of the mightiest genera in the daisy family is *Aster,* with a complex and bewildering roster. Some groups have driven even botanists around the bend, for the plants often cross and interbreed in a great variety of habitats and can become a taxonomic nightmare. Typical prairie species are the smooth aster, sky-blue aster, willow aster, many-flowered aster, and the prairie aster *A. turbinellus.* The central disk of wild asters is usually bright yellow, with rays of white, pink, blue, purple, or lavender. They are hardy flowers, and on some eastern Oklahoma prairies in favorable years the wild asters may continue blooming in November, long after the taller fall flowers have ripened and died.

Coming into late summer, the tall prairie erupts with coarse, strong composites whose heights may challenge the tallest of the grasses. The great common sunflower may grow to fifteen feet. Beneath it are a host of others; the prairie sunflower, Maximilian's sunflower, the stiff sunflower, and probably twenty other species that flourish in the openlands, edges, and prairies of mid-America. All have brilliant yellow rays — providing the generic name *Helianthus* — with central disks of yellow, brown, or brownish purple. With the sunflowers come the native goldenrods: the Missouri goldenrod, stiff goldenrod, the showy and field goldenrods, and others. Sunflowers and goldenrods — like dandelions and most other composites — are so hardy and common that they're generally held in low esteem. Many of the goldenrods would be valued as ornamentals if they were delicate or rare; indeed, these native American flowers are carefully planted and reared in many European gardens. Over here, they are seldom admired and often falsely accused. Yet, the goldenrods are not a source of hay-fever pollen; their pollen is spread by insects, not by wind, and has never been proved to be an important cause of hay fever. But the showy blooms are

ASTER

NEEDLEGRASS   PRAIRIE GENTIAN

damned by the company that they keep, consorting in weedy edges and open waste places with the ragweeds.

No single flower family has the corner on beauty or form, and each stage of the growing season has its own rich spectacle. But if all the prairie flowers were put to popular vote, the winner might well be *Liatris,* the blazing-stars of the composite family.

Like many of the composites, it's a confusing group with enough similarity between members to throw most casual naturalists for a loss. But it makes no real difference; when the August prairie is lit with the blossoms of *Liatris,* such things as technical pedigrees lose their importance.

They may be called blazing-star, gayfeather, or button snakeroot. Their rose-purple blossoms may vary in arrangement — some ranked on eighteen-inch stems in little floral buttons, others in glowing spikes six feet above the ground. One of the most common is button snakeroot, *Liatris spicata,* a showy form whose dense spike contains up to twenty individual flower heads and usually occurs in upland prairies and well-drained ground. The flower heads of others are distinctly stalked along the upper part of the leafy stem, as in *L. scariosa,* the large button snakeroot that may grow nearly six feet tall. Drier, western parts of the true prairie are home range of *L. punctata,* the dotted gayfeather. It is named by the tiny, dotlike glands on its leaves, which are translucent when held against a bright sky. Even a modest stem of blazing-star will draw attention. And once in a lifetime, with luck and patience, you may wander into one of August's rare spectacles — a lost patch of original tall prairie that is a solid bed of gayfeather, *Liatris pycnostactya,* in glowing masses of head-high magenta.

A balanced tallgrass prairie is rich in wild legumes, with the prairie clovers, many-flowered *psoralea,* silver-leaved *psoralea,* numerous violets, and wild indigos and vetches. One of the most typical and conspicuous legumes of the prairie uplands is leadplant, *Amorpha canescens*. One reason for the common name is said to be the belief that the plant indicates bodies of lead ore — but a better reason is the grayish, leaden color of the leaves, especially when the plant occurs in dense colonies. Through the heart of summer, this bushy legume produces long spikes of tiny purple flowers that are sparked with golden stamens. Leadplant may grow as high as four feet in the southerly parts of its prairie range, and usually about half that farther north. Wherever it's found, it is part and parcel of the bluestem prairies and is generally associated almost exclusively with the *Andropogon* grasses. With it are the white and purple prairie clovers, each slender stem crowned with a silver thimble that wears a fringe of white or purple flowers — a floral circlet that progresses up the seed head with the passing days.

The prairie saves some of its best for last.

During late August and September in the "hanging bogs" of northern Iowa and southern Minnesota prairies, sods between the strange little bog pools may produce a dainty brook lobelia. A flower of the north, *Lobelia kalmii* is about a foot high with small light-blue flowers with white centers. Nearby there may even be a few fringed gentians. At the margins of such an alkaline fen there is often a calcareous crust, or "tufa," that is packed with parnassias whose delicate stems bear small white flowers streaked with green or yellow veins.

Down in the wet swales of the autumn prairie, sometimes even surviving in frost pockets, is the bottle gentian with its closed, tubelike corolla that never opens. This is the gentian that must be forced open by a bumblebee for pollination, a spring-loaded blossom that requires considerable muscle to enter. Of all the autumnal flowers, only the gentian can prosper in the lowest understory of the tall grasses.

Higher on the midslopes and prairie uplands is the superb downy gentian with its five broad, pointed corolla lobes of deep purple-blue. Sometimes flowering into November in southerly parts of the true prairie, this magnificent gentian opens its blooms only in bright sunshine. Like the pasque-flower at the other end of the seasonal spectrum, the downy gentian blooms fully only in weather when pollinating insects are abroad — the warm, bright times that grow more and more infrequent in the wane of the year.

At best, this chapter is only a skimpy bouquet of the prairie's flowers. There may be at least one hundred and fifty species of native flowers in the open prairie, and many are showier than most of the ones mentioned here. My only alibi for not including more of them is that the ones discussed are representative of families, forms, and seasons.

Yet, some of the most interesting of the prairie forbs do not have showy flowers. The rattlesnake-master is one — a member of the parsley family with yuccalike leaves that give it the specific name *yuccafolium*. It's an odd plant, sometimes as much as four feet tall, with its leaves like yucca, a head like a thistle, and second cousin to the carrot. I can't recall ever seeing one of these plants except on expanses of quality prairie, and this specificity adds to its appeal — at least, to those of us who like genuine trademarks of genuine country. A decoction of *yuccifolium* leaves and roots was supposed to be useful in treating snakebite, and there's also a tale that rattlesnakes carefully avoid the plant. On the other hand, an old prairie farmer once told me that the presence of rattlesnake-master in a field of "wild hay" was a sure sign of massasauga rattlers. His granddad had told him that, so it had to be true.

Unlike grasses, which are wind-pollinated, the prairie's flowers depend on insects for pollination — a process rewarded with pollen and nectar and inspired by the brilliance and fragrance of the floral displays.

The showy blooms of the daisy family are generally open to all comers, as are many members of the rose, lily, buttercup, and parsley families. The mints and snapdragons, with their trick nectaries and complex forms, are often reserved for only a few specialized pollinators. The monarch butterfly is drawn to the milkweed that it helped name, and a certain twilight moth seeks out the delicious spurs of the white-fringed orchid. The painted lady butterfly has a special fondness for thistle blooms. The bumblebee is one of the few insects brawny enough to get into the bottle gentian, and this huge bee also serves the gorgeous blue flag — that stately wild iris of the wetland edge. Most of the pollinators are butterflies, moths, bees, and flies. But certain soldier beetles, which resemble brightly colored fireflies, often feed on goldenrods and carry their pollen from plant to plant. Hummingbirds do their part, especially on certain wild lilies and the trumpet creepers of the woodland edges. But while some insects work overtime to provide fertile seed, others work to limit the production. The ripening capsule of a single downy gentian may produce thousands of tiny seeds that are nearly all destroyed by small beetles that cut through the ovary wall. I have opened hundreds of wild indigo pods seeking seeds for garden planting, and in most cases small black weevils had gotten there first.

The big show is almost ended by the first hard frosts. Although the tall grasses provide an encore with their rich burst of golds, winey russets, and shades of bronze, the great host of prairie flowers now exists only as dried stalks with stripped seed heads, and a few pods clinging to frost-blighted stems. Then even the grasses begin to bleach and fade; the prairie is assuming winter dress, a sere monotone with all life gone underground to await another spring.

I've never found this depressing, although some people do, and I like to return to the November prairie for some of my hunting and just to see that everything has been properly put to bed. For another year in the infinite procession of years, it has all worked out O.K. The wreckage of the great vegetative tides still functions in behalf of the prairie biota — providing deep forms and snug coverts for the foxes and coyotes, prairie chickens, quail, pheasants, rabbits and hares and meadow mice, and all the beleaguered little critters that must stay awake through the winter and so desperately need shelter from the sharpening, never-ending wind. Nothing has been wasted; nothing has really died or gone. The prairie pendulum has swung to one limit, and has already begun to return, and in a few bleak months there will be pasqueflowers again.

❧

Like the grasses, these wild forbs are finely adjusted to the grim facts of prairie life — meaning fire, drought, and the incessant attacks of insects.

A leaf of rattlesnake-master, for example, has strong cords of lignified cells running along its margins and veins, and a caterpillar or grasshopper has a tough time handling it. The jaws of an insect work from side to side, and not up and down, and a grasshopper chewing the edge of a rattlesnake-master leaf finds it almost impossible to make a meal of it. I can't recall ever seeing a rattlesnake-master leaf that had been badly damaged by insects, and they seem to get through the entire summer looking fresh and new. Furthermore, the pores in the upper surfaces of rattlesnake-master leaves are sunken, reducing loss of water vapor during critical drought periods.

Such drought resistance is evident in the root systems of many prairie forbs; they are likely to have deep, heavy rootstocks that drive far into the earth to subsoil moisture supplies. The taproot of an old compass-plant may be as thick as a man's wrist just below the surface of the earth — and although it may be less than an inch in diameter only three feet down, this main root may drive almost fourteen feet into the prairie earth.

Of the various blazing-stars, the dotted button snakeroot is characteristic of westerly parts of the true prairie and is the

one most resistant to drought. In rather light prairie soils the roots of this beautiful little plant may penetrate sixteen feet. Professor John Weaver of the University of Nebraska found that such a plant may have few lateral rootlets until an extreme depth is reached, and then it fills the soil with small, silvery-white rootlets. This is one of the last prairie forbs to suffer in severe drought, while some of the more easterly blazing-stars are among the earliest forbs to die. Large button snakeroot, with a root system that may extend only two feet into the prairie soil, is unable to endure prolonged drought and is generally confined to the moister regions of the true prairie.

Although not really a forb, the "half-shrub" prairie rose also has a mighty root system; the roots of one older plant were found to extend almost straight down for twenty-one feet. Most upland prairie forbs have numerous lateral rootlets just beneath the surface, but the purple coneflower differs from these by having a thick, fleshy taproot that is almost unbranched and may reach eight feet into the prairie soil. Even the little white and purple prairie clovers root deeply. They may have relatively few absorbing roots and rootlets in the upper two feet of soil, but their root systems often extend downward almost six feet and branch widely at the lowest levels.

The rootstocks of some prairie plants gave pioneer plowmen trouble. At best the roots made plowing difficult; at worst they might damage plows and injure draft animals. Leadplant could be a problem, although a plowpoint usually tore through its rootlets with a sharp snapping sound that caused the plant to be known as "prairie shoestring." The taproot of an old compass-plant might prove bothersome to a light plow, but none could compare with the main rootstock of New Jersey tea, or redroot, the "pest of the plowman." The plant frequently produces huge, burl-like rootstocks that defied a light breaking plow and ox team, and was probably

the reason that some old wetplate photographs show axes or shovels strapped to the plow handles of homesteaders. Not long ago I heard of a small western Iowa prairie patch that had been left uncultivated because of the problem that a colony of redroot presented even to modern, tractor-drawn plows! One of the most vivid terms I've ever heard was that of an old eastern Nebraska farmer who told me that his father had simply called New Jersey tea "rupture root" — which just about says it all. I have a hunch that the heavy burls of redroot may develop at least partly as a result of long-term burning — much like the infamous "oak grubs" of southern Wisconsin.

Since native tallgrasses are preadapted to a fire ecology, it's inevitable that climax prairie forbs be equally well adapted. No fire-sensitive forb or shrub could possibly thrive in a landscape that consists of highly flammable tinder for at least half the year. Most climax prairie forbs are perennials whose underground parts assure a continuum of life and vigor, penetrating deep into moist subsoils. Such underground reserves cannot be reached by fire and may even be strengthened and stimulated by the surface fires that unlock mineral content of above-ground plant parts and remove deep, insulating surface litter.

There's a certain Iowa prairie in which we always find some white and purple prairie phlox in late June and early July. But although phlox is reasonably common in that summer prairie, there's usually nothing remarkable in its abundance. Then, one April, part of the eastern portion of the prairie was burned in a management program. When we visited it in early July, the burned portion of the prairie was a storm of white and purple prairie phlox in broad beds and patches. There is no doubt that the phlox was released by that early burn, and such associated species as larkspur and butterfly-weed also prospered. The same thing apparently happened in a little sand prairie in eastern Iowa. It always

has some stands of *Liatris,* but following an early spring burn it erupted in rich masses of great gayfeather that we couldn't have believed if Carl Kurtz hadn't photographed it.

In Green County, Wisconsin, there's a place called "Shooting Star Hills" — a small tract of rather undistinguished ground that had never been plowed or heavily grazed. Still, there had apparently been enough interference to weaken the native prairie species there, and the little area had been overwhelmed with exotic weeds from adjacent farms. It was acquired by The Nature Conservancy, and in early spring it was carefully fired by University of Wisconsin ecologists. The results were surprising and spectacular; invading plants were either killed outright or fatally retarded, and by August the place was vivid with native flowers that had been thought to be extinct there.

It's not surprising that native prairie forbs are usually perennials and the shallow-rooted annual aliens have such a hard time invading established prairie. The competition with native perennials that sap upper-level moisture supplies is problem enough, but prairie fire can be deadly to an alien invader with no underground reserves. Most introduced farm weeds are annuals that can swiftly occupy lesions in native prairie and flourish temporarily on gopher mounds, neglected plowing, and other disturbed areas. But tough and adventurous as they are, they're unable to prevail in any fight in which native prairie species have frequent fire as an ally.

❧

The leaves, stems, flowers, fruits, and roots of many prairie forbs had colorful pioneer uses — some genuine, some imaginary.

The horse Indians used to feed their ponies the rootstocks of blazing-star to increase speed and endurance. The roots of butterfly milkweed were sometimes used as an emetic, and as a treatment for pleurisy — thus the term "pleurisy root."

Pasqueflower, for a similar reason, was called "headache root." Wild indigo was sometimes used as a cathartic and emetic. The roots of black samsom yield the drug *echinacea,* which is a stimulant and diaphoretic, and the roots of New Jersey tea contain *ceanothin,* which promotes blood clotting in wounds. The rhizome and root of the yellow lady's-slipper orchid contain tiny quantities of a material that has been used as an antispasmodic and a mild nervous stimulant. Some larkspur seeds contain materials that were used as mild insecticides and were said to destroy body parasites. Yarrow was another old wound-cure, and its technical name *Achilles* derives from the legend that Achilles first discovered this use.

In the rude pharmacopoeia of the prairie wilderness, some of these uses were of real effect. And even in cases where a forb's medicinal value was largely imaginary, the pioneer might not have done much better if he'd been back home in Old York State. You simply made do, and died if it weren't enough, and even the bitter tea of some obscure rootstock might alleviate helpless despair if nothing else.

But aside from plowing and potions, we wonder what the flowering prairie meant to those who found it in virgin fullness — those half-desperate sodbusters and their worn drabs who were committed to survival in a land that they scarcely understood.

We can never know. Many of the florid descriptions of summer prairies were affected exercises in letter-writing, or done by promoters making capital of any resource that the prairie offered. To the earliest prairie settlers, the wild gardens may have been just another face of the same old enemy, and such people would take little serious interest in anything that couldn't be reduced to granary, smokehouse, root cellar, or mill. Theirs was a hard mission, and they surely reserved their real admiration for cleanly broken ground with crops and livestock safely under fence.

Yet, even then, a man or woman would have had to be

blind to not see the doomed beauty of a summer prairie. And in the pride and hope of cutting a long, arrow-straight furrow through flowering sod, was there ever regret for tearing up a patch of blazing-star or burying a bright bed of prairie phlox? There's no doubt that there were a few men who had learned to love the wild face of what they were destroying, and some of them reserved little patches of prairie that they would never plow. They might rationalize this as "jest savin' some good hay ground," but would defend it from land-hungry grandsons with a vehemence out of all proportion to any hay value. Such old-timers would probably never admit that they liked to walk over ground that was still the way they'd first found it, when they were young and strong and the land was too. The first prairie farmers never forgot that they were the first, and they never got over the fierce pride of it, and a few of them kept little scraps of their original homesteads as other men keep war medals.

But the deeper feeling for flowered prairie must have been held by the women. They were not doing direct battle with the land as their men were, and they surely had a gentler vision and an abiding hunger for "somethin' nice." In the attic corners of old farmhouses there may yet be pictures that grandma made with dried prairie flowers, and a yellowing volume of a county history may hold a pressed gentian — still showing traces of prairie sky.

A friend once told me of meeting an old lady who had spent her childhood on a prairie farm. One of her midsummer chores was bringing her grandmother a perfect wild orchid each morning. A fleeting vignette, but one revealing a gallant and sensitive woman determined to have beauty in a harsh daily grind. What was her legacy to that granddaughter? A Rocky Mountain quilt, maybe, or a prized spool bed brought all the way out from Lancaster. And certainly, and best, a sense of beauty that remained dew-fresh and blooming after nearly eighty years.

The flowered pageant of summer prairie gentled the grass-lands, and must have helped gentle the lives of those who shared it. And as often as not, it even passed a final benediction.

Of all the relict prairies I've known, none was as poignant as the scrap I found years ago in the center of an intensely farmed Iowa land section. It was a small, lost graveyard, all that remained of a tiny settlement that had been almost wiped out by diphtheria. About a dozen weathered stone markers leaned and lay in a patch of original bluestem. Among the graves were those of a young mother and her children, and when I found the place in late summer their graves were set about with a few tall magenta torches of blazing-star, stateliest of the prairie flowers. It was part of an original place and time, and held fitting memorials. There were flowers of gayfeather to lift the spirits of beauty-starved women. There was bluestem for the men, for their wild hay and prairie-chicken hunting. For the children there was compass-plant, with its wonderful chewing gum, and wild strawberries hidden in the grass.

That patch of tall prairie was a more enduring memorial than the stones that stood there, and infinitely more appropriate. Today, our memorials reflect our values, and we will probably be interred in manicured "memory gardens," our graves decked with plastic blossoms that are imitations of tameness.

And that, too, may be appropriate.

5

Prairyerths

IN *Huckleberry Finn*, Mark Twain has the Child of Calamity sitting there on the raft and telling about rivers. Not just any rivers, but the clear Ohio that drained the timbered country and the muddy Mississippi that drained all that prairie country. The Ohio just had no body to it at all, compared to the Mississippi, which was good, thick, nutritious water and if a man drank it he "could grow corn in his stomach if he wanted to." The Child of Calamity knew this, because:

> "You look at the graveyards; that tells the tale. Trees don't grow worth shucks in a Cincinnati graveyard, but in a Sent Louis graveyard they grow upwards to eight hundred foot high. It's all on account of the water the people drunk before they laid up. A Cincinnati corpse don't richen a soil any."

The Mississippi is all that nutritious because it drains such mighty nutritious land — and even carries some of that land along with it just to keep its strength up. It's land that the prairie farmers have always bragged on, and they still yarn about it. Herb Shriner used to say that folks around his part of Indiana weren't much worried about the Bomb. They figured that any bomb dropped on Indiana wouldn't do much but just lay there and grow. That's what everything else did.

And just about everything should — for anything planted

in the deep mellow prairieland lies in some of the richest soil ever known, a bank of incredible fecundity that produces nearly half the world's corn, much of the wheat and soybeans, and a billionweight of meat each year, and radiates a deep and steady power that helps drive the work of a half-billion people. The energies of our other black fuels, coal and oil, are rather modest, short-term sources of power when compared to the great black loams of the American midlands.

❧

Prairie loams, like all their poorer relatives, spring from ancestral materials that are derived from rock.

One of the commonest parent materials is loess, the rock flour that was ground in the mills of the Pleistocene ice-rivers and left behind in outwash deposits. Fine-grained and light, it was easily picked up by wind as aeolian dust and often blown great distances before being dropped in beds that sometimes grew hundreds of feet thick during centuries of sheet erosion.

Named for the Loess district of Germany where it was first studied, and pronounced "luss," it has few peers as a soil base — light, fine-grained, and containing a complex wealth of plant nutrients whose major component is often calcium carbonate. It's odd stuff with a strange ability to stand in smooth vertical banks when cut by road-building machinery, although it loses this ability once it is disturbed, loosened, and piled elsewhere. At first glance it may appear to be just another clay cutbank, but its fine texture, lightness, and high permeability by water are unlike any clays.

Airborne loess was often trapped by elevations and wooded streambanks that ran generally north and south at right angles to the prevailing westerlies, and the deepest deposits are usually along such west-facing streamsides. This is the material comprising many of the eastern shoulders of midwestern rivers — and forms the "west coasts" of Wisconsin, Illinois, and Iowa. The timbered loess ridges above some prairie streams were called "white oak soil" in the early days of settlement and were eagerly sought and cultivated. It was fertile land and easily tilled, but tended to "wear out fast" — a character probably due to reduced soil humus under trees, and the high permeability of the loessian base that allowed organic nutrients to leach rapidly away.

Loess is probably the most extensive parent material under the world's northern prairies, with glacial till ranking second in importance. Ranking still lower in order of importance are silt deposits from streams and ancient lakes, wind-and-water-laid sands, soft shales, and sandstones.

Glacial till is the vast load of rock debris brought down

from the north and dumped in great beds and moraines. Much of the northern prairie today is underlain with this unreconstructed glacial drift — broad deposits of boulders, gravels, sands, cobble, and clay that may average one hundred and fifty feet thick, often penetrated by ground waters that run in deep, cold aquifers. Over much of this lies the mantle of loess, a coverlet of rich windblown dusts that varies from a depth of a few inches to more than three hundred feet.

Through the millennia, some upper portions of this glacial transport have weathered and broken down into component minerals. Soil formed from glacial drift is likely to be much better than that derived from native bedrocks, for the till has more soluble mineral matter for available plant food and contains a great variety of rocks with a corresponding variety of minerals. Prairies south of the glaciated regions may be formed from unconsolidated rock debris broken away from the bedrock beneath, but such native bedrocks seldom possess the varied mineral abundance found in the glacial drifts. No prairie soils are formed from granite bedrock — nor from any other extremely hard rock, for that matter.

The degree of this glacial wealth depends on many things, such as its proximity to the farthest advances of the glacial lobes and the length of time since glaciation. The more recently glaciated the prairie region and the "newer" its parent materials, the more likely it is to be rich in available minerals. This can be seen in the "black prairie" of northern Illinois that was covered by the last stages of glaciation. Farther south, in Illinois's "gray prairies" where glaciation occurred much earlier, rain and snowmelt have had much more time to leach drift minerals from the soil.

The abundance and variety of available minerals in the most recently glaciated regions exert strong influences on the production of certain plants and animals — the ring-necked pheasant, for example.

In the Midwest, the most successful introductions of ring-necked pheasants have been generally within the boundaries of the Wisconsin glaciation that brought immense loads of pulverized limestone from the Manitoba region. The gaudy ring-neck apparently depends on the existence of readily available calcium carbonate in the northern prairie soils. More than most native gamebirds, the imported pheasant feeds heavily on corn and other plants that have relatively low calcium content, and the pheasant's diet may meet only about half of its calcium needs. The rest must be met by calcareous grit or calcium-rich soils; indeed, a ring-neck's choice of grit appears to depend first on the need for calcium and secondly on the need for grinding materials.

Although there are native limestones and limestone soils far south of the pheasant's primary range, the calcium in these materials may be chemically locked with such elements as magnesium, and may not be physiologically available to the pheasants. This is not the case in the most recently glaciated regions, where calcium is likely to be readily available both physically and physiologically.

That's only one theory for the mysterious northern limitation of the ring-neck and there are a number of exceptions to it, but the fact remains that the pheasant is most prosperous on the prairie soils of the Dakotas, Nebraska, southern Minnesota, northern Illinois, and Iowa — all of which lie within the southerly extensions of the last glaciation.

※

Out of the raw, lifeless stuff brought by glaciers and winds, rich soils were slowly formed in a complex melding of organic and inorganic agents that was monitored by the master hand of climate.

Although the prairie climate is called "temperate," it has strongly defined seasons that swing from intemperate cold to blazing heat, from periods of prolonged rainfall to times of acute drought — including the ultimate drought of fire that regularly swept the tall prairie and instantly mineralized its produce. The prairie soils that were built under tallgrasses are distinct from those of most other grasslands, largely because of temperature and precipitation ratios that produced immense tonnages of organic materials and reduced those materials to humus and component minerals in a wonderfully controlled, balanced conversion.

As the base materials were broken down, the invading grasses began their long work of modifying and infusing them with organic richness. Grasses and other herbaceous plants moved in on the parent materials, the dense matrices of their roots and rootlets locking the mineral soils into place. Roots grew, spread, penetrated, and died. Their remains were attacked by fungi, bacteria, earthworms, millipedes, and the myriad small animals that live in soil, breaking down the organic materials and converting dead plantstuffs to organic humus.

Burrowing animals and worms stirred the young soil, moving and mixing it in prodigious quantities and further enriching it with their own remains. Surface litter was broken

down by unhurried decay during periods of warmth and moisture when bacteria flourished. Deeper-rooted grasses and forbs sent their underground parts into the rich mineral subsoils, bringing more nutrients to the surface where they were released from the plants by decay, fire, and the feeding of animals.

It was a slow beginning that gained momentum, the pioneering grasses and forbs pouring their life forces into the mineral soils for centuries, gradually establishing an equilibrium between bacteria and other organisms and the plants themselves. It was the recruiting of an infinitely complex work force, and once that work force was organized the soil formation proceeded apace. Accumulations of organic soils deepened and richened until a maximum content of organic material was established. This often required hundreds of years, eventually leveling off in a rough balance between the formation of soil humus and its breakdown into mineral matter.

For a long time it was a process of net gain to the developing prairies, with plants returning more to the maturing soils than they were taking. Year after year, the prairie substrate's rich mineral matter was further modified and charged with organic energy.

The minerals provided the basic building materials for the new soil, with the sun pouring radiant energy into plant tissues that combined the simple minerals into complex organic compounds — waxes, resins, fats, sugars, proteins, starches, and cellulose. In time, all would be food for the biomass above the ground, and for the swarming host of microflora and microfauna that lived below. The organic substances synthesized by the plants through photosynthesis and absorption would undergo a total return to their mineral ancestry — the process of mineralization that is the ultimate fate of any plant.

The world of the prairie grassroots is a teeming lifeswarm.

One gram of loam from the surface of fertile prairie may contain as many as 2,000,000 protozoans and 58,000,000 bacteria on which some of those protozoans feed. Of the biological and physical agents that shape and influence prairie, none is greater than the least — the soil bacterium.

Among the key groups of these bacteria are those that convert nitrogen compounds to forms usable by plants. Nitrogen is an essential element of plant cell protoplasm and is vital to vigorous plant growth, but since plants are unable to take free nitrogen from the air they must rely on nitrogenous compounds absorbed from the soil. Nitrates are being constantly lost by leaching and absorption in plant tissues, and their constant renewal is essential to the prairie community. Bacteria provide that renewal. There are some species that can take free nitrogen from the air and combine it in organic compounds. Others can oxidize the ammonia that is liberated during the breakdown of plant proteins — a process of ammonification that produces nitrates useful to plant metabolism. Still other soil bacteria are capable of fixing nitrogen in the root nodules of certain plants, notably legumes, and such bacteria and their hosts are of huge importance to prairie balance and fertility.

Because of bacteria the prairie's upper solum is a region of dynamic processes, a tension zone of life forces doing herculean labors that result in deposits of the dark, amorphous, organic residues known generally as "humus."

This material is a warehouse of mineral plant nutrients tied up in organic debris in all stages of decay — a rich compost that may hold from sixty to three hundred tons of organic carbon per acre, with six to thirty tons of nitrogen and about the same amount of various mineral nutrients. Heavy content of organic humus is largely responsible for the dark-brown, almost black color of typical northern prairie soils. Although any dark soils are generally regarded as highly productive, this isn't always true. Darkness may be due to some mineral, or to inadequate drainage in humid regions. But in the northern prairies, darkness of soil usually signifies a high content of humus that is laden with such nutrients as nitrogen and calcium.

Humus conserves basic plant nutrients and also regulates their release to plants — slowly metering them out in available forms. In young, growing prairie soils, it tends to accumulate faster than it is broken into its mineral parts. But as soil develops maturity, a stability is reached in which new humus is formed no faster than the older humus is mineralized; from then on, the two processes of humification and mineralization are likely to proceed at more or less equal rates depending on rainfall, temperature, and other factors, and the soil is said to have reached equilibrium with its climate.

A rich reserve of plant nutrients in humus form is characteristic of temperate climates where the rate of plant decomposition is relatively slow and measured, permitting accumulation of humus. Grassland soils in cool regions have more organic matter than those in warmer climates. From south to north, the nitrogen and organic matter within grassland soils is likely to double or even treble with each 18° F decrease in average annual temperature. And within regions of equal annual temperatures, nitrogen and organic content of grassland soils increases with rises in humidity. North Dakota soils almost invariably have more humus and nitrogen than east Texas soils under similar annual rainfall, and eastern parts of the tall prairie are likely to have more humus and nitrogen than drier westerly prairies that lie in the same general temperature belt.

The ultimate in humification can be seen in certain cool, wet regions where organic matter is produced so much faster than it decays that deep peat beds are formed, and semidecomposed plant materials are held in limbo. The other extreme is in tropical forests with such a high, constant rate of decomposition that little, if any, true humus is formed. Some of these low-humus soils may be fertile, but they lack reserves. And without a warehouse of humus to conserve and meter nutrients back into the soil, their fertility is often short-lived.

Ideal humus balance exists in the temperate tallgrass prairies, with production and destruction functioning in a smooth and fertile cycle. Yet, even in the heart of the tall prairies there are low-humus soils that differ greatly from the grassland soils around them.

The alluvial soils of some prairie bottomlands are rich enough — usually fertile silt underlaid with sand and gravel — but this fine-grained silt is often solidly packed by the frequent flooding that also washes away accumulations cf dead tree leaves that are the only real source of humus in such places. This silty soil is likely to be heavy and poorly aerated as well, and too wet for ants and earthworms that might otherwise stir it and lighten its structure, giving the soil coarser texture and more pore space for air. Heavy alluvial silts may grow huge, soft-wooded bottomland trees but do not usually produce heavy stands of grasses and forbs.

A prairie region's forest soils differ from those of adjacent grassland largely because of the types of organic matter produced by trees and grasses, and the distribution of that material. The total plant production of a patch of hardwood forest and an equivalent stand of tall prairie may be remarkably similar — the difference exists in the location of plant matter. In forest, most of the plant community's weight is aboveground, or rather evenly divided between earth and air. In prairie, the great bulk and weight of organic materials are buried.

An acre of oak timber in southern Wisconsin may raise ninety tons of dry plant weight above the surface of the land, with another eighty tons of organic materials in the top forty-two inches of soil. A nearby acre of tall prairie may have only three tons of standing grass, but there may be several more tons of grass litter on the surface and another 150 tons of organic material in that top 42 inches of soil. And in terms of fertile depth, it's no contest. For even though a particular forest soil may have good proportions of humus and nitrogen, these are likely to be concentrated in the extreme upper level of the soil horizon. Virgin prairie soils are several feet deep, with high levels of nutrients and a wealth of organic stuff all the way down to the subsoils.

This superficial character of a forest soil's organic content is due to the fact that nearly all a forest's annual return of organic materials to the soil is a surface process. Dead leaves, twigs, branches, and fragments of bark lie on the ground where they combine with mosses, ferns, lichens, and a few grasses and forbs to eventually form the soft, yielding "mold" of the forest floor. Nothing much is going on at lower levels to enrich and lighten the mineral subsoils; organic residues resulting from deep, rotting tree roots are only a small part of the annual residue of forest life. And although all tree roots eventually die and return their components to the soil's mineral bank, such roots are too widely distributed at all levels in the soil to develop a zone of concentrated richness.

In contrast, the roots of grasses are packed into the upper soil levels in dense organic masses, and their decomposition distills and re-distills fertility where it can be easily exploited by successive plants, animals, and man. A forest's richest soil may be little more than leaf-layer deep, while the basic fertility of balanced prairie is of uniform richness extending as deep as the root systems of the grasses, and beyond. The amount of true humus in a forest soil may vary from 20 to 50 tons per acre; an acre of nearby prairie may have 250 tons of humus.

Grasses return huge quantities of dead organic materials to the top levels of prairie soil each year, for the roots of grasses decay rapidly. Dead switch grass and needlegrass roots are almost entirely decomposed within three years. The roots of big bluestem and Indian grass decay somewhat less rapidly and may still show some tensile strength after three years, but their rate of decay is far faster than that of tree roots. In western Iowa and eastern Nebraska, even the relatively long-lived big bluestem may annually contribute over 500 pounds of raw organic material per acre to the top six inches of prairie soil. In one year, decaying roots and surface litter of all kinds may add up to 900 pounds of organic matter per acre to the entire soil profile of a prairie.

However, prairie-like soils may develop under hardwood forests that have large earthworm populations. The worms help stir leaf parts and leaf mold much deeper into the soil than those materials could normally penetrate, giving the soil properties similar to those caused by decaying grass roots. But even then, the grass soils are likely to be superior. There is usually a higher percentage of mineral plant nutrients in the organic remains of grass than in those of forestlands. For every ton of dry matter produced, grasses return more calcium, potassium, and other bases to the soil than do trees.

Because of its short growth cycle and annual renewal, prairie soil has a quality of eternal youth. It is difficult to say how "old" a prairie soil may be. In one sense it may be incredibly ancient; in another sense, it celebrates an infinite series of first birthdays. However, the soil of a glaciated northern prairie may stabilize its plant production, humification, and mineralization in three hundred years or less.

There has been a tendency among some workers to regard prairie soil as a natural body that was once young and growing, and then passes through a period of maturity into a long and gradual aging process. They point out that a soil's mineral content is sure to be depleted during long centuries of leaching rain, and chemical processes form subsoil clays that tend to impede a free exchange between ground water supplies and surface plants. But other pedologists are inclined to regard prairie as an open system in which soil forms, matures, and continues in an equilibrium almost indefinitely under an unchanged climate.

※

Soil classification is heavy going, and this is probably as much as you'll ever want to know about it. It's damsure as much as I ever want to write about — especially after pondering the most recent system of American soil classification. In that system, prairie soils are generally lumped under "Mollisols," taken from the Latin term *mollis*, meaning "soft." In the older system, most of the tall prairie's northern soils were classed as Brunizems and Chernozems — with the Brunizems found in the more humid easterly portions of the tall prairie and the Chernozems in the somewhat drier western parts, then grading off into the paler soils of the Great Plains. These are Russian terms, by the way, dating back to the first soil-classing system made near the turn of the century. It was probably necessary that we develop an American name system, for many of our native soils are unique and should bear their own identities. But in a stroke of scientific shorthand, the soils of our central grasslands are sometimes called simply "prairyerths." For our purposes, as good a term as any.

The prairyerths that many of us still regard as "Brunizems" are those of the eastern parts of tall prairie that receive over 25 inches of precipitation annually. Both soil surface and parent materials are usually moist. The upper part of the soil, or "A horizon," is often about eighteen inches deep, rich in humus, and has a granular structure. The subsoil, or "B horizon," usually extends down to about three feet below the surface and may have a relatively high clay content. In the heart of the Cornbelt, the Brunizem soil type reaches from the prairie peninsula westward through Iowa and into eastern Nebraska and the eastern Dakotas, where it begins to be replaced by the other major prairyerth, the class of Chernozems.

These are soils developed under less than 25 inches of rainfall each year. Quite similar to their neighbors just to the east, they are neutral or slightly alkaline with a limey layer of carbonate salts concentrated several feet deep at the lower limit of water penetration — a situation that develops because generally not enough rainfall penetrates the soil profile. Water falling on such land picks up solutes of calcium carbonate, penetrates the soil, and finally peters out at that point in the subsoil where the water has begun to evaporate back into soil air or has been picked up by plant roots.

In contrast, precipitation in the eastern reaches of the tall prairie provides enough water each year to pass entirely through the soil profile, and Brunizem soils are slightly acid and have lost some of their original calcium carbonate content through the leaching of heavier annual rainfall. As a result, the Chernozems of Nebraska are inherently more fertile than the Brunizems of northern Illinois — but not much. Any differences are almost negligible in terms of crop production, for the higher rainfall on the somewhat leached Brunizems is more favorable to agriculture than the lesser rainfall on the relatively unleached Chernozems. It's largely academic; both of these tallgrass prairyerths are immensely fertile, and each is superbly endowed by climate and topography to produce high yields of meat and grain.

☙

In terms of plant production, and particularly crop production, the basic productivity of soil is only partly a matter of fertility and available minerals. It is also a matter of soil structure, or "tilth," and the balanced humus content of the true prairyerths combines with humid and subhumid climate to impart a finely granular, crumblike structure to the soil, with high porosity and much space for air and water vapor. Easily penetrated by plant roots, the humus-filled, granular soils of the tall prairie may be only 50 percent soil by actual volume — the rest consists of pore space. Since the content of soil humus in the upper level of a mature prairie may range as high as 10 percent and since half of the soil volume is pore space, only about 40 percent of that prairyerth is composed of relatively solid parent materials and mineralized soil.

This gives virgin prairie soil a soft, almost fluffy character. Springy and light, it never packs under heavy rains because the humus content is highly absorbent but relatively insoluble. A man jumping off a haywagon onto virgin prairie sod may see the tremor of the impact for several feet around, and you easily notice this soft resilience while you walk across native prairie. Even if the prairie has been burned and all surface litter removed, it feels somewhat the same underfoot as if you were walking on the carpet of a pine forest. By comparison, the black loams of adjacent cornfields are heavy and solid. Much of their original humus content has vanished. A cubic foot of long-farmed prairie soil may weigh almost twice as much as that soil originally did.

Humus is the self-perpetuating reserve of the great prairyerths. Let black prairie be invaded by trees, and this equilibrium begins a reversal because the annual increment of humus resulting from the rapid turnover of plant parts no longer exists, or is greatly reduced. The same thing can happen under a relentless agriculture, even though crop roots are left in the soil and some upper plant parts are regularly plowed under. It doesn't usually happen fast, for prairie soils are strong. But for all their strength, they cannot survive indefinitely if the great natural processes that formed them are entirely suspended.

In central Missouri, a tract of undisturbed prairie soil was once compared to an adjoining field that had been cropped with small grains for sixty years. Little erosion had occurred in that cropland, but 38 percent of the organic material in the soil had been lost. The field soils were heavier and more compacted than those of the neighboring prairie, a density that hampered circulation of soil moisture and soil air, hindered the soil's role in plant nutrition, and made actual tillage more difficult. In a little over half a century of grain farming, more than one third of the organic matter in the upper soil — representing centuries of accumulation — had been destroyed.

Basic fertility is also sapped, although the sturdy prairyerths are likely to remain productive long after lesser soils are exhausted. Come to think of it, I can't remember any large quantities of commercial fertilizer being applied to the cornlands around home until after World War II. Up until then, most of the fertilizer put into corn ground consisted of livestock manure and some limes and phosphates. But the synthetic, high-powered fertilizers were on their way — superphosphates began to appear in about 1948, and were soon followed by almost universal use of liquid anhydrous ammonia and specialized commercial fertilizers that sometimes contained trace elements. It was inevitable change. Unlike a horse, what a tractor takes from the soil it never gives back.

❦

Speaking of soils and men, most of the prairie farmers I've known have been cautious, conservative types who know that even a gift horse can kick. They aren't likely to offend the fates with premature rejoicing about anything, if you follow me. Although the very nature of their calling stamps them as optimists, they reflect a quiet pessimism and feel that just when things seem to be going best is when they're most likely to start going wrong — especially if the legislature is in session. It's summed up pretty well by the story of the Iowa farmer who hit everything just right one year, but seemed glum. A friend asked him:

"What's ailin' you, anyway? You had your biggest corn crop ever, sold most of it for the highest price you ever got, and fed the rest to cattle and hogs that brought top market. What does it take to make you happy?"

"Mebbee that's all so," said the farmer, "but think of what it must have took out of the soil."

Like most anecdotes meant to illustrate regional character, that has a core of truth. Many of the men born and rooted to prairie soil have an abiding concern for it, and often burn with sullen resentment as they see old family farms being consolidated into cash-grain factories owned by absentee investors who, like their great machines, take much from the land but return little. As one old farmer told me: "The family farmhouses around here are gittin' so damned far apart that we've had to start keepin' our own tomcats!"

Such farmers have never read Gibbon and would scoff at being compared to the hardy Roman centurions of the Punic Wars — a period when much of the raw vitality of the early Empire flowed into the legions from small family farms.

Nor have they read of how the tie between Rome and the land came to be broken, when the landowners moved into cities and farmed *in absentia* with slaves and bailiffs and regarded the soil as something to be drained of revenue. The old wellsprings of strength, emanating from the home soils and the men who grew there, waned and vanished as those men lost their roots. It was not the heartland soils of the Roman Empire that failed, but the men who farmed them. Which is something that the farmers of our own heartland needn't read about to understand.

6

A Prairie Bestiary

As THE OLD TROPICAL FORESTS of the Tertiary Period shrank under a cooling, drying climate, the land opened to the sky. It was a new beginning — climate was shaping the great grasslands and savannahs, which in turn began to shape new plants and animals.

The grasses that replaced the Tertiary forests were better adapted than trees to cooler, drier conditions, to more extreme temperature changes, and to winds of the opening landscapes. Furthermore, they did not lock up nutrients in woody, inedible cellulose, but offered nourishment in both leaves and stems, as well as in seeds that were remarkable bundles of superbly balanced nutrition. All of this was easily available, and the great pastures began to draw plant-eaters out of the shrinking forests and into the open, followed by a multitude of creatures that shared their prosperity.

Among these were certain primates. The one that would evolve into man had its origins in forest, but it was in the opening grasslands that the animal was to be refined, forced to stand more erect in order to see better, and put its hands and brain to new uses.

Prehuman *Australopithecus*, in the broad savannahs of south and east Africa, had already learned to supplement his diet with meat — and the great herds of grass-eaters must have been immensely attractive to the agile, erect little primate. He left his larger cousin *Paranthropus* grubbing toward extinction at the forest's edge, and moved out into the open. He grew there, his wits incessantly sharpened by hunting, and put down the roots of his cultural beginnings. The Old World's grasslands gave man the ancestors of his domestic stock — cows, horses, sheep, camels, and dogs. In grassy lowlands he would find the big-fruited grasses that were ancestors of his modern grains. The grasslands and their tantalizing horizons led him wandering, to populate the earth as he followed the wild herds.

The importance of grassland to us may be overstated here; it certainly is oversimplified. Yet, our origins did coincide with grass. We are products of convulsion, born to an era of geologic and climatic turmoil — and so was grass. We have returned to the forest sometimes, to live there for long periods, but it was open country that first shaped us as humans, and it has been in open country that we have advanced. Our progress seems to lag in pure forest, to resume only when that forest is opened up and the sky let in. Our genesis was in grassland; perhaps our Garden of Eden was prairie.

❦

The grassland shaped many creatures besides man, giving them the indelible stamp of open country. It molded their teeth, eyes, legs, and life patterns, often in subtle and special ways. Adapting to light, space, and distance, they grew bolder in the bold realm of openness.

Some became runners, specialists in moving swiftly and easily on firm open ground. The horse is a grasslands development, with lungs, legs, and heart developed by open country, its teeth adapted to grinding grasslike foods. A classic example of another grasslands runner is our pronghorn antelope, molded in North American grasslands. On slender, laminated leg bones that are stronger than a cow's, with shock-absorbing hooves, a heart twice as large as a sheep's and a trachea larger than man's, the little goat-antelope runs with mouth open, drinking the wind at sixty miles per hour — the swiftest hoofed animal in the world.

The open grassland gave some creatures speed. It also sharpened eyes. Visibility is high in the open country, and the visual acuity of its animals is often developed accordingly. The little diggers of prairies and plains are neither swift nor large, but they make the most of what they have. All ground squirrels of the American grasslands share the "outlook" habit of sitting upright in order to broaden their field of vision. The little thirteen-striped spermophile takes its common name of "picket-pin" from this, posing as rigidly erect as the stake to which a plainsman tethered his horse. The same erect sentry habit occurs in grassland rodents in all open parts of the world, such as the tarbagan of central Asia and the viscacha of South America.

Prairie mammals have certain characters that are trademarks of the open country. A forest mammal may or may not share some of these. But if a mammal was born to the grassland life, it is certain to have two or more of these traits: the ability to burrow, sharp long-range vision, swift movement, tawny coloration, largely plant-eating habits, the ability to do without much water, and the likelihood that the main daily activity is in early morning, evening, or even at night.

The stamp is just as strong on the grassland's birds. The songs of prairie birds are usually clearer and louder than their forest cousins'. Their long-range vision is keen, they are able to endure intense heat and lack of water, and they can live and fly in strong winds.

Typical forest birds rarely sing from the wing; they sing from perches. Grassland birds commonly sing from the air, for there is little other choice. The prairie horned lark, lark bunting, lark sparrow, bobolink, meadowlark, dickcissel, and

several longspurs all sing while flying. Only about 20 percent of the forest birds build nests on the ground; about two thirds build nests in standing or fallen trees. But over half of our typical grasslands birds build nests on or near the ground, and a third of all prairie birds use low shrubs or weeds for nesting.

There's another thing about open-country creatures: their tendency to congregate in large life groups. Not all do; some are loners. But the most spectacular massing of North American mammals occurs in open country: the bison and antelope herds that numbered millions of individuals, and such prairie dog towns as the rodent megalopolis that sprawled across the high plains of Texas in a band 100 miles wide and 250 miles long.

The deeper the forest, the more mammals seem inclined to go it alone. Animals of forest and forest edge — such as the white-tailed deer — are likely to congregate not from any social urge, but because they are drawn together in a limited habitat such as a wintering yard. This may be true of some prairie creatures as well, but the fact remains that most forest mammals are not inclined to group together, while bison, antelope, elk, and prairie dogs are.

The flocking habits of prairie and forest birds show some contradiction. Such forest birds as the Carolina parakeet and passenger pigeon flocked in huge numbers, while many prairie birds — especially the passerine or "songbirds" — pursue a rather solitary life. Yet, the greatest flocking among American birds is likely to be in open country. The prairie chicken is a flocking bird; its forest analog, the ruffed grouse, is inclined to be solitary. This flocking character is even more marked among waterfowl, cranes and shorebirds that are chiefly citizens of open-country wetlands, and not even the passenger pigeons matched their numbers.

It seems to resolve to this: The original forest was the home of a multitude of individuals. The great open grassland was the home of individual multitudes which, in the aggregate, was an American biomass that was staggering by forest standards.

❧

The tallgrass prairie was a great faunal crossroads — the eastern limit of some wildlife species, the western limit of others.

There was no sharp break between the great deciduous forests and the edge of the North American grasslands. The Prairie Peninsula drove deep into the East, and outriders of eastern forest ran out into prairie drainage systems as timbered stream valleys, or as islands of woodland deep in the tallgrass country. Neither forest nor grassland ceased abruptly at any special meridian, nor did the creatures indigenous to each.

Far out into the prairie, tongues of prairie forest harbored such eastern forest creatures as the black bear, ruffed grouse, white-tailed deer, eastern wild turkey, and timber rattlesnake. But as the proportion of timber to prairie dwindled, so did those forest species, being replaced by more typical grasslanders such as skunk, coyote, and plains pocket gophers. The prairie forests also held some eastern birds, but as woodland was increasingly overwhelmed by grassland there were more Cerulean warblers, greater prairie chickens, swallow-tailed kites, turkey buzzards, and sandhill cranes.

Much of the intergrading of East and West occurred in the narrow, vital zone between trees and grass.

An axiom in wildlife biology is that the ability of land to support wildlife depends in part on the variety of habitats found there. Biologists use the term *carrying capacity* to describe a place's total life-support capability, and the term *edge effect* describes the influence of vegetative transition on the habitat's total carrying capacity.

A great edge effect was exerted where tallgrass prairie and forest met, and its carrying capacity for many types of wildlife was immense. At the juncture of forest and grass there were long edges of hawthorn and wild plum, sumac, dogwood, snowberry, coralberry, and other shrubs, with rich understories of edible forbs and shade-tolerant grasses. It may have been one of the most productive wildlife habitats in the New World. It swarmed with life. It was home base for great herds of elk that would drift out into the grassland for grazing, drawing back into the woodland in midsummer and winter. For white-tailed deer it must have been paradise; they are most prosperous in edge situations, and they flourished in the browse-rich "brush in the sun" situation presented by the margins of prairie woodlands. Even flocks of prairie chickens, so closely bound to grassland, sought shelter on winter nights in the edges of the woods. It was in these prairie-forest zones that bobwhite quail were found, and countless small mammals. This is where crows lived, and many hawks and owls, nesting just within the trees but foraging out into the open.

In this rich confusion of life there were few distinct "prairie species." Many of the creatures that inhabited tall prairie either extended farther out into the plains or back into the great forests, and sometimes both; but few species were confined to the precise limits of the prairie itself. Environmental conditions of true prairie just weren't different enough from eastern forest or western plain to mold a distinct fauna, although some species such as the greater prairie chicken, the plains pocket gopher, and the bullsnake were probably as "pure" prairie species as it's possible to be.

The division between "eastern" and "western" animals fell somewhere between the 97th and 99th meridians in our central grasslands. Of 73 species of wildlife studied in Oklahoma, 30 percent were distinctly eastern species that reached their western limits there, and 30 percent were western species that reached their eastern limits in Oklahoma. The remaining 40 percent, presumably, were prairie creatures that might drift successfully in either direction.

Our knowledge of this overlap of eastern and western animals in the true prairie is hazy, for the great biomes of forest

and grassland were fragmented long ago and their original
creatures have been shuffled and disrupted. Long before the
bull-tongue plows began breaking prairie sod, there were
breaks in the wildlife populations of the tallgrass country.

❦

For two hundred years the French *coureurs de bois*, with the
help of Indians, had hunted and trapped in the heart of the
tall prairie. By the time the early settlers arrived in Iowa,
most of the otter and beaver had vanished down trade routes
that were old before the first covered wagons appeared. It
was much the same with prairie bison, which were nearly
gone before the first real waves of settlement appeared in the
Midwest.

There's reason to suspect that tallgrass prairie was always
marginal bison habitat, and that the bison had arrived in the
East late and had left early. In all the sites of the early Mound
Builders living east of Illinois, a single thigh bone of a bison
in the top layer of a midden near Muskingum, Ohio, is the
only record of the presence of buffalo. It may not have been
until 1000 A.D. that real buffalo herds appeared east of the
Mississippi.

They were there when the first colonists arrived — no
doubt of that. There were buffalo reported on the banks of
the Potomac in 1639, and frontiersmen crossed the Appalachians into Kentucky's Dark and Bloody Ground on old buffalo roads, such as the one that led through the Cumberland
Gap. Other great buffalo roads pointed into the West — one
ran from the Potomac cross-country to the Ohio River, and
another led into northern Ohio and was eventually followed
by the New York Central Railroad.

There were many buffalo in the Upper Mississippi Valley.
Nicolas de la Salle once reported: "The number of bison is
almost beyond belief. I have seen twelve hundred killed in
eight days by a single band of Savages . . ."

In 1680 he saw the prairie near modern Morris, Illinois, "alive with buffalo." Even today, buffalo sign can be seen in some parts of Illinois as faint wallows and paths through flood-plain forests. Buffalo on the northern and western Missouri prairies were never plentiful, occurring only sporadically even before white settlement. Much of Iowa's prairie — particularly the poorly drained glacial plain in the northern parts of the state — was probably too wet for optimum bison habitat. Although buffalo were hunted in Iowa in the earliest days of settlement, Iowa bison may have drifted farther west before the pioneer era.

In view of what the first settlers found in the tall prairies, early French reports of the abundance of bison have the ring of fiction. Yet, there's no reason why bison shouldn't have done well on true prairie. An acre of such prairie, growing well over a ton of forage per year, could easily have supported a buffalo for two months or more — leading to one estimate that there could have been 12 million buffalo on the original prairie, or one bison on every 20 acres. But if this were true, it was never recorded in later journals. Whatever the pristine abundance of prairie bison, it faded swiftly with the first inroads of settlement.

There were buffalo in the prairie openings of southern Illinois and western Kentucky, and apparently in good numbers. In about 1700 an early French trader named Juchereau set up a trading post and tannery on the north bank of the Ohio River near modern Grand Chain, Illinois, and is said to have collected 13,000 buffalo hides in one year.

This must have meant considerable commercial hunting in that region, for it is doubtful that the few settlers in the trans-Appalachian country of 1700 could have produced 13,000 hides as a by-product of personal meat-hunting. Surely, under the fading rumble of the eastern bison herds, there was a steady clink of pounds sterling and louis d'ors.

Combine the factors of some commercial hunting, growing waves of meat-hungry settlers, and marginal bison range, and the result is a buffalo-empty East.

Eastern bison scarcely survived into the nineteenth century. The last buffalo in Pennsylvania was killed on the final day of the eighteenth century: December 31, 1799. Bison were gone from Ohio by 1802, from Kentucky by 1810, and the last Wisconsin buffalo perished in 1832.

In Illinois there is a persistent legend that most of the herd there was killed by a savage blizzard in about 1775. Maybe. Bison did die in plains blizzards farther west, their magnificent survival equipment notwithstanding, but it seems doubtful that any blizzard in eastern parts of the true prairie could wipe out bison herds on a grand scale — because of the proximity of sheltering timber, if for no other reason. It seems more likely that the easterly bison herds, in spite of their reported "locally large numbers," really existed in a rather fragile relationship with essentially marginal range. And any species on marginal range is far more vulnerable to stress than if at home on its primary range.

The bison's early disappearance from Illinois is probably not due to blizzard so much as to the fact that Illinois buffalo range was bordered and split by three main trading routes that ran down the Upper Mississippi, along the Ohio, and down from the Great Lakes via the Illinois River. These routes all converged at St. Louis, which was a thriving settlement and trade center at the time Illini bison were vanishing.

Elk were more at home east of the Mississippi; originally, they were the most widespread of any American hoofed species. Elk, or more properly "wapiti," thrived in eastern forests and the Prairie Peninsula. If they lasted longer in their eastern range than the bison, it was because they were more successful in the woods. But there was no escape from the swelling tide of settlement and the rifles of hungry pioneers.

The Great American Elk Hunt was the essence of history's

bloodiest hunting spree. Beginning in a little cluster of British colonies on the Atlantic coast, it surged across the continent and recoiled from the Pacific to finally sputter out in a few pockets of Rocky Mountain wilderness over two hundred years later. In New York's Genessee Valley, elk had lingered until about 1847. The last Pennsylvania elk had been killed in 1867 by a Seneca Indian, and the final Tennessee elk was probably killed near Reelfoot Lake in about 1849. Indiana elk vanished as early as 1818.

The end of the Iowa elk came in winter. As prairie settlements grew on the Iowa frontier, so did unrestricted hunting pressure. For deer and elk that was bad enough, but weather dealt the final blow. Big game populations in south-central Iowa had been hard-hit by the blizzards of 1848 and 1849, and the terrible winter of 1856–57 finished deer and elk in northern Iowa — the last stronghold of big game.

Storms had left snow three feet deep in northern parts of the state. There was a slight midwinter thaw and then a cold snap, enabling men and dogs to move easily on the crusted drifts, while elk and deer broke through with their sharp hooves. A pioneer writer left a vivid picture of the slaughter:

> Another lamentable effect of the ice cap of that winter was the cruel and wanton destruction of game. Prior to that season the groves bordering the streams in northern Iowa were well stocked with deer and elk. The ice drove these out from sheltering timber to seek food about the farmers' stacks. Men and boys with guns made savage onslaught on these. The sharp feet of the larger game cut through the ice [crust] and rendered escape impossible. In some instances they were run down by men on foot, with no other weapon than the family butcher knife, which was all too effective.

That winter broke the big game populations in prairie Iowa. Elk were exterminated, deer herds would not be the same again for ninety years, and one of the last buffalo in the region came wandering into the little settlement of Iowa Falls where it was summarily butchered. By the time author Hamlin Garland arrived with his parents to settle in northern Iowa, the prairies there were strewn with the "bleaching antlers of great stags" — a lingering token of game herds that had faded under the merciless combination of pioneer hunting and the worst winter in human memory.

The most spectacular members of the prairie bestiary were shot into oblivion. Others passed more quietly, fading with the original grasslands and vanishing by default rather than human intent. They lingered in widening croplands, their margin of survival shrinking, until they were buried forever by corn and commerce.

❧

As a young man in the early 1880s, my grandfather Eli Posegate made a certain fall journey each year in central Iowa, going from his farm in Story County to the coal fields of Boone thirty miles away.

He and a neighbor would hitch team to wagon and head cross-country along lanes and over unbroken prairie, keeping to high ground as much as possible and avoiding wet swales. It would probably be after corn-picking time when great flocks of prairie chickens traded between the picked fields and their prairie roosts. One man drove while the other walked ahead, shotgun in hand, flushing and shooting prairie chickens on the way. By the time they reached Boone — a mildly notorious railroad town on the main stem of the C&NW — the wagon would have a respectable cargo of prairie hens. These were sold in Boone for as much as 20¢ each, cleaned and dressed, packed in barrels, and shipped east.

The two farmers then drove to the mine, bought as much coal as wagon and team could manage, and headed for home. It was the sort of business deal that my granddad must have

relished: one that entailed a bit of sport, a night in some of
Boone's better watering places, a low initial investment, and
the rich sense of getting something for nothing. And perhaps
knowing, as he toasted his shins at a coal fire, that Diamond
Jim Brady might be eating those prairie hens at Delmonico's.

As the tall prairie filled with settlers, and the first trans-
Mississippi railroads followed, market hunting for prairie
chickens became a useful way to earn a cash dollar — always
a rare commodity to the prairie granger. For a change, it was
apparently a toll that prairie wildlife could afford to pay.
There were countless greater prairie chickens or "pinnated
grouse" on the original prairie, and they increased with the
coming of settlement. They flourished with early farming
that created new habitat types in the original unbroken
grasslands. The birds learned about corn and wheat, and their
food supplies expanded enormously. Yet, enough native
grassland remained for their courtship, nesting, and brood-
rearing.

When Abe Lincoln was learning to split rails, an Illinois
hunter had to hustle to kill a dozen prairie chickens a day.
Forty years later, in the 1870s, a hunter might kill up to a
hundred chickens in a day. Improved shotguns, with choke-
bored, breech-loading barrels, had a lot to do with that. But
it's likely that there were just more prairie chickens. There
were single flocks of hundreds of birds in late fall, swarming
over shocks of corn and even mounting assaults on the corn-
cribs. The typical corncrib of the day was made of willow
poles and thatched with sloughgrass; it was highly pervious
to enterprising prairie hens and some farmers exploited this,
setting big box traps on the roofs of their cribs. A western
Iowa farmer named Jim McGee caught as many as fifty birds
at once. Cleaned and salted, they brought 25¢ each in the
Council Bluffs market.

The greater prairie chicken was a true bird of the tall
grasslands, ranging east in the Prairie Peninsula up to the

wall of forest as far as Ohio. It was a creature of the open, and as Indiana forest was cleared for cropland, the birds spread into entirely new range. Much the same thing happened in Wisconsin and Michigan. The prairie chicken moved north with pioneer lumbermen, taking advantage of openlands that followed the cutting and burning of original forest. Prairie chickens pioneered all the way into Michigan's Upper Peninsula — some three hundred miles north of their former range. At the same time, the birds were prospering in their home country as corn and wheat came to the prairie.

The heyday was brief. In parts of Indiana, Wisconsin, and Michigan, forest succession began to choke some of the newly created prairie chicken range. The birds lingered for years in eastern parts of Michigan's Upper Peninsula, but are now gone. The Illinois prairie chicken peak came shortly after 1860 with an optimum balance of prairie and cultivated land, and the same thing probably occurred in Iowa in the 1880s. As cropland overwhelmed grassland, the pinnated grouse began to fade. A few birds clung to the richest prairie until more than 85 percent of the land was broken into grainfields — surviving in small, isolated bands that eventually vanished.

Remorseless cultivation, coupled with long, deadly hunting seasons, had a cumulative effect on prairie chickens in the richest parts of the true prairie. When Ohio officially closed its prairie chicken hunting in 1903 it was only a formality — the birds were gone. Indiana ended its chicken hunting in 1909, when only a few birds remained along the Kankakee River. Protection helped, for a time. Indiana prairie chickens began to increase again, and by 1912 the population was estimated at over 100,000 birds. That was the highwater mark for Hoosier prairie hens. By 1941 they had dwindled to about a thousand birds, and ten years later Indiana prairie chickens survived in only three counties. By 1969 they were gone.

Farther north, in central Michigan, a handful of prairie

chickens survive on range created by forest cutting, where Michigan's remnant flocks are marooned with no real southern Michigan grasslands to which to return. Wisconsin prairie chickens have been cut back to the middle of the state, to the partly drained Buena Vista and Leola marshes. The only remaining Illinois prairie chickens cling to a few scattered refuges in the southeastern corner of the state — nine flocks given a reprieve by a handful of concerned citizens.

These, then, are the three remaining outposts on the eastern frontier of the greater prairie chicken: Michigan, Wisconsin, and Illinois, with a total of something fewer than 700 surviving birds that are as out of place as wampum on Wall Street. They are relicts that have long outlived the original prairies that brought them into being. They now exist on artificial prairies that are their final strongholds east of the Mississippi — little reliquaries of flocks that once spanned the prairie horizons.

West of the Mississippi, the prairie chicken is almost entirely gone from Iowa. In 1946 there were about two hundred birds in southern Iowa in small flocks or as stray singles. Then the postwar farm economy began to soar toward bigger things than simple prairie chickens, and by the spring of 1956 there was only one report of an Iowa prairie chicken — a single cock bird on the old booming ground south of Corydon.

The birds have lasted in western and southwestern Missouri, where state lands have been held in grass. Today's Missouri prairie chickens may number from 7,000 to 10,000 birds, and are apparently holding their own.

There are still greater prairie chickens in the eastern Dakotas and eastern Nebraska where grasslands persist, and they occur in huntable numbers in the Flint Hills of eastern Kansas — the great prairie ridge that has survived because the soil is too shallow to plow.

There was a winter evening last year in the Flint Hills

when my son Chris, our old friend Bob "He-Dog" Henderson, and I had given up on our coyote hunting and were walking back to the road. It had been a clear day, but the weather was turning and a rising wind cut through the white parkas and numbed our mittened hands. I was walking with head slightly bent — in the rapt introspection that comes with hunger, cold, and a bitter wind in my face — when He-Dog called out: "Look! Heading for timber!"

Above and around us, low over the Kansas prairie, came the flock of prairie chickens. They had started from some high open ridge ahead and were on a long, fast slant toward a belt of creek timber a mile behind us. Alternately beating and gliding, they passed swiftly — the only gallinaceous birds I know that fly so far and fast, flashing downwind toward a haven of dark trees, going to roost on a January evening. Some passed within twenty yards of me and I could hear

wind in their pinions and clearly see the transverse barrings
of brown and white. The flock was lined out, in swift direct
passage, backlit by the last of the winter sunset, clear and
vivid with each feather in sharp focus. Then they were gone.

It is usually so, with prairie chickens and me. Whenever I
see them, on their April dancing-grounds or over winter prairies, they materialize from nowhere and wholly occupy stage
center for a time, then vanish into nowhere again before I
can fix them in my mind so that they will stay. I have
watched them for hours on end, and again for split seconds,
and it is always the same. I think I have them fixed where I
can keep them awhile, but they pass in and out of my aware-
ness like one of those vivid scraps of dreams that are said to
last only a heartbeat.

That is the way it was this day. One instant the winter
prairie had been bleak, iron-hard, and white, lifeless and

without feature. Then it was infused with a wild burst of life and energy that ceased as swiftly as it came. But the wake of its passage remained — as an afterimage of dark speeding birds, and an impression that the prairie was not dead, and never empty, but beating with a pulse that measured other lives than our own.

The pulse beats in all seasons but is loudest in spring, and loudest of all on the age-old dancing-grounds of the prairie chicken. Yet, it is passing strange how few prairie people really know that. When Bob Henderson sets up his plywood blind at the edge of some dancing-ground, in spring, he must sometimes explain that he does so to watch the courting of the prairie chickens. There are old men in the Flint Hills who have lived their lives on the land without seeing this — strangely blind to the rites of April.

Long before full dawn, the male birds begin coming to their dancing-grounds to set up their sharply defined territories and attend to the most urgent affair of their year. Often, but not always, they choose well-exposed ridges, possibly because such places are in short grass and have the best visibility. These are often traditional sites, used spring after spring, possibly for hundreds of years. When there is hardly enough light to see, the males tune up for their main serenade with some routine dancing and booming. By dawn, the first hens demurely pick their way into the booming ground — affecting utter boredom and idly wandering through the ranks of excited, displaying, dancing males.

On each side of the male prairie chicken's neck is a bright orange air sac almost hidden by stiff feathers. During the courting dance, these feathers are raised until they resemble horns — the "pinnae" of the pinnated grouse. The tail of the cock is raised and fanned slightly; his wings spread and cupped. Displaying to the hen, he rushes frantically about, wings spread, head low, tail and pinnae stiffly erect, orange neck sacs inflated and glowing in the early sun, his feet beating staccato on the hard sod. He suddenly stops and utters the hollow howling *whoom-ah-wh-o-om* that can be heard for a mile through the still prairie dawn. Adjacent cocks may begin hopping high into the air, cackling as they jump, to finally join battle on the boundaries of their territories. There are brief, furious fights in which neither bird is really hurt, and then the drumming begins again. In the half-light of an April dawn it is a strange, stirring performance. The Indian, who knew good dancing when he saw it, adopted the grouse dance step for step, posture for posture. He could have done much worse; the prairie chicken is a master choreographer.

Someone wrote that the prairie chicken's booming was of great comfort to the pioneer. I can't imagine why. Many things can be said of prairie chicken noise, but by no measure is it a comforting, civilized sound. It is a lonely, wild sound made by a lonely wild bird. It has the quality of an ancient wind blowing across the smokeflap of a wickiup — companion noise to an Indian courting flute and the drum of unshod pony hooves on bluestem sod. In all of modern America, there is no more lost, plaintive, old-time sound than the booming of a native prairie chicken.

And when it is gone, it shall be gone forever. All our television will not bring it back to us, and none of our spacecraft can take us to where it vanished. It is the last fading voice of the prairie wilderness, echoing after the lost clouds of curlews and plovers, crying farewell.

❧

Ducks and geese are not generally regarded as "prairie birds," but they meet the criteria about as well as any. They existed in incalculable numbers on the rich, wet prairies of the northern Midwest before draglines and clay tiles bled off most of the original prairie waters. Yesterday and today, the northern prairie states and the Canadian prairie provinces are the premium nesting range of North American ducks, geese, and shorebirds.

It was because of the last glaciation, a gargantuan bulldozing that planed the northern prairie regions, scouring and tearing, heaping up vast moraines of ground rock and soil, changing the northern face of a continent. Huge lake basins were torn out of bedrock, and other basins appeared behind the terminal moraines of the glacial lobes. Vast blocks of ice were driven into the glacial debris; left behind by the retreating glaciers, the melting ice blocks formed small lakes, ponds, and "potholes" in a wild assortment of sizes. In the northern Dakotas today, a hundred or more of these basins per square mile are common.

Poorly drained on the level glacial plain, the potholes filled with water. Only a few were fed or emptied by streams; most were filled with snowmelt and rain, and emptied by seepage and evaporation. There were millions of them once, pocking nearly half a million square miles of North America. Most were in southern Canada, but over 60,000 square miles of pothole country lay in the Dakotas, western Minnesota, and northern Nebraska and Iowa.

The prairie potholes, rich in food, nesting sites, and brood cover, were incredibly attractive to waterfowl. And although they have been mercilessly drained and dried, the remnant is still premium waterfowl habitat. The prairie pothole country today includes only ten percent of the available duck-nesting habitat in North America, but produces half of all our ducks.

The original northern prairies were strewn with small lakes, potholes, and marshes and veined with tiny creeks that ran over beds of bright glacial pebbles, hidden beneath arching grasses. Through spring, summer, and fall these regions were darkened with clouds of waterfowl of all kinds. The land teemed with ducks, geese, pelicans, sandhill cranes, whooping cranes, bitterns, egrets, and swans. Shorebirds came in a vast spring tide; in March and April, golden plovers began arriving from Argentina on their way to the arctic, and they would always stop on the prairie. These plovers (settlers called them "prairie pigeons") hunted the burned prairie hillsides for grubs and insect eggs, and the ashy slopes were spangled with moving gold and silver as the great flocks of plovers fed.

Swans and geese arrived in squadrons to graze on new bluestem shoots, and with them came huge, loose wedges of Eskimo curlews, long-billed curlews, and upland plovers. But spectacular as the spring arrivals were, they must have paled before the immense autumn concentrations when staging areas for the fall migrations drew local birds and northern migrants as well, and the great arch of the prairie sky was filled with waterfowl to all horizons.

Old-time Iowa hunters revered the Duck Special, a Northern and Western Railway train that ran between Des Moines and Spirit Lake. It consisted of engine, coach, and a combination baggage car that doubled as a saloon. The old Duck Special was a wildfowler's dream come true. It ran through a hundred miles of wet prairie into northwestern Iowa, through the colorful market-hunting towns of Mallard, Curlew, and Plover. If ducks appeared along the right-of-way, the train was stopped and passengers and train crew alike grabbed their scatterguns and shot holes in the schedule. It sometimes took the Special several days to make a run that can now be traveled in a few hours, and many hunters had all the shooting they wanted before they arrived at Spirit Lake. The conductor of the Special once said that "more ducks was shot at Gun Barrel Slough alone than our engine could have pulled in one load."

Waterfowl still travel the route of the old Duck Special, but the great expanses of wet prairie are gone from Iowa, and waterfowl no longer nest there in real numbers. The migration tides are only trickles now, flying farther and farther north to find dwindling nesting habitat. Yet, there are still some echoes from the old days.

One of these echoes comes in mid-March, when blue and snow geese pour up the Missouri River's valley en route to their nesting grounds in the Hudson Bay country.

They precede the ducks and most Canada geese, advancing in three great waves from their wintering grounds along the Gulf Coast. They leave the balmy marshes of the Sabine and the Chenier du Tigre, fly entirely through spring, and catch up with the last of winter in western Iowa. Their passage is halted by the thirty-degree isotherm, and the birds pile up on the threshold of winter around Forney's Lake, Kellogg Slough, and Lake Manawa, south of Council Bluffs. The entire snow and blue goose migration of central North America may mass in an area ten miles long and a few miles wide, waiting and feeding on new sprouts of winter wheat and waste corn from last fall's harvest.

On the wall beside me, as I write this, is my wife Dycie's painting of massed blue and snow geese against a spring moon. Most people who see it assume that some artistic license was practiced there, but the picture's truth couldn't be greater if it had been a photo. It was as I described it to her, telling of the night when I walked out on a sandspit of the old Plum Creek Washout near the Missouri River, where the sound of geese settling down to sleep was like a distant rumble of white water. I stepped out of concealment and clapped my hands and shouted, commanding the clamor to be silent. It was, for one blank instant, and then a clap of thunder replied and a vast wall of geese eclipsed moon and sky. There was the gusty roar of a hundred thousand wings and the bedlam din of geese rising into the night.

They were gone by late March, as they almost always are. The last barriers of the prairie winter were collapsing, and the ranks of geese advanced north across the Dakotas, over the Canadian wheatlands, and on to the reeking mud flats and barren tundra of Baffin and Southhampton islands. Their coming had been a promise of spring; their departure was a guarantee of it.

❧

The native components of the true prairie included about three hundred species of birds, but the roster was not clear-cut. Over a hundred years of interchange between forest and grassland have shuffled the deck so thoroughly that it is difficult to say: "This bird was of the original grasslands; this one was not." Forests became fields, and the prairie was filling with groves, before modern ornithologists were at work. Richard Brewer, a Michigan biologist, has listed some of the birds that probably characterized the eastern grasslands of 150 years ago. In his estimate, summer birds of the Michigan prairies included the swallow-tailed kite, red-tailed hawk, marsh hawk, sparrow hawk, prairie chicken, bobwhite quail, sandhill crane, upland plover, mourning dove, short-eared owl, nighthawk, short-billed marsh wren, loggerhead shrike, bobolink, eastern meadowlark, dickcissel, grasshopper sparrow, Henslow's sparrow, and the vesper sparrow.

Typical winter birds in Brewer's list are the red-tailed hawk, rough-legged hawk, marsh hawk, sparrow hawk, prairie falcon, bobwhite, mourning dove, snowy owl, short-eared owl, northern shrike, common redpoll, common tree sparrow, Lapland longspur, and the snow bunting.

Some vanished quickly with settlement and landbreaking. The swallow-tailed kite was one, preying on frogs and snakes in the true prairie. As the virgin grasslands vanished under the plow, so did a critical part of its feeding ground. In 1872 a shy, gifted naturalist named Robert Ridgeway visited the Fox Prairie in northern Illinois and wrote:

> As we came well out of the prairie, a beautiful and unlooked-for sight appeared; in short, we were completely transfixed by the to us novel spectacle of numerous exquisitely beautiful swallow-tailed kites floating about on buoyant wings, now gliding to the right or left, then sweeping in broad circles. Soaring lightly above them were many Mississippi kites, of which one would now and then close its wings and plunge downward as if to strike the very earth, but instantly checking the velocity of its fall by sudden spreading of the wings. When two or more passed one another at opposite angles — as frequently happened — the sight was beautiful in the extreme.

Twelve years later Ridgeway visited this prairie again:

The change which had taken place in the interval was almost beyond belief. Instead of an absolutely open prairie some six miles broad by ten in the extreme length, covered with its original characteristic vegetation, there remained only 160 acres not under fence.

The kites had vanished as well.

There were some grasslanders that benefited by the change, however, prospering as the prairie was put to the plow and the nearby forests were cleared. For a time, the greater prairie chickens increased. Horned larks apparently did well, and the savannah sparrow liked the prairie groves. Even the prairie bobolink, in some cases, thrived as native grasslands were broken. But the birds that prospered most were the original birds of forest and edge, extending their ranges far out into regions once forbidden to them.

Some early prairie women sorrowed at leaving their eastern songbirds behind in the forests of the Old States, but this began to change as homestead windbreaks of soft maple, box-elder, and willow matured. The "timber birds" did some pioneering of their own, and joined the settlers out on the prairie. Many prairie-born children could easily remember the first robins that they ever saw — an event marked not only by a brand-new bird, but by the delight of their parents.

One of the prairie originals is the meadowlark — our true American lark — and probably the most abundant songbird on the virgin prairies. Yet, it breasted the transition well, and may be as abundant as ever. There were both eastern and western meadowlarks in the true prairie. They are almost identical, but the western bird sings a longer and more tuneful song than his eastern cousin. It is a freer, wilder song, and what power to evoke memories it has!

Sitting here, gray-haired and Responsible, I can softly whistle the cadence of the western meadowlark and conjure up an instant vision of utter freedom many years ago. A green-gold morning, the dust cool and soft under bare feet and the road running arrow-straight between fencelines shaggy with bluestem. I am 12 years old, rejoicing in the heady miracle of shedding both shoes and school — hurrying toward the Skunk River and into a summer that had six Saturdays in every week. There on the fence, dressed to the nines in gold and black and shouting his howdies to every newly freed schoolboy in Iowa, perched a meadowlark. Inspired, I whistled back. My first try was almost perfect, and I've never forgotten how. The western meadowlark and I sang the same song that morning, and we still do.

I am grateful that the western meadowlark waited for us boys, bridging the time between my granddad's wild prairie and the tame cornfields of my youth. Some of the prairie birds couldn't wait.

I never saw the clouds of long-billed curlews — part of the pure essence of tallgrass prairie. My grandfather's plow and gun did them in long ago. These great curlews, or "sickle-bills" (their curving, seven-inch bills named them), once haunted the true prairie in huge numbers. The largest curlews in the world, they had ceased nesting in Illinois before 1880 and were largely gone from Iowa, Minnesota, and probably eastern Nebraska before the turn of the century. There are still some long-billed curlews in the Great Plains and along the West Coast, but they no longer exist east of the Mississippi. They were prized by gunners and heavily hunted. Although warier than most shorebirds, they were not hard to decoy and their flocks seemed strangely reluctant to leave any downed companions, wheeling over the guns with long legs down.

The smaller Eskimo curlew was hit even harder by early gunning. Called "dough-birds" because of their plumpness, these little curlews were one-pound bundles of sweet, fat flesh. They were shot in huge numbers by prairie hunters who not only sold them, but coveted the birds for their own tables. The fat curlews were commonly preserved by parboiling, then packed in jars or crocks and covered with melted butter or lard. They were easy to shoot; Eskimo curlews could be approached closely on the ground, and often flew over the prairie in massed flocks so dense that a gunner could simply "shoot into the black" and make multiple kills. One early hunter killed thirty-seven dough-birds on the rise with his repeating shotgun — and in such cases a retreating cloud of curlews might drip with wounded birds for half a mile.

There are still sickle-bills in the West and Southwest, but the little dough-birds were part of the Great Dying. By the turn of the century they were failing rapidly, and since then the sporadic reports have grown fewer and more infrequent until, in the late 1960s, the reports ceased entirely.

There's no doubt that such birds were mercilessly and wastefully hunted. Yet, there was something else. The gun was the most spectacular agent, but not the only one and perhaps not even the deadliest. Some lost prairie birds were in deep trouble before the real peak of hunting pressure. Other birds, such as ducks, geese, and prairie chickens, survived it. For example, the last nesting record of the long-billed curlew in Illinois was in 1873, when the prairie chicken was at its zenith. The gun may simply have tipped the balance for species already doomed by sweeping destruction of native grasslands, for no gun that ever boomed over the prairie could match the deadly killing efficiency of plow, cow, and dragline.

For three seasons of the year, the tall prairie teemed with birds. In the fourth season it lay silent and empty, much of its life gone underground or south with the sun.

The great hosts of prairie birds were migrants, and their passage each spring and fall was marked in the billions. There was nothing in the Old World like it, for nowhere else does such an immense, open corridor invite free migration. It was a limitless airway with no ocean or mountain barriers, reaching from the Canadian subarctic to the Gulf Coast, and on deep into eastern Mexico. The curlews and plovers traveled farthest. Small wonder that the Eskimo curlew was a ball of fat by late summer — it needed maximum fuel reserves for its journey from the Canadian barrens to the southern end of South America. It traveled as much as 16,000 miles each year, and from Nova Scotia to the Brazilian coast some curlews might never touch land. Golden plovers made a similar journey, sometimes logging a round trip of 20,000 miles annually, and flying nonstop over open sea for 3,000 miles.

Such vast travels demand early departure from the northern nesting grounds. Last July, on the Kalsow Prairie in northwest Iowa, I might see as many as ten male bobolinks at once, their bubbling calls floating over the tall grasses. A few weeks later, by mid-August, there was not a bobolink to be seen; like other great travelers, some had made an early start for Argentina.

Since the bulk of the prairie's birdlife was migratory, the birds' departure each autumn left a silence broken only by the ceaseless wind passing through dried grasses. This was the beginning of the hard time — the cruel test for the true prairie birds that had stayed behind.

Probably few birds actually wintered on the prairie; many drew back to the brushy edges of the prairie timber, for winter food supplies on the prairie were scanty after wind had stripped grasses and forbs of their seeds, and snow had choked the low cover. Even the rugged prairie chicken would shift toward timber, and might move fifty miles across the prairie to better winter quarters. The depths of the prairie itself were largely left to the wind and the hungry hawk, and to clouds of snow buntings that whirled and blew like the snowflakes for which settlers had named them.

The winter birds are superb professional survivors, living

from one crisis to the next by exploiting the smallest advantages. One cold afternoon in January I walked across a stretch of ragged Iowa grassland. The place seemed lifeless, appearing to offer no real food or shelter to birds. But from the cutbank of a tiny creek, just under the overhang of shaggy grass, I flushed two short-eared owls that went wafting out over the prairie like scraps of windblown cloth. They had been sheltering there in a southern exposure, snug and out of the wind, in as good a place as any. A little farther on, a small flock of mourning doves was feeding on tiny marijuana seeds that were dusting down on the crusted snowdrifts of a fenceline. Finally, a red-tailed hawk swung overhead — expert testimony to the fact that not all of the small mammals were asleep underground.

Then, one day in late February or early March, the migrants began returning to the old prairie. They brought spring with them, and a surge of life and excitement. Up from the southern swamps and savannahs, Gulf Coast marshes and the sandspits of the Laguna Madre, from subtropical Mexican forests, and finally from the farthest reaches of South America, they came — serried flocks of ducks and geese beyond number, and endless wedges of curlews and plovers. With them came herons and kites, trumpeter swans and giant cranes, and a multitude of small minstrels — warblers, larks, singing sparrows, longspurs, redwings, and a host of others, all trigged out in brightening nuptial plumage. The prairie pulse quickened; it was spring again, with the birds come home.

❧

There were fewer kinds of mammals than birds on the prairie (possibly 90 species as compared to 300), and most of those mammals were small. But for every bison that loomed on the prairie, many bison-weights of rodents and tiny hunters lurked unseen in the tall grasses.

The grassy flats and ridges teemed with little critters. The jumping mouse and Franklin ground squirrel usually held close to the prairie-timber edge, but of all American ground squirrels, the Franklin was the one most closely linked with true prairie. It is the only ground squirrel that consistently lives in grass that it cannot see over, its gray pelage in perfect harmony with clumps of gray and weathered grasses. It is large, as ground squirrels go, somewhat resembling the gray squirrel of the dense forests but with a shorter and less bushy tail, and smaller, rounder ears — as befits a proper digger. Franklin ground squirrels are still fairly common, but aren't commonly seen — they may spend 90 percent of their lives underground in deeply grassed fencelines, and their clear whistle is usually mistaken for a prairie bird's.

More obvious are the thirteen-lined ground squirrels, or spermophiles, which like short open grassland and often teem on neglected golf courses, airports, and pastures. Like the Franklin, these ground squirrels key their above-ground activity to bright light, and may never emerge at all in cool and cloudy weather.

The little "picket-pins" swarmed in the wild grasses that adjoined newly broken fields, and could dig out a settler's corn almost as fast as he planted it. They were often the first game that prairie boys hunted, spreading nooses of twine around the burrow entrances and waiting for the "stripy gophers" to stick out their heads, or by laboriously toting endless buckets of water to drown them out. This can be done, and I've done it, for one penny per picket-pin. But it calls for a handy water supply, several boys and several buckets, and a sublime ignorance of business principles. It is not a practical way to turn a penny.

Some early naturalists remarked that the plains pocket gopher was the tall grassland's analog of the prairie dog of the plains, which is to say, in a classic jumble of nomenclature, that the plains pocket gopher was as typical of the prai-

rie as the prairie dog was typical of the plains. Still, the
pocket gopher is one of the most typical prairie diggers, generally limited to the tall-prairie region that lies between the
Great Plains and the Mississippi. Found almost anywhere in
the true prairie, it has a special kinship to deep, moist soils in
general and windblown loess in particular — the fine-
grained, stoneless soil that is easily worked.

There is a prairie white-footed mouse, close kin to the
woodland white-footed mouse of the East — a sprite that is
usually abroad only after dark, and even shuns bright moon-
light. Possibly the most abundant of the small rodents is the
prairie meadow mouse, or prairie vole, a stocky little animal

with an outsized head, short legs, and no tail worth mentioning. One of the most prolific mammals known, with a gestation period of only twenty-one days, it can build up to averages of 250 mice per acre. They are cyclic, as such fecund creatures often are, operating on a general boom-and-bust schedule based on the four-year cycle.

These and other chisel-teeth battened on a limitless supply of grasses, forbs, seeds, fruits, and roots. In turn, they fed a large and active citizenry of foxes, coyotes, minks, weasels, shrews, badgers, skunks, snakes, owls, and hawks.

Of all those prairie hunters, the badger and coyote were the most typical — western forms that rarely existed in eastern timberlands. They were two of the great common denominators of our original grassland biome, together with bison, antelope, and buffalo wolf — all classic grasslanders. The buffalo wolf is no more, the bison are relicts, and the badger and antelope have been trimmed back to the Great Plains — but the coyote goes on, far and forever.

The lobo wolf was almost universal in wild America, and its prairie form was the great gray "buffalo wolf" — a magnificent hunter that once prowled most of our native grasslands. The coyote might be called "prairie wolf" — a point of confusion, for the two are wholly different. The confusion persists today largely because men want it to. It is not uncommon to hear a midwestern hunter tell of shooting a "brush wolf" or of going "wolf-hunting." And if it gives him an illusion of wilderness, why not? But although a northern prairie coyote, *Canis latrans,* may bulk large by desert standards — weighing as much as thirty-five pounds — it is a watchfob edition of the great buffalo wolf, *Canis lupus,* that sometimes scaled over a hundred. To be precise, the lobo and the songdog are (or were) both prairie wolves. The coyote was simply much the lesser of the two.

There is some concern over the future of the American coyote, particularly among those who deplore the tireless

persecution of a classic American predator. But I'm inclined
to share Bob Henderson's hunch that the coyote is master of
his own fate.

Bob knows as much about the coyote as any man living,
and he aired his opinion late one December afternoon while
we were dressing out a buffalo cow about fifty miles south of
Abilene. We were making a careful job of it, for this was to
be much of our winter's meat, and our work was being monitored by a squad of coyotes that perched out there on the
prairie and crooned to us. I had said something trenchant,
like: "Robert, we are engaged in an act of the past, watched
by anachronisms." He-Dog paused to stone his knife, and
opined that there would be coyotes long after we were gone,
and they'd probably be using the artifacts of our technology
as scent posts, which was a damned good idea. It resolved to
this: Coyotes are simply more efficient at tuning in on environmental changes than we are, learning fast, applying it
sensibly, and succeeding without waste.

And so the little songdog sings on. Highly mobile, geared
to a universal diet that includes virtually anything edible, and
equipped with a diamond-bright intellect, he has spread far
beyond his original prairies all the way into the north woods,
New England, and Maine.

The coyote's sometime hunting partner, the badger, is a
squat, powerful weasel that hasn't done as well. He needs
open grassland for his hunting and digging, and is a more sta-
tionary target than the coyote. His survival kit doesn't include much in the way of speed, mobility, or smarts. A coyote
can exist in an area *incognito*, but a badger's presence is so
obvious that even the average farmer grows aware of it.
Tireless diggers after rodents, badgers leave prairie pastures
riddled with their prospect holes, and they are notoriously
tough on farm dogs.

Once every few years here in southwestern Illinois, there is
a news feature about some farmer who has heroically de-

fended his hayfield against a badger. However, such reports grow rarer. There are still badgers east of the Mississippi, but they are highly uncommon there. They are almost as rare just west of the River, for cash grain and agribusiness have cut them back to the permanent grasslands of the Great Plains. Oddly enough, the badger may be the only animal that's had any real influence on the prairie's form. In Canada, where a great belt of aspen lies between the evergreen forests and the prairie, badgers breaking the prairie sod make it possible for snowberry to grow on their earthen mounds. Snowberry, known in Canada as "badger willow," is often succeeded by aspen and allows woodland to invade the inviolate grasses — until the next fire.

There were, of course, tree-country furbearers in and around the true prairie: beaver, bobcat, puma, lynx, black bear, and otter. Some of these must have stretched their bond with the forest quite thin, for they were sometimes found in groves and creek bottoms well out on the prairie. I've jumped white-tailed deer from grassy swales in eastern South Dakota miles from the nearest real timber. The last black bear in my home county in central Iowa was killed in the 1860s along a tiny creek that was fringed with a skimpy stand of timber.

A few grizzlies were in the true prairie, but in only the extreme western limits of the tall grasslands in eastern Nebraska, the eastern Dakotas, and western Iowa. There are no good records of grizzlies in the prairie portions of Missouri, Kansas, or Oklahoma; and it's possible that the great silvertips were rare transients that drifted down the Missouri River's valley. The same may have been true of mule deer, which were reported from the eastern Dakotas and northwestern Iowa, and which surely occurred in eastern Nebraska. Such movement along the Big Muddy's long corridor still occurs, for in recent years mule deer have been seen near St. Louis.

The pronghorn antelope, which was anything but a river

valley traveler, simply came overland and was checked by
some unknown habitat deficiency in the tall prairie. Our little goat-antelope came as far as eastern Nebraska, the eastern
Dakotas, western Iowa, and extreme northwest Missouri, but
no farther.

In some ways the prairie mammals have fared better than
many prairie birds. Deer are more numerous in our midlands
today than at the time of white settlement. Franklin ground
squirrels still whistle in the fencelines, and farm boys still re-
capitulate the frontier by trapping picket-pins. The otter and
beaver are back and the coyote never really left — all of
which, sadly, is more than we can say of the Eskimo curlew.

❧

Those showy flowers in the tall prairie were a sure sign of
countless insects, for most blossoms depended on butterflies,
moths, and bees for pollination.

Insects not only inspired this floral riot, but complemented
it with life and color of their own. Big clumps of butterfly
milkweed, with their masses of red-orange blooms, wear
clouds of monarch butterflies. The monarchs have a special
affection for this milkweed, just as the painted lady flirts with
thistle flowers, and brightly colored soldier beetles seek out
goldenrod.

Some prairie plants welcome any insect that happens by.
The composites — coneflower, daisy, dandelion, compass-
plant, and many others — are open to all comers. It is the
most abundant flower family on the prairie, and attracts the
widest range of insect visitors.

Other prairie flowers are more particular, and may be
served by only certain insects. The large white orchid *Habenaria leucophaea,* with its gorgeous spurs over an inch
long, emits a delicate fragrance only at dusk and is pollinated
only by sphinx moths. The wild iris or "blue flag" of the prairie wetlands is pollinated by bumblebees, while trumpet vine

and red columbine are fragrant invitations to hummingbirds.

Pollination is not just a job for beauty; it may require brawn. Monarch butterflies and bumblebees are two of the commonest insects visiting butterfly milkweed because they are strong enough to pull their legs free of the flowers' pollen traps. And the bumblebee needs all his strength and skill when he visits the bottle gentian in early fall.

This striking gentian never entirely opens its lovely flowers. The sepals are clamped together to form a graceful, swelling tube. The bumblebee — drawn to the gentian by his favorite color, blue — can enter the closed sepals by pressing on their apex, to which he is guided by the color pattern. However, it's a one-way entrance, opening only from the outside in. Any insect entirely within the blossom is likely to be trapped there. So the bumblebee pushes only the front half of his body into the gentian's "bottle," holding the entrance open behind him with abdomen and rear legs. It's not easy, but it must be worth it to bee and flower.

The contract between flowers and insects is most tenuous in early spring and fall, when the few available flowers must be as receptive as possible to a small number of insects. The hardy little pasqueflower, often blooming before Easter, when the raw prairie wind cuts with a wire edge, must shield itself from bad weather — but cannot risk being overlooked by insects. At night, and on cold, lowering spring days, the pasqueflower's sepals bend up and in, covering the green carpels and golden anthers and exposing only the furry backs of the flowers to the keen wind. On fair days, when insects are abroad, the lavender bloom opens wide. It's all a matter of physiology, of course, and has to do with such dull stuff as differential turgor pressure within the pasqueflower's cells. But to the flower and the fly it means that their periods of dormancy and activity coincide, and that is enough. At the other end of the year, the gentians react in the same way to cold autumn nights and bright days.

Native bees were everywhere on the prairie; almost a thousand species can be listed for the main prairie region. Some were social, but many were loners that built solitary nests. The summer prairies droned with *Bombus*, the great black-and-yellow bumblebees that nested in the ground, and woe to the farmer who drove the point of his walking-plow into their nests. All of the native bees can sting, and unlike the honey bee, they can withdraw their ovipositors after stinging and do not die.

Honey bees were usually not far from timber, although I've seen them working blossoms at least a mile from anything that could have been a hive tree. This bee was a gift from our founding fathers; it was not native to North America, but was introduced by early colonists. Spreading like wildfire across the new land, it was established and waiting when the first of the prairie settlers arrived — at least, so claimed Washington Irving in 1835.

By late August there might be ten million insects in an acre of tallgrass prairie. Two of the dominant orders are the true bugs and flies, *Hemiptera* and *Diptera*, which occurred in vast numbers. I once spent a winter dissecting samples of old bluestem sod, laboriously counting chinch bug eggs in the hollow stems. Every stem in some of those foot-square samples contained eggs, and must have represented hundreds of thousands of potential chinch bugs per acre.

Flies abounded. Some, such as the bee flies and robber flies, were conspicuous prairie insects that were easily seen in flight — like typical prairie birds. Robber flies of the genus *Promachus* were especially bold; preying on other flying insects with remarkable rapacity and skill, they are the falcons of the insect kingdom.

Biting and stinging flies plagued men and animals at some seasons, especially in poorly drained prairies within the last glacial advance. I've suffered sorely enough from mosquitoes in the Everglades and Louisiana swamps, but never so sorely as on the wet prairies of southern Minnesota. There were certain "greenheaded flies" in prairie swales that drove men and livestock beyond endurance, and inspired good Methodist settlers to supreme heights of sulfurous invective. These were probably tabanid flies of the horsefly group, crescentheaded terrors to anything warmblooded. One Illinois settler wrote home in 1821:

> I became acquainted this year with the prairie flies, about which I had heard so much in Vermont. The smallest kind are a beautiful green about twice the size of a common housefly. Another kind is about twice as large as these, of a slate color. These, this season, in riding on the prairies, would entirely cover a horse, and when fastened they remain until killed by smoke or by being skinned off by a knife, and then the horse will be covered with blood. The only way of riding a horse by day is by covering a horse completely.

But of all the insect tribes on the prairie — and there were many representatives of most groups — none was more typical than the great order *Orthoptera*, which included the grasshoppers.

They belong more to grasslands than anywhere else, their forms and functions wonderfully adapted to grass and sun. Kansas has 118 genera and 301 species of grasshoppers, twice as many as New Jersey's 60 genera and 152 species. Most of these prairie grasshoppers are of little general interest, but there was one that wrote history.

Its formal name was *Melanoplus spretus*, its common name "Rocky Mountain locust," and it fell like a Biblical plague on the fields of some prairie pioneers. Over the long run, chinch bugs may have been more damaging to human interests. But for a few short, terrible years, the Rocky Mountain locust was a crushing calamity.

This grasshopper is not native to the tall prairie; it hailed from farther west, from the high, dry grasslands at the eastern foot of the Rockies. Most of the time it was just another grass-hopper. But there were periods when the Rocky Mountain locust was far more successful than usual. Say, when a partic-ular fall with warm temperatures allowed long periods of egg-laying, followed by a cool spring that delayed the hatch until there was adequate food for the young locusts. Say that this occurred for several consecutive years, with an astro-nomical pyramiding of numbers as the full reproductive po-tential of the insect was realized. Something happened then; some inherent biological instability asserted itself, transform-ing a rather sedentary insect and impelling it to swarm and travel. It was then that the Rocky Mountain locust, on long wings and riding the prevailing westerlies, came out of the Great Plains as a cloud of destruction.

It often happened at the loveliest time of the year, at the start of the ripening time. To German and Scandinavian set-tlers — newly arrived on the prairies of the Dakotas, Iowa, Minnesota, and Nebraska and still confused by the great sweeps of open country — it must have seemed a terrifying affliction. O. E. Rölvaag, in his masterpiece *Giants in the Earth*, described a grasshopper invasion of South Dakota in the early 1870s:

> From out of the west layers of clouds came rolling — thin layers that rose and sank on the breeze; they had none of the look or manner of ordinary clouds; they came in waves, like the surges of the sea, and cast a glittering sheen before them as they came; they seemed to be made of some solid murky substance that threw out small sparks along its face . . .
> The ominous waves of cloud seemed to advance with terrific speed, breaking now and then like a huge surf, and with the deep dull roaring sound as of a heavy undertow rolling into caverns on a mountain side . . . But they were neither breakers nor foam, these waves . . . It seemed more as if the unseen hand of a giant were shaking an immense tablecloth of iridescent colours . . .
> The next moment the first wave of the weird cloud engulfed

them, spewing over them its hideous, unearthly contents. The horses became uncontrollable ...

And now from out the sky gushed down with cruel force a living, pulsating stream, striking the backs of the helpless folk like pebbles thrown by an unseen hand; but that which fell out of the heavens was not pebbles, nor raindrops, nor hail, for then it would have lain inanimate where it fell; this substance had no sooner fallen than it popped up again, crackling and snapping — rose up and disappeared in the twinkling of an eye; it flared and flittered around them like light gone mad; it chirped and buzzed through the air; it snapped and hopped along the ground; the whole place was a weltering turmoil of raging little demons; if one looked for a moment into the wind, one saw nothing but glittering, lightninglike flashes — flashes that came and went, in the heart of a cloud made up of innumerable dark-brown clicking bodies! All the while the roaring sound continued.

From 1874 to 1877 the locusts ravaged the prairie frontier. Rölvaag wrote: "The devastation it wrought was terrible; it made beggars of some, and drove others insane; still others it sent wandering back to the forest lands, though they found conditions little better there, either."[1]

The locusts left vast areas as barren as if seared with flame, leaving not even ash. In many places the only clue to where plants had been were holes in the earth. Trees were stripped of leaves and green bark, and often killed. The insects covered fields, houses, and barns in a vast, clicking, metallic tide, devouring every green and growing thing on the landscape.

A Nebraska witness to one of the great plagues estimated its magnitude. In places the locust swarm, measured with surveying instruments, was nearly a mile high — and swept into Nebraska on a 100-mile front that was 300 miles deep. With an estimate of twenty-seven grasshoppers per cubic yard, it was calculated that the living cloud contained

[1] Rölvaag, O. E. *Giants in the Earth.* New York: Harper & Brothers, 1927.

twenty-eight million grasshoppers per cubic mile. The swarm persisted in that density for at least six hours at the observation point, moving eastward at about five miles per hour. There were thought to be over 124 billion locusts in the invasion.

Then, inexplicably, the plague would vanish.

We now know that the Rocky Mountain locust cannot maintain itself in relatively low, humid regions. The hordes of insects that reached the tallgrass country had great vigor but this was not transmitted, and although the migrants laid eggs in infinite numbers, the young grasshoppers invariably died before reaching maturity. The locusts usually vanished within a year from their deepest eastern penetrations: the western halves of Iowa and Minnesota, the western tier of Missouri counties, and Kansas, Oklahoma, and most of Texas. Nearer their point of origin — in the Dakotas, the western half of Nebraska, and the northeastern fourth of Colorado — they persisted longer. But even that close to the Rockies, they lasted for only a few years.

The prairie climate resisted them, and so did the prairie creatures. Birds exploited this windfall, gorging themselves and consuming locusts by the millions. This was seen in 1875 in eastern Nebraska, where some areas had over a hundred locusts per square foot. In one 320-acre creek bottom near Lincoln, which "harbored an immense number of locusts," the birds counterattacked. Quail, horned larks, bobolinks, yellow-headed blackbirds, plovers, curlews, and prairie chickens zeroed in on the bounty, and within a month hardly a locust remained.

But more than any other factor, breeding conditions on the locusts' native heath must have undergone changes and were never again so favorable. Something, too, had happened to the insect itself. *Melanoplus spretus*, the terrible traveler, may have sunk into a quiescent phase to become *Melanoplus mexicanus*. It may even have become extinct, for no specimens of *spretus* have been taken for more than fifty years. Its passing has evoked no grief among prairie farmers. Yet, the Rocky Mountain locust was undeniably part of the old prairie time — a rich balance of the bitter and beautiful. The plague locust was a special creature of a special world, as surely as the bison or curlew. In its own way it was a hallmark of quality, and passed with the floral and faunal excellence of the lands that had shaped it and given it life.

7

The Great Weathers

ON ONE OF HIS INFREQUENT JOURNEYS into the hinterlands, William Cullen Bryant saw his first prairie — an Ohio "barren" that was an outrider of the main grasslands several hundred miles farther west. It was a gentle encounter, as most of his encounters with nature were, and he returned home to pen some gentle lines:

> These are the gardens of the desert, these,
> The unshorn fields, boundless and beautiful,
> For which the speech of England has no name —
> The Prairies.

Which was true as far as it went. However, it went no farther than Ohio and October. If it had gotten as far as South Dakota and January, the poem would have lost some of its dreamlike quality. Out in Iowa a man named William Haddock — who had come to the prairies in 1855 — adapted Bryant's style to a fuller reality:

> These are the terror of the settlers, these,
> The Arctic blasts, howling and freezing,
> For which the land of England has no name —
> The Blizzards.

Blizzard must be a coined name; at least, it seems to have no roots in either English or French. The origin of the word is unknown, but its meaning is clear enough. The blizzard is a cyclonic winter storm characterized by high winds, extreme cold, and moderate-to-heavy snowfall.

In northwestern Canada there gathers a pole of intense winter cold, a sort of coalescence of deep frost similar to those in Greenland and Siberia. From this center a wide mantle of heavy, frigid air sinks southward. As it approaches the United States it deflects eastward in a class of winds called "the polar easterlies." When these collide with the warm Gulf and Atlantic air masses that are moving northward into the midcontinent, there is meteorological havoc. Differing greatly in temperature and humidity, and stirred and driven by the polar-front and subtropical jetstreams that encircle the northern hemisphere, these great air masses join in a tempestuous marriage with wild wind systems and unstable atmospheric pressures. The meeting ground of these major air masses is a region of storms and crazy weathers, of rapid and violent change, and the cyclonic wind systems that spin about centers of low atmospheric pressure in winter to create blizzards covering hundreds of thousands of square miles.

Since its primary component is wind, the classic blizzard is essentially a phenomenon of the open lands — particularly the prairies and plains, where the topography offers little resistance to moving air and the great storms can run almost unimpeded. There may be more snow in northern and eastern forest regions, and certainly as much cold. The difference between winter storms there and the classic prairie blizzard lies in the intensity of unbridled wind that plunges the chill factor to deadly lows, drives a blinding smother of snow during the actual storm, and continues as ground blizzards and white-outs long after snow has stopped falling. Depending on snowfall and wind, the storm may leave drifts three times as

tall as a man and is usually followed by calm, silver-blue days
of burning cold.

Not every prairie winter is a blizzard winter. Even on the
northern prairies, winters may be open, warm, and without
any severe or spectacular weather. During some Dakota
years the grass may still be green at Christmas, the winter
seeming to be a long extension of late fall. The days are se-
rene and mild, with a few gentle snowfalls and an uneventful
winter that melts placidly into the fretful days of early
spring. A prairie farmer knows that such winters are sent on
credit and must be paid for sooner or later — often at exorbi-
tant interest. And since a prairie farmer is wary of anything
gotten on credit, he goes about his chores on a balmy January

day with one eye on his work and the other on the western horizon, watching for the grayish-white pall that lifts and thickens with a deepening of temperature.

For if there is one constant in a prairie winter, it is inconstancy. In 1930, at Webster City, Iowa, between February 15 and 24, the temperature ranged from −34° F to 72° F — a fluctuation of 106 degrees in only nine days. An even wilder fluctuation occurred on January 22, 1943, when a warm winter wind or "chinook" blew into Spearfish, South Dakota, and the temperature rose from −4° F to 45° F in two minutes! And, of course, the opposite may occur when a vast eddy forms within the general prevailing wind patterns in a brief, violent episode that becomes a record blizzard and the temperature plunges from a high positive to a low negative in a matter of hours.

The sharpest, deepest drop in which I've been involved was one of almost 70 degrees that occurred in about sixteen hours during the Armistice Day Blizzard of 1940. A great mass of warm, moist air had swept up from the lower Mississippi Valley at about the time a particularly strong, cold air mass began pressing south from Canada. The cold air underran the tide of warm air and created a vast low-pressure system that moved swiftly across the upper Midwest.

In central Iowa, that November 11 had begun as a gray, damp day, somewhat warmer than usual. John Cole and I had walked our mile to Ames High School wearing light jackets and no caps on our brilliantined heads. By midmorning the temperature stood at almost 60° F, which was a very fine thing because that afternoon our vaunted team planned to mop the home field with our hated rivals from nearby Boone. A pep assembly was held late in the morning, but the assemblage was thoroughly de-pepped when told the great game was being called because of weather. So were afternoon classes; our balmy, misty day had vanished and we'd just begun to be clobbered by a sizable blizzard.

The mile home at noon was longer than it had been that morning. The temperature had dropped thirty degrees and a rising wind was driving in from the northwest. By the time Cole and I reached home, our brilliantine was like iron and a full hurricane couldn't have ruffled a hair. Being young, tough, fairly weatherproof, and not encumbered with an excess of good judgment, we figured this as an ideal day to jumpshoot ducks on the Skunk River near home. Now let it be said that we knew our way around that section of boondocks as well as we knew the route to the supper table, and were accustomed to about every kind of weather that our Iowa prairies offered. Or thought we were. We would learn new things that day.

On the way home from school we had faced wind that was beginning to drive wet gray featherduster puffs of snow that plastered our fronts and the north sides of trees and houses. But by the time we were out on the river an hour or so later, and the temperature had fallen another ten degrees, the snow was becoming hard and granular. The wind was now a more or less steady forty miles per hour, sometimes gusting at fifty. Not even our hunting fever could temper that wind. We worked north into it, and the day resolved itself into small compartments of suffering. The world about us was closed out by an encircling wall of wind and snow; we moved in the center of a circular arena whose radius shrank as the afternoon wore on and the storm rose. There was a strange intimacy to this — a tearing microcosm of cold and gale, occupied only by Cole and me and the tiny stretch of visible river that traveled along with us, and the masses of ducks that cowered under the north banks.

The storm had overtaken a main waterfowl migration over the Midwest and bludgeoned countless ducks down into sloughs, creeks, ponds, and rivers. We saw mallards beyond number. Each sheltering bend and cutbank had its huddled flock, sometimes a hundred or more. We would lean and stagger across a sandbar toward them and they would rise into the noisy grayness, only to be battered back down into the river. We would fire at the rise and the sounds of our heavy 12-bore guns were muffled thuds swept away on the wind.

Neither of us had hip boots. I remember wearing heavy blanket-wool breeches with short shoepacs and two pairs of thick woolen socks, and wading for the ducks up to my hips. Coming out of the water into that wind I would be quickly sheathed in ice that sloughed off in plates as we walked. Yet cold as it was, there was no great sensation of cold; the wind was not getting through my thick breeches and woolen underwear, and the sensation was rather one of unpleasant clamminess. The greatest discomfort was not of cold, but the ice particles driven at gale force into our faces; that, and the labor of simply moving into the wind, faces averted, ramming our way through that gray wall with thick stocking caps. I had worn a heavy muffler tied over the lower part of my face — not so much to protect against cold as to permit breathing in that dense smother of wind and snow — but it got to be a mask of ice and a nuisance, and Cole and I walked with faces partly turned from the wind, noses and mouths shielded with mittened hands so we could breathe.

The visible world shrank and broadened with the wind gusts and snow flurries; at times we could scarcely see each other a few yards away, and then visibility might open to several hundred yards, revealing another mass of ducks that drew us on. At the time, our labor kept us from suffering from the cold. But we were spending our energies prodigally, as young hunters do, and extending ourselves too far. We hunted all the way to Templeton's Bridge, at least seven river miles, and by the time we turned south again it was nearly dark and we were almost spent. Each of us with a thirty-pound bundle of ducks slung over his shoulder with bits of fence wire, and that terrible wind pushing us homeward.

Cole and I have forgotten many parts of that day, even parts that we might be expected to remember — such as where we found the ducks and who shot well, and who missed. Still, one can't be expected to remember what he never knew, for we shot at some of those ducks at places we could not recognize although they were as familiar as home. But never forgotten is the warm, quiet, blanket-fold snugness of being in a house again — a deep sense of shelter that was, oddly enough, not entirely pleasant. I also remember the exhaustion that came over me as the warmth began to take hold, and of dozing while pulling off frozen boots.

Another thing is clear and full-remembered, even after forty years: that tearing wall of gray that we leaned into but never through, dragging twenty yards of our little visible world behind us and pushing twenty yards of it ahead, the wall blasting us with horizontal spicules of ice, and making its sound. I don't recall that as a howl, but as a hissing moan whose sustained timbre hardly wavered, a deep hum that drove through our ice-sheathed caps and mackinaws as if we were traveling between the tines of a great tuning fork. It was the cry of winter with all its furies marshaled in one level, sustained force of deepening cold and energy — a weight of heavily frozen, syrup-thick air driven at gale force.

Fifty miles away, west of Fort Dodge, my old friend Frank Heidelbauer had gone hunting alone that day, jumpshooting ducks along Lizard Creek on the open prairie. It was a wet, foggy morning with light drizzle, and quite warm. I asked Frankie if he remembered that day, and he replied:

"I left the car about half a mile from the creek. I was wearing hip boots and a knee-length rain parka; it was warm, so I wore only a light sweatshirt under the parka. I struck the little creek after cutting across a half-mile of picked cornfield and started hunting its many bends, working upstream. It soon became apparent from sign that a trapper had been ahead of me, probably flushing any ducks using on the stream, but I continued to hunt out each bend of the creek working north and west.

"I had hunted about three miles of this stretch of Lizard when a large flock of mallards hooked in out of the murk and landed almost in front of me — I took about two steps and they were back in the air and I folded one for each of my three shots. It was while I was picking up these ducks that the wind suddenly thundered down on me out of the northwest.

"In all my days I can't recall such a rapid change in weather. With the wind came an almost unbelievable drop in temperature, and the drizzle changed to heavy wet snow that the wind would slam onto trees and fences in great wet gobs that immediately froze. I turned my back to the storm and started downstream. Thank God for that rain parka — it kept out the wind.

"Where there were no ducks before, the creek was now full of them and they were obviously worn out. I would step up to a bend protected from the wind and a flock would go up from behind its north cutbank — I would shoot, and the flock would slowly hover downstream for maybe no more than three hundred feet and land under the next protecting cutbank.

"By the time I limited out with my tenth mallard the storm was really raging, and I was at least three miles from the point on the country road where I had left my car. I'll never forget that walk, and those huge gobs of wet snow — some as big as my two hands. If I turned into the wind it would plaster onto my face and stick there. At times, clouds of fine, misty snow would engulf me and make breathing very difficult; then there would be small breaks in which I could briefly see for some distance, followed by more onslaughts of wind and snow.

"When I had reached the edge of the cornfield a half-mile north of my car the snow was knee-deep and drifting, and

those ten mallards were becoming almost more than I could
manage. On my way through that half-mile of cornfield to my
car I saw six big gray geese curve out of the storm and appear
to land only a short distance ahead of me. I dropped my
heavy bundle of mallards and went in the direction I had last
seen the geese. But although I cast about the area I failed to
find them and the raging storm became so heavy and thick
that at times I could hardly breathe. Born and raised on a
northwest Iowa farm, I had heard the old-timers tell of the
dangers of snow-mist blizzards, and I knew that I'd better be
getting the hell out of there. I almost didn't find the mallards;
only a couple of orange feet protruding from a drift marked
the spot where I had dropped them.

"Heading down the cornrow in the direction of the car, I
finally hit the fence and then found the car with its north side
plastered with ten inches of rime ice. Luckily, I had a heavy
wool sweater and a lined hunting coat in a duffel bag in the
trunk. When I finally got partly thawed, I had to jack up the
hind wheels and put on chains. The storm was raging worse
than ever, and as I lay on my back under the car hooking up
the chains, the fine-driven snow would be so smothering that
I would pause to cover my face with my hands in order to
breathe. It took me three hours to cover the few miles back
into Fort Dodge, and only the fact that a snowplow had just
passed the corner as I reached the highway made it possible
at all.

"Do I remember the Armistice Day Storm of 1940? Ol'
Coon, I'll *never* forget it."

Tough as that day was on the prairie creeks and marshes, it
was deadly on some rivers and lakes. Hunters died by the
score on the Upper Mississippi, Illinois River, and the big
lakes. Caught by the storm with little warning, they drowned
as they tried to reach land, or stayed in their duck blinds as
waves tore them apart, or simply died of exposure that night
on the river islands out of reach of help from shore. At least
85 hunters died that afternoon and night: 49 in Minnesota, 23

in Wisconsin, and 13 in Illinois. That doesn't include the ones that died on the Iowa side of the Mississippi. On storm-wracked Lake Michigan, 73 sailors died as their ships were driven onto rocks in winds that were clocked at 80 miles per hour at Grand Rapids. At least 158 people died between one noon and the next.

From then on it was a rather normal winter — neither much worse nor better than most. That one storm made it a standout, and set a record for November prairie weather.

Just as some prairie winters are long, balmy bridges between autumn and spring, others are interminable chains of successive storms — each more bitter than the one before. For many years in the tall prairie country, the standard by which other winters were measured was that of 1856–57. Beginning in early fall, recurrent blizzards were followed by slight thaws and severe cold. The deepening of winter intensified the suffering of men and animals. A typical account is that concerning the young Williams brothers, who lived on a prairie homestead near Clear Lake in northern Iowa.

On the morning of December 28, 1856, they were working near the inlet of the lake cutting a water hole for thirsty calves. The morning had begun clear and cold with no hint of the storm that struck at noon. Caught in the open nearly a mile from their cabin, the brothers took shelter in a creekside thicket of crabapple and willow. It was a bit quieter there out of the wind, and the young men spent the afternoon and night walking in circles through the thicket. Just before daylight, with the thicket deeply choked with snow, they decided to try for the cabin. They never found it; instead, lost and exhausted, they were found by rescuers that morning when "it was so cold that the air seemed fairly blue, and struck into the flesh like steel." The rescue party happened to see the toe of a new red-topped boot in a heavy drift, and although both boys lived, they "were crippled for the rest of their days."

This was the Massacre Winter that wiped out the last of

northern Iowa's elk and deer — and at least one frontier settlement. By February 1857, the prairie frontier was in critical
straits. Even the Indians, with all their disciplined understanding of prairie winter, had grown desperate. In February
fifteen starving Sioux renegades drifted over into their old
northwestern Iowa hunting grounds from the hunger camps
of South Dakota. They were the hard core of frontier violence, led by the notorious Inkpadutah, or "Red Tip," with
such tribal outlaws as Old Man, Mysterious Father, Putting-
On-Walking, and a Sisseton thug with the heavy name
Man-Who-Makes-A-Crooked-Wind-When-He-Runs. Instead
of finding river forests and lakeshore groves with herds of
wintering elk and deer, the Sioux found new settlers who had
not only occupied their old hunting grounds and wiped out
the game, but had the temerity to move into sacred country
by the lake called *Minne-Wakon*. The enraged Sioux worked
from cabin to cabin and massacred thirty-eight people — the
entire settlement at Lake Okoboji and Spirit Lake.

When the news reached Fort Dodge near the head of the
Des Moines River, a relief column was dispatched to Okoboji.
Most of the dead were found and buried. On the return
march, the poorly equipped column was struck by an April
blizzard. Two of the militiamen froze to death, several became snowblind, and two went insane. That storm left drifts
that lingered in some sheltered ravines until late May.

I grew up with interminable vignettes of children per-
ishing on their way home from country schoolhouses, of
guide ropes stretched between house and barn, and of the
farmers who made the last small mistake and died only a few
yards from the door. Of cattle lost until spring, when thawing
drifts revealed carcasses in the swales and along lee slopes.
It's all part of the required prairie folklore — one contingent
on the assumption that the winters were colder then, the
blizzards fiercer and longer, and the snow deeper — which,
in essence, may have been true enough. There were some

hellacious winters in the early periods of prairie settlement, but much of their severity surely reflected inexperience of the settlers. With the primitive facilities of the pioneer era and corresponding ignorance of blizzard behavior and prairie winter, it's little wonder that so many settlers had a tough time of it.

In a letter home to Norway, Ole Nielsen of Estherville, Iowa, wrote in 1870:

> Between January 15 and 16 we had a terrible snow storm, which claimed a life among us Norwegians, namely the second oldest son of Tollef Nedgaarden, Ole, who froze to death out on the prairie. He was as close to the nearest house as the distance from Tollef Hagene to your farm when they found him. At the burial banquet, a Jew functioned as cook, and he managed very well, in the American manner, of course.

This was not an unusual thing; death in winter by many causes was commonplace enough, and death by freezing seemed to excite no special comment. In a March 1887 edition of the Napoleon (North Dakota) *Homestead* were such chatty items as:

> This winter is being compared to that of 1848 . . . Our railroad boom is getting brighter and nearer. Bro. Streeter of Williamsport will set up the cigars if the O.B.&N.W. does not build through here by September . . .

> *   *   *

> With the event of the closing of the Steele Bank, another saloon opened up. The Steelites will thus still have some place to leave their money . . .

> *   *   *

> Miss Kate Bardill froze to death on the prairie near LaMoure.

> *   *   *

Of such stuff were great-granddad's winters, and each was remembered for some special event or character: a particularly savage or early storm, interminable periods of cold, prolonged and unrelenting snowfall and drifting, a wave of diphtheria, or all combined into one five-month visitation of misery, ruin, and death.

The winter of 1848 was another of the bad ones on the northern prairies. So was that of 1855–56, when the grasslands were struck with the first real snow and cold on New Year's Day, and severe cold and snow continued almost unabated through March. The Massacre Winter that followed began in earnest on December 1 and continued much longer, and the winter of 1880–81 was the almost endless siege so eloquently described in Rölvaag's *Giants in the Earth*. The special character of that winter was the October storm that struck the eastern Dakotas. It was not particularly cold, but was notable for the huge fall of wet snow that literally leveled the prairie world, filling hollows, creek bottoms, stream valleys, and the multitude of small and large depressions that characterize rolling prairie until the whole land appeared to be graded into a uniform elevation. And from then on, the weather got bad.

The winter of 1886 virtually ended the days of open range in Montana. It had been a dry summer with poor grass, and the unfenced public and private ranges were badly overstocked and overgrazed. The herds went into the winter of '86 with no forage reserves to speak of, and no defenses against the savage blizzards and waves of bitter cold that ravaged the northern plains and prairies for months. Cattle perished by the hundreds of thousands, and the ranchers who survived put their hayfields and pastures under fence and turned to winter-feeding.

The deep cold extended into Illinois and beyond; 1886 was one of the few winters that the Mississippi has ever frozen bung-tight at St. Louis, and an entrepreneur set up business on the approximate center of the river and sold bottled heatstroke from a saloon mounted on runners. By sledding his saloon from one side of the channel to the other, he evaded the authorities and tax assessors of Illinois and Missouri while profiting from the chilled citizens of both. The whole thing is said to have been complete with Keystone Kops on skates, and it must have gotten pretty lively out there on the ice. Which was about the only funny thing that happened around there that winter, what with the cold weather, and Mark Twain gone off to live in the East, and all.

In my own time I remember the winter of 1936, which was notable for prolonged periods of clear, bitter cold — and certain heroic schoolmates who were kept at home with frozen ears and noses. Whatever torments they suffered were salved by friends who stopped after school to gaze awestruck at crimson ears that ballooned out at right angles, and noses that looked like W. C. Fields's. Some kids had all the luck. Most of us just had chronically peeling ears and raw cheekbones — the walking wounded who fought on without hope of glory or respite. There was no such thing as school closings because of weather. A little thing like fifty degrees of frost wasn't allowed to waste tax money. Even so, we kids might have swung a few school closings if we'd hung around home whimpering and snuffling instead of joyously hurling ourselves down snow-packed hillsides. The bitterest weather, we found, was more suitable to our needs than the gray, thawing days of late winter. When the snow creaked underfoot and whined and sang under sled runners, not even the radio exploits of Jack Armstrong could keep us indoors.

❧

Were winters tougher in the old days, Daddy? Why, of course they were. And they surely grow progressively worse as we retreat further into memory and the earliest days of settlement. To many prairie people today, a severe winter or even a savage blizzard is likely to be more inconvenience than hardship — precluding any failure of electricity, of course.

But let one component of our culture fail, or be overlooked, and there can still be hell to pay.

As I'm writing this in late January, the northern prairie states are digging out in the wake of "the worst blizzard in 35 years." There was never a great deal of snow in the storm that has just ravaged the eastern Dakotas, western Minnesota, and northwestern Iowa, but there were reports of 70 mph winds that built 20-foot drifts and drove the chill factor to almost 100 degrees below zero. Des Moines recorded the lowest barometric reading in 53 years. A week after the storm, metal detectors were being used to find cars stalled in some Iowa road ditches — cars totally buried under drifts that were wind-packed until they were as solid as a floor.

Almost fifty people died in the northern Midwest in this storm; there were twelve deaths in North Dakota alone. There are stories of people trapped in their cars for over forty hours — some of whom lost toes, feet, or legs from frostbite. A pair of youths, stalled by drifts on Interstate 90 in South Dakota, took their sleeping bags and struck out on foot. They were found several days later by a snowplow, frozen in their sleeping bags. Another youth, far luckier, was stalled in his van several miles east of Sioux Falls where a big drift had built across the highway. Just ahead of him, stalled by the same drift, was a small car driven by a young woman. They prudently retired to the van and bundled together in a sleeping bag until the storm had passed.

Livestock losses were immense. Cattle died by the hundreds in open feedlots or simply walked over the packed drifts that had buried fences and moved for miles with the wind until they froze to death standing up. Some North Dakota deer, turning from the wind, had masses of ice build up on their hindquarters until the ice's weight pulled it away, tearing off long strips of skin and flesh. Some of these deer were blinded by the driving ice crystals, and had to be shot. Even the Hungarian partridges suffered heavy losses — and any storm that kills off Huns has got to be a blue whistler.

It was another grim reminder that men should never take prairie winters lightly. As long as our adaptations function, there are not likely to be great problems. But what of central heating when electricity fails? Of what value is an interstate highway and a new automobile if there are ground blizzards and 20-foot barrier drifts?

As things are, we're infinitely better able to survive (and even enjoy) severe prairie winters than were our great-grand-dads. But please, Lord, don't let the thingamabob bust. If it does, Nature will get in!

※

The continental weather that sweeps the tallgrass prairie region is a raw, unrefined climate, untempered by any large bodies of water that might serve as reservoirs of warmth in winter and coolness in summer. Frostbite one month, sunstroke the next. There are places in North America that are colder than the prairie Midwest, and some that are hotter. But I'll stack our prairie country against any as the hottest cold place, or the coldest hot place, on the continent.

In a switch on Sam McGee's famous cremation, a story is told of the old Nebraska farmer who had died in retirement in San Diego. The mortal remains were trundled into a crematorium and subjected to an hour of white-hot flame. When the furnace was opened the old man stepped out, a healthy flush suffusing his weathered cheeks. He wiped the sweat from his forehead with the edge of a calloused thumb, looked up at the sky, and said:

"Shore good to be home again. But by God, another couple weeks of this and we ain't gonna get a corn crop this year!"

It has always seemed incredible that only a few sheets of the calendar separate the prairie winter from summer. Some prairie years have a temperature range of nearly 150 degrees, beginning with the land lying numb and silent under its iron sky, melting into weeks when that land is stunned by the full weight of summer, parboiling in transpired vapor that rises in shimmering waves from fields where corn leaves droop and curl.

Given a choice of being parboiled or baked, I favor the latter. I have hoboed through midsummer in the Mojave and Sonoran deserts where the afternoons were a white blaze and nothing geared to desert life would be abroad; the wild hunters waited until evening, and travelers had made their day's journey by noon. And yet, that heat was not exactly uncomfortable — it was simply untenable in the full sun. It had an odd purifying effect, seeming to shrink tissues and burn away unneeded juices until a man was fired into the igneous conformity that the desert world requires. To one accustomed to the sweltering prairies, it wasn't half bad.

Summer deserts notwithstanding, I can think of no purer form of hell than threshing oats in the old way, and stacking straw under the blower of a steam-driven threshing machine on a July afternoon in central Iowa or Nebraska. The stacker worked directly under the blower, tramping the center of the growing stack to give it the proper rounded shape that would not only shed water readily, but which was also the mark of a good farmer. He labored in a midday twilight of dust and blown straw, his face a mask of grime and sweat, consuming vast quantities of water or "stichel" — the ginger-and-water mixture that some old-time threshers preferred. Almost as bad was the job of spreading straw through the barn lofts or "haymows," working under airless, dust-choked eaves in a torment of itching chaff and smothering heat. It was a labor often complete with the afflictions of Job — I can recall the "thrashers" who did such work while tortured with carbuncles on their necks and wrists, fierce occupational boils that were aggravated by dirt and sweat. No, the working definition of heat is not to be found in the Mojave but in prairie fields with the afternoon standing at 102° and a relative humidity of 80.

The sun blazes, weighing unbearably on the enduring men.

The air is thick and heavy and they are drenched with sweat that cannot cool them. Their work is fevered with special urgency; low on the western horizon is a dark wall of weather that heightens and swells into thunderheads that roll eastward across the land on flickering legs of fire. The front grows taller and darker as the men glance over their shoulders, the storm coming on swiftly now, rising blackly over the summer fields. The long, sullen rumble begins to resolve into individual salvoes of thunder; in the east the land is still flooded with heavy sunlight, but a dark veil is screening fields in the west. Running before the storm is a long, cold, level wind that is delicious against drenched chambray shirts; over in the next section the soft maples and box-elders of a farmstead toss and bow, flashing white as the wind turns up the pale undersides of the leaves. Men and horses quit the fields and head for the buildings, hurrying through that blessed draught of cool wind, the first heavy drops cratering the dust of the home lane. Then the driven sheets of rain are upon them, a pounding deluge lit with thunderflashes of white light and freighted with ozone. The men take shelter under booming shed roofs, not talking a whole lot but sometimes speculating on what landmark trees are being riven, and whose windmills are running wild and destroying themselves.

It passes quickly, the ear-splitting crashes of sound flowing together as before, beginning to deepen with distance as the rain pours down straight and undriven by wind, and then the nearer fields begin to slowly emerge and the vista lifts and lengthens. The western sky goes from slate to ragged gray, and then to pearl that dissolves into windows of watery blue. The sun begins to come again, pale at first but strengthening, and now without weight. There is the fresh dawn-smell of wetted dust and deep coolness, and trees and fields glow with a clear translucence against the dark banks of the fading storm. It is one of the best of summer times, a gift of coolness and beauty with the memory of sweat and heat only an hour old. The farmer looks at his neighbors. "Well, now that we're

washed off we might as well go to the house and find some
pie 'n' coffee."

Such a time is always heightened by the sense of relief that
the thunderstorm was no worse, and that it didn't bring a
"cyclone." Our Grandmother Posegate was a most unflappa-
ble person, but those days would make her nervous as a cat.
She would putter around the house with make-work that
kept her near windows where she could see westward. It was
usually during a "spell" of particularly heavy, breathless heat
when a threatening black weather line would appear along
the western horizon. As it rose toward us, dark and towering,
we might see that it wasn't the usual thunder-front but one
colored like a great bruise, with sullen green and sulfur tones
against the slate of the storm, and strange green flickers of
lightning. At which point Grandma Tut hustled everyone off
to the cellar. It was almost always just another bad thunderstorm. But the old lady had lived through the Grinnell tornado of 1882 — which killed 100 people — and she never
took "cyclone weather" lightly. Nor do any prairie folk who
have been through a real twister.

The tornado is the most violent, abrupt, and unpredictable
wind on earth. It is a "cyclone" in the sense that any cyclone
is wind rotation around a low-pressure area. The tornado is
the distilled essence of cyclone, associated with a violent
thunderstorm and often occurring in afternoon or late in the
day when the hottest time is just past.

Dr. John Stanford, an atmospheric physicist at Iowa State
University, tells us that tornados may occur in Europe, Aus-
tralia, and parts of Asia, but are more likely to occur in the
American Midwest — and with greater violence — than anywhere else in the world. No other region has such classic tornado ingredients.

In simplest terms, there are three basic conditions that
cause the violent thunderstorms that spawn tornados. One is
a warm, moist layer of air extending from the ground to
about 5000 feet. Under certain conditions this warm layer is

prevented from rising by a "lid" of cool, dry air. An extremely unstable condition — especially as the base layer continues to receive additional heat and moisture carried northward from the Gulf and is heated by the sun as well. Dr. Stanford compares this to a pressure cooker, with a lid holding it near the earth as its forces build.

An explosive release of this swelling energy can be provided by the third condition: a cold front advancing from the northwest. This mass of cool, dense air tends to wedge under the layer of moist, heated air and force it upward through the temperature inversion and the heavy lid of cool air. When the masses of extremely warm, wet air are driven up into the chill regions of the upper atmosphere, spectacular forces are triggered. That cold front has, in effect, lit the fuse of atmospheric dynamite. Powerful thunderstorms result — and if enough energy has been built up in those lower layers of heated air, the sudden release of that energy may produce tornados.

The formation of the tornado funnel itself has been described as a localized updraft of the warm, moist air that rises at great speed while developing a twisting effect as more air pours in from all sides. This vortex of rising air spins violently amid heavy rain, salvoes of lightning, and sometimes hail. L. Frank Baum, describing the tornado that spun into one of childhood's greatest adventures, wrote in *The Wizard of Oz:*

> From the far north they heard a low wail of the wind, and Uncle Henry and Dorothy could see where the long grass bowed in waves before the coming storm. There now came a sharp whistling in the air from the south, and as they turned their eyes that way they saw ripples of the grass coming from that direction also ... The north and south winds met where the house stood, and made it the exact center of the cyclone.

Not bad, considering the primitive condition of meteorology in 1900. It makes you wonder if there might not be a lot of truth in the rest of the book as well.

The nation's main tornado zone coincides closely with the central and southern parts of the tallgrass prairie country, extending down from eastern South Dakota into eastern Kansas and Oklahoma and on through eastern and south-central Texas. Branching eastward from this north–south configuration, the infamous "Tornado Alley" extends through southwestern Missouri up through St. Louis, through southern Illinois, and into west-central Indiana. Many people have died in that deadly corridor; in the past 80 years, more than 400 persons have been killed by tornados in St. Louis alone. It was along this route that the nation's worst tornado swarm struck in mid-March 1925, moving from southeastern Missouri across southern Illinois and killing 689 persons. Another tornado zone, somewhat isolated from the others, occurs several hundred miles farther south, where the "Dixie Alley" develops in southern Tennessee, northern Mississippi, and off across northern Alabama and Georgia.

The probability of tornados decreases westward across the Great Plains and virtually ceases at the Rocky Mountains. West of the Rockies, tornado occurrence is extremely low. The East Coast reports many tornados — although their number is small compared to the Midwest's and their intensity far lower. The world's most violent tornado belt lies in the midwestern region of the United States, and the greater number of these storms occurs in southerly parts of the region. For example, Oklahoma is likely to have about twice as many tornados each year in a given area as is Iowa.

Tornados are treacherous, unpredictable, and highly variable — sometimes traveling only a few yards along the ground, or perhaps cutting a swath of destruction for a hundred miles at forty miles per hour. The funnel of a classic tornado, extending down from the low ceiling of storm sky, may be a straight-sided cylinder nearly three hundred yards in diameter. Or it may be a slender, crazily twisting rope that swings and writhes between clouds and earth. Sometimes the

funnel is a ponderous elephant-trunk, or a searching tentacle. The winds within the edge of such a tube are inconceivable — the most powerful winds known. In the past, some meteorologists have estimated tornado wind velocities at 600 miles per hour or more — far more powerful than the strongest hurricane wind — but no one was really sure of this. The winds destroyed the instruments that might have measured them. Recent estimates have been more conservative, putting wind velocities at a mere 300 miles per hour.

There have been authenticated accounts of men's having looked up into the heart of a tornado's funnel. One was of a farmer named Will Keller, of near Greensburg, Kansas, who paused at the door of the family storm cellar and took a last look at an approaching tornado:

> . . . Two of the tornados were some distance away and looked to me like great ropes dangling from the clouds, but the near one was shaped more like a funnel with ragged clouds surrounding it. It appeared to be much larger and more energetic than the others and it occupied the central position of the cloud, the great cumulus dome being directly over it. As I paused to look I saw that the lower end, which had been sweeping the ground, was beginning to rise. I knew what that meant, so I kept my position. I knew that I was comparatively safe and I knew that if the tornado again dipped I could drop down and close the door before any harm could be done.
>
> Steadily the tornado came on, the end gradually rising above the ground. I could have stood there only a few seconds but so impressed was I with what was going on that it seemed a long time. At last the great shaggy end of the funnel hung directly overhead. Everything was as still as death. There was a strong gassy odor and it seemed that I could not breathe. There was a screaming hissing sound coming directly from the end of the funnel. I looked up and to my astonishment I saw right up into the center of the funnel, about 50 or 100 feet in diameter, and extending straight upward for a distance of at least one-half mile, as best I could judge under the circumstances. The walls of this

opening were of rotating clouds and the whole was made brilliantly visible by constant flashes of lightning which zigzagged from side to side. Had it not been for the lightning I could not have seen the opening, not any distance up into it, anyway...

A tornado funnel is horror itself, and its setting compounds the effect — a witches' sabbath of storm, the stricken countryside glowing eerily under that bruised sky of angry green, deep saffron, and purple in a fearful half-light. Accompanying this is what used to be described almost universally as "a roar like a thousand freight trains," an analogy that was brought up to date by one of our Kansas friends who compared it to "every jet in North America doing Mach II at low level across the prairie." The ominous, elemental roar of air gone mad.

Most tornados do little damage. But when they do swing briefly through towns or farmsteads, their havoc is incredible. Structures are torn to matchsticks by the tremendous winds, and it has been speculated that buildings may also be exploded by the great differential of air pressures within the tornado and the buildings. It has even been speculated that this may be responsible for de-feathered chickens that are sometimes found wandering, naked, and confused, in the wakes of tornados. That is, it was thought that their feathers may have been blown out by an instant reduction of air pressure. In an effort to learn more about this, a chicken was once fired from a cannon at 340 miles per hour. The chicken lost all its feathers but its body was torn in the process — something that might not have happened in a tornado in which the bird might be stripped but otherwise undamaged. Anyway, it was concluded that a chicken's feathers are more likely blown *off* by a tornado than blown *out*. I don't believe this work ever received a Nobel nomination.

The internal and external ballistics of a mature tornado have created a folklore that is no less remarkable for being largely true: stories of straws driven through wooden planks, and of the plank driven so deeply into a tree trunk that a man could stand on the free end and spring on it. In 1964 in Campbell County, South Dakota, a tornado peeled back several hundred feet of blacktop surface on Highway 10.

I've never seen a tornado funnel touch down, although I've watched several spawning at once, but I will never forget walking through what had been a prosperous midwestern farmstead. House, barn, and outbuildings had simply vanished, their components strewn like chaff across nearby fields. The thing that struck me most forcibly was not being able to find two boards still joined together. It seemed that every rabbet, dovetail, and nailed joint in two large buildings and one smaller one had been torn apart in an explosive fragmentation that may have lasted only seconds, as if an initial blast had hurled debris into peripheral winds of huge velocity. I have seen V-2 rocket hits on London buildings that did not work such thorough structural dissection.

Still, I wouldn't mind seeing a harmless tornado one of these summers. One that doesn't hurt anything, of course, but just tools around an empty pasture long enough to make its noise and kick up the dust. It's got to be one of the greatest shows on earth, belonging on the same playbill with such primal forces as erupting volcanos and farm wives who find feedlot mud on their kitchen floors.

❧

Much has been made of the wild vagaries of the prairie climate with its high summers and deep winters. An old cliché declares: "There is no usual weather in Iowa; it is all unusual." And there's something to that. On the same date in May, in different years of course, Iowa has had a high of 100° F and a low of 20° F. My home clime in central Iowa has been broiled at 120° F and congealed at −40° F, with a lot of wild stuff in between.

But in spite of such extremes, and the wild episodes of blizzard and tornado, the fact remains that the midcontinental weather of the prairie country is essentially temperate. It averages out to dry, cold winters, hot summers, moderate levels of precipitation, and temperate weather patterns that greatly outweigh the intemperate. That old cliché is somewhat misleading; most prairie weather is just plain usual, and at any time of year there's better weather somewhere else.

Even the best of our prairie weather may not be anything very special in itself. I wouldn't care to get into an autumn contest with New England, nor match springs with most places in the Rockies. The special quality of fine prairie weather isn't necessarily one of intrinsic merit, but of contrast with what has gone just before. Sprinkled through the prairie year are certain very fine times that are usually moderations of unbearable extremes, or which come as refreshing novelty after a long run of dull. The oppressive, wet-wool heat of early August is relieved overnight by a set of sparkling, green-gold days with a sharp decline in humidity and temperature. Or a gray, bitter blizzard sequence is interrupted by silver times of blue-enamel sky, with just enough promise of spring to give new hope but not so much as to drop the bottoms out of country roads. There's another old cliché, truer than the first one: "Iowa is the place where it always rains — and just in time." The same applies to fine weather.

In most of this chapter, I plead guilty to having stressed the theatrics of prairie extremes and of emphasizing the unusual. If I were a climatologist I might be more concerned with means than with extremes — but as a wildlife worker and long-time prairie rambler, the violent extremes of our prairie weather are of the keenest interest

Between these Great Weathers, however, is that broad set of temperate conditions that not only define the prairie climate, but which have largely created the prairie itself, building tall grasslands and deep, fertile soils within a specific band of rainfall and temperature. It is a finely tuned adjustment that favors the prosperity of tallgrasses, including such tame grasses as corn. In *My Ántonia* Willa Cather wrote:

> July came on with that breathless, brilliant heat which makes the plains of Kansas and Nebraska the best corn country in the world. It seemed as if we could hear the corn growing in the night; under the stars one caught a faint crackling in the dewy, heavy-odoured cornfields where the feathered stalks stood so juicy and green. If all the great plain from the Missouri to the Rocky Mountains had been under glass, and the heat regulated by a thermometer, it could not have been better for the yellow tassels that were ripening and fertilizing the silk day by day . . . The burning sun of those few weeks, with occasional rains at night, secured the corn. After the milky ears were once formed, we had little to fear from dry weather.

Those "occasional rains at night" are likely to be convectional showers, often strong but brief, caused by excessive surface heating of unstable Gulf air. These are the "heat thunderstorms" of the corn country, and when they come at night they provide an ideal condition for growing corn — a maximum degree of exposure to sunlight for the amount of rain that falls. June is usually the rainiest month in the Upper Midwest, often followed by a dry late July and August that sets the corn.

Down through the long belt of subhumid tallgrass prairie country that extends from eastern North Dakota and western Minnesota into south-central Texas, rapid and irregular changes in temperature are more frequent in winter than in summer. Most of the region's precipitation comes during summer when water-laden tropical air masses move north from the Gulf of Mexico, literally pumped up the Mississippi Valley by pressure differentials of the Bermuda High. This is the real source of prairie moisture; the polar air masses that prevail in winter are much drier, and as a result the prairies get far more moisture in the form of rain than of snow. Nearly three fourths of the year's precipitation falls during the growing season and about half of this comes during May, June, and July — an optimum arrangement for the production of tallgrasses.

In terms of total rainfall, the tall-prairie belt is a transition between the semiarid Great Plains and the humid forest lands of the East. The easterly margins of the prairie may average only one dry year in twenty; where the western prairie edge merges with the Great Plains there may be ten or more dry or semiarid years in each twenty. On the average, the subhumid lands in the heart of the tall prairie are likely to have only a few years out of twenty that are so lacking in rainfall as to be classed as dry or semiarid.

There was an unusual succession of dry years during the Dust Bowl of the 1930s, when a severe seven-year drought began in the summer of 1934. During this period the western edge of the tallgrass prairie shrank eastward, replaced by the midgrasses of the traditional mixed prairie, which were, on their western edge, replaced by shortgrasses of the plains. This was sharply reflected in the drought's effects on grain crops, as well. The wheatlands of the main Dust Bowl, in what had been mixed prairie and plains, were wiped out by desertification. A little farther east, in what had been the westerly edge of the true prairie, corn was similarly affected — for its climate was actually being converted to a wheat climate. Deep within the subhumid prairielands of eastern Iowa and Illinois there were no bad crop failures that I can recall, but the shadow of drought was felt there, as well.

Winters in the northerly reaches of the tall prairie country run at least 50 degrees colder than in the prairielands of south-central Texas. The midwinter months in eastern North Dakota average about 5 ° F, increasing to about 30 ° F in eastern Nebraska and Kansas, and averaging as much as 55 ° F in the grasslands of south Texas. The contrast of summer temperatures is less great, and a North Dakota July may average 65° F while south-central Texas has a July mean of about 85° F. So the great variance between northern and southern prairie temperatures exists less in hot extremes than in cold ones. A south Texas year may range from 0° F to 110° F, which is wide enough, but a North Dakota year can vary from −60° F to as much as 118° F — a total range of 178 degrees! Latitude is part of the reason for this great differential, with the upper prairies lying far enough north to feel the full weight of the polar easterlies but not so far north as to escape the furnace winds of the Southwest in August. Add to this the fact that the northern prairies lie deep within the midcontinental climate with no modifying influences of large water bodies. Lake-bound northern Michigan is on about the same latitude as North Dakota, but rarely has the extremes of heat and cold that commonly occur on the prairies.

Altogether, the prairie climate is not remarkable for any special extremes of precipitation. The more spectacular extremes of the grassland country are likely to occur in terms of temperature range, and in the abruptness and violence with which changes may occur. For the tall prairie is an ancient warring-place of the subtropical and subarctic, each seeming to strive for its old sovereignty in a conflict of great continental weathers. It is a region where giant airs wrestle at the outer edge of the montane rain shadow, filling the skies with fury that always spends itself and abates in periods of peace and beauty, tempering and strengthening the land below.

PART II
THE PEOPLE

8

Grandfather Country

IF THE EXPRESSION "Land of Beginning Again" seems folkish
and trite today it is through no fault of its own, for there is
still no better way of saying what it meant. But it expresses
something that has no real contemporary meaning, and with
which we can no longer identify — the ineffable spell cast by
new lands on a people weary of the old.

It was the main chance of which men had always dreamed;
more than just hope, it was hope susceptible of attainment. It
blew in on the west wind from empty lands that they had
never seen, fanning their youth and awakening old dreams
and plans that had slumbered among the forested hills of
eastern farm valleys. Ole Rölvaag spoke of it in his *Giants in
the Earth:*

> And it was as if nothing affected people in those days. They
> threw themselves blindly into the Impossible, and accomplished
> the Unbelievable. If anyone succumbed in the struggle — and
> that happened often — another would come and take his place.
> Youth was in the race; the unknown, the untried, the unheard-of,
> was in the air; people caught it, were intoxicated by it, threw
> themselves away, and laughed at the cost. Of course it was possi-
> ble — everything was possible out there. There was no such
> thing as the Impossible any more. The human race has not

known such faith and self-confidence since history began . . . And so had been the Spirit since the day the first settlers landed on the eastern shores; it would rise and fall at intervals, would swell and surge on again with every new wave of settlers that rolled westward into the unbroken solitude.

Romanticized, of course. But in spite of costs that no sane man or woman would laugh at, and however their first exuberance would gray with later reality, there is no gainsaying the hope and excitement that drew the people up the west wind.

Rölvaag knew only one broad cultural category of prairie people. There were essentially two, as unlike as trees and grass: the pioneers who sought permanence on the land, seeking to put down roots in rich soils of their own choosing, and the frontiersmen whose goals were as ephemeral as the frontiers that would always fade off before them. One group sought new lands because they held the main chance; the other sought newness alone, and as the newness wore away so did the land's attraction.

The early thrusts of midwestern pioneers originated in the piedmonts of Virginia and the Carolinas, moving over the Appalachians into Kentucky and Tennessee and then into southern Illinois. It was a fiercely independent breed that customarily moved ahead of the main waves of settlement — perhaps driven by a desire for cheap land or the wish to live in nonslave territory. But more than anything else, they sought to escape the pressures and disciplines of established communities. They were hunters first and farmers a long second.

One early writer who had been "sent to the Illinois" commented that many of the first settlers on the fringes of the Illinois prairies were "idle fellows that are too lazy to cultivate lands, & invited by the plenty of game they found, have employed themselves in hunting, in which they interfere much more with the Indians than if they pursued agriculture alone . . ."

In his *Letters from an American Farmer,* Crèvecoeur wrote: "Thus are our first steps trod, thus are our first trees felled, in general, by the most vicious of our people."

The irascible Dr. Timothy Dwight expanded on this in 1821:

> A considerable part of all those who begin the cultivation of the wilderness may be denominated foresters . . . These men cannot live in regular society. They are too idle; too talkative; too passionate; too prodigal; and are too shiftless; to acquire either property or character. They are impatient of the restraints of law, religion and morality; grumble about taxes, by which Rulers, Ministers and School-masters are supported. After displaying their own talents, and worth; after censuring the weakness, the wickedness, of their superiors; after exposing the injustice of the community in neglecting to invest persons of such merit with public offices . . . they become at length discouraged; and under the pressure of poverty, the fear of a gaol, and the consciousness of public contempt, leave their native places and betake themselves to the wilderness.

Such men were often called "Pikes" in the prairie country and beyond, for they frequently originated in some Pike County or other. This could have been many places. There's a Pike County in eastern Kentucky, another in southwestern Arkansas, and there are neighboring counties Pike in northeastern Missouri and western Illinois, separated by the Mississippi River. Anyway, this archetype of the prairie frontiersman wasn't content with whatever Pike County he happened to hail from. Crowded out into the open grasslands by increasing settlement of the forest and the prairie edge, he was among the first to cross the plains into California, where he was arbitrarily dubbed "Pike" and described by Bayard Taylor:

> He is the Anglo-Saxon relapsed into semi-barbarism. He is long, lathy and sallow; he expectorates vehemently; he takes naturally to whiskey; he has the shakes his life-long at home, though he

generally manages to get rid of them in California; he has little respect for the rights of others; he distrusts men in "store clothes," but venerates the memory of Andrew Jackson. That's what a "Pike" is.

But for all that, he was among the first — as Crèvecoeur had said. He was certainly the most colorful of the prairie-comers, and made some unique contributions. By rough definition, Jim Bridger, Kit Carson, Davy Crockett, and even Abe Lincoln came from families of "Pikes," and Sweet Betsy and her tall lover Ike gave Pike County a lilting place in American folk music that would never be shared by the solid farmers who put down roots in prairie counties and never found much reason to sing about it.

The first real prairie settling of any magnitude was in Illinois, of course, for that was the first-met of the real prairies. The vanguard of upland Southerners began drifting into the forested southerly parts of Illinois shortly after the Louisiana Purchase. The second major contingent — the Yankees from New England, New York, and Pennsylvania — began arriving in force during the late 1820s and 1830s. These later arrivals were in the minority of Illinois settlers during the early days, but they rapidly increased and became the most significant part of the population. They were generally better educated than the woodsman-hunter-farmers who had preceded them; they were invariably better farmers, with more cash and better equipment, knew more about Illinois before they had begun their journey, had more regard for plow than rifle, and had generally come to stay. These were the real prairie pioneers, or would become so.

Few were actually frontiersmen. They were pioneers in the sense that they had no real taste for unmapped vastnesses nor wilderness, and certainly not for fighting Indians and living off the land. They simply wanted good ground on which to settle — and the prairie country offered nearly unlimited land, and almost for the asking. Not all were farmers, of course. There were blacksmiths, merchants, circuit-riding exhorters, politicians, and a sprinkling of lawyers and doctors. But whatever their plans might be, those plans always included good cheap land.

In 1840 the American frontier lay at the eastern margins of the tall prairie. The first period of American settlement, that of the eastern forests, was drawing to a close. The second major period, the taming of the great grasslands, was just beginning. It was a dynamic time, with a sort of cultural interface existing between the two periods — an "institutional fault" at which ways of living were changed. Many of the institutions carried across it were broken, remade, and broken again in a dramatic reshaping of agriculture, tools, weapons, lifestyles, laws, and even political philosophy. For two centuries the symbols of American frontierism had been the axe and the log cabin. Men were accustomed to judging land by the kinds of timber that grew on it — not by the kinds of grasses. But by 1840 the eastern forests were at their backs, and they were being confronted by the real prairie in its full magnitude.

During the preceding twenty years or so, midwestern settlement had been more or less limited to the oak openings and prairie enclaves of Ohio, Indiana, Wisconsin, Michigan, and eastern and southern Illinois. But as these areas were settled by farmers or claimed by speculators, new pioneers had little choice but to head out into the heart of northern Illinois's Grand Prairie, or over into the empty new lands of interior Iowa.

Many emigrants in the 1840s and early 1850s were second-generation pioneers who had grown up in parts of Indiana or Illinois where there was no longer room on the original homesteads for big pioneer families. With the best farmlands already claimed or settled, the landless sons and daughters of the original pioneers began to roll forward in a new wave of prairie settlement. In 1850, almost three fourths of the Iowa settlers were native-born midwesterners from Illinois, Indiana, and Ohio. This began to change later in the 1850s when the proportion of New Englanders and foreign-born pioneers increased greatly, and the wave of Scandinavians that would settle northern Iowa, southern Minnesota, and the Dakotas was just beginning. Some of these, incidentally, had a strangely naïve conception of the new land. As Ole Rynning wrote in his *True Account of America,*

> It is a general belief among the common people in Norway that America was well populated a few years ago, and that a plague — almost like the Black Death — has left the country desolate of people. As a result they are of the opinion that those who emigrate to America will find cultivated farms, houses, clothing and furniture ready for them . . .

The new land wasn't free for the claiming. In fact, the federal government was largely financed for a half-century by the sale of its public lands, at a going rate of about $1.25 per acre. A new arrival chose an area and drove claim stakes, blazed trees, or marked rocks at the corners, put up some kind of shelter, and began cultivation. This established his claim. He was required to pay for his claim at the nearest land office — in gold. Soldiers in various wars were paid in part with land warrants that were as good as gold at land offices. (Abe Lincoln used his land warrant from the Black Hawk War to acquire land in Iowa.) Such warrants were originally nontransferable, but that was changed and land speculators began to buy up many of the warrants. There may have been as much original prairie acquired with land warrants as with gold.

The actual prairie pioneering spanned only about fifty years from first to last. The first trickle of real prairie settlement into grassland Indiana and Illinois began no earlier than about 1820. The prairielands of those states were largely claimed and tamed in little more than two decades. The pioneer era in Iowa extended from the opening of settlement in the mid-1830s to the beginning of the Civil War, and most of the pioneering of the tallgrass regions of the Dakotas, Nebraska, Kansas, western Missouri, Oklahoma, and central Texas was over by 1875. In one lifetime the great tallgrass reaches of middle America had been opened, broken, and inked onto deeds. It was all deceptively swift and easy; in reality, it was one of the world's great revolutions — a vast reordering of what men felt they knew about land, a discarding of old traditions and methods, and a painful learning process in which men adapted to a new system of grassland existence.

❦

Whenever they could, they settled " 'cordin' to wood 'n' water."

They preferred the prairie region's timbered country and clung to "oak openings," upland groves, and timbered stream valleys, for all their experience related to forestland farming and they chose to deal with what they knew. They certainly knew woodlands — and besides, some of them nursed the suspicion that upland prairie soils weren't all that danged good, anyway.

There were excellent reasons for stopping in the prairie's woodlands. These timbered regions offered fuel and building materials, good game supplies, shelter from blizzards and prairie fires, and often ledge-rock for cabin foundations and fireplaces. Water was readily available, either in streams or in the shallow wells of flood-plain water tables. Out on the prairie uplands it might be necessary to dig a hundred feet or more to reach water, and there was rarely any stone with which to line the wells. A man living on open prairie in the early days had to depend on creeks and ponds, or waste valuable time hauling water casks from streams that might be some distance away. Prairie well-drilling would come much later, and even then it was expensive.

Then, too, the remote prairies lacked major waterways for

transport and trade. Early settlement in Illinois had begun in the south because of the excellence of the Ohio River as a travel route; from there, settlers moved northward along the Wabash, Illinois, Kaskaskia, and Mississippi. By 1820, the 55,000 people in Illinois were practically all living within forested regions where running water, fuel, and building materials were available. The large prairies were settled last because they lay on remote divides between major watercourses. Northern Illinois prairies were virtually inaccessible until the development of transportation facilities on the Great Lakes in the late 1830s. These great interior prairies could be reached only by overland travel — and prairie schooners came to northern Illinois years after the first keelboats and rafts had brought settlers to southerly parts of the state.

Early pioneers could afford to be fussy about how far they lived from timber, if indeed they lived away from it at all. In 1819 an Illinois man wrote: "At present a new settler builds his cabin at the edge of the timbered land and fences in the prairie ground, sufficient for his tillage, which he has no trouble in clearing. But the great distance between the timbered land in many places, it being from 12 to 20, 30 or 40 miles, will leave it thinly settled in places for some time." In 1833 an English observer in Illinois noted: "A settler regards a distance of half a mile from the forest as an intolerable burden."

But as prime timber sites were claimed, this attitude was steadily modified. In 1837 Judge James Hall said:

A farmer had better settle in the midst of prairie and haul his rails and fuel five miles, than undertake to clear a farm in the forest. The farmers of Illinois are beginning to be aware of this fact, and there are now many instances of farmers having purchased a small piece of land for timber, in the woodland, and make their farm at a distance, in the prairie.

Settlement proceeded in ringlike waves toward the center of the prairie. The most desirable farmsteads (once the value of prairie soil was known) contained both timber and prairie — although there was much disagreement over the relative size of each portion. The first prairie farmers might have their homes in upland groves or wooded stream valleys, with most of their farming done in adjacent prairie. Later homesteaders would live and farm on the prairie itself, but own timbered plots not far away. At the very last, settlers of the great open prairies might be forty miles from the nearest big timber.

The value of woodland was scaled in its proportion to the prairieland in which it lay. Most farmers soon knew that prairie soils were far more productive than timber soils — but there was prairie everywhere, and wood was a rare commodity. During the 1830s in Illinois, the value of timber to prairie was roughly seven to one — with forested land bringing about $35 an acre and prairie selling for $5 an acre. As late as 1867 in Marshall County in central Iowa, prairie was selling for as little as $3 an acre while good timberland brought as much as $50.

So in spite of the great superiority of prairie soils, timberland had the advantage of sheer utility. And even though grassland soils were inherently richer and more durable than those of the woodlands, the prairie sods and loams presented some special problems.

Clearing a forest farm was a low-capital project that required more manpower than animal power. A good man with an axe and a team could "set up" in forest farming; it took time and patience and heavy labor, but once the trees were girdled, or felled and burned, the light forest soil could be easily plowed and cultivated.

Not so with prairie.

The crests of ridges weren't too bad, with their stands of little bluestem; and weakened prairie sod near forest borders wasn't bad, either. But out on the flat, open prairie in the realm of big bluestem, cord grass, and Indian grass, the heavy sod that lay between the settler's boots and the treasure of deep loam was a formidable barrier. It demanded special attack by huge breaking plows and oxteams; if the settler didn't own the necessary stock and equipment, he had to hire it. Either way, it demanded a sizable investment to break a quarter-section or more of native prairie.

The first sodbusting was done with a clumsy, heavy, unmanageable plow that might have a 14-foot beam and a 125-pound plowshare, perhaps rolling on a pair of cartwheels and pulled by as many as seven yokes of oxen. It might require three men; one guiding the lead oxen with a goad, another holding the plow handles, and a third sitting on the long beam in order to hold the plow to its work if it were necessary to rip through stands of hazelbrush or patches of redroot. Some massive breaking plows would turn a furrow 26 inches wide and a mile long, the lines of oxen leaning into their wooden yokes and rolling their eyes in effort. Breaking new ground was often the work of small groups of local men who "hired out" with their teams and plows, laboring on new claims miles from any house. It wasn't uncommon for them to live off the land, taking rifle or shotgun out into the prairie to shoot their food.

Breaking a native quarter-section might cost as much as $600 — a staggering sum on the money-poor prairie frontier. And even after the native sod was broken and turned, a new set of problems emerged. The cast-iron or wood-and-iron plow blades that had worked so well in light forest soils and the rocky fields of New England proved unsatisfactory for most prairie plowing because the rich prairie loam clung to the moldboards like glue, and the plowman had to stop every few yards and scrape off the clotted loam with a wooden paddle. A new way was badly needed.

The breakthrough began in 1833 when John Lane, Sr., of Lockport, Illinois, came up with the idea of making prairie plows of polished steel, to which the loam could not adhere. He made his plowblades of old steel mill saws, and the plows were soon in such demand that not only was the supply of old sawblades used up, but new blades were being converted to plowshares. However, Lane never patented the idea nor made his plows in large quantities.

The idea was improved in 1837 by a Grand Detour, Illinois, blacksmith named John Deere. Late of Rutland, Vermont, where he had earned a reputation for brightly polished hay forks and shovels, Deere not only designed an improved plowshare that he made to order, but built up supplies of the new plows that he took out into the countryside to sell. By 1843 he was ordering special rolled steel from England, and was soon making a thousand of his new prairie plows each year.

These were the beginnings of a whole lineage of prairie plows. In 1868, John Lane, Jr., developed a three-layer plowshare and moldboard of two thin outer plates of polished steel with a center layer of soft iron that lent strength without brittleness and was not so likely to snap under sudden strain as were earlier plows of pure tempered steel. Each model was more efficient than the one before. They were uniquely American, these plows, with that special grace that marked the Lancaster rifle and the curved-helve American axe — light, artistic, but supremely functional and answering needs unique to a new land. In her poem "The Land," Sackville-West sang somewhat prematurely:

> Homer and Hesiod and Virgil knew
> The ploughshare in its reasonable shape,
> Classical from the moment it was new
> Sprung ready-armed, ordained without escape,
> And never bettered though man's cunning grew,
> And barbarous countries joined the classic reach . . .

But the plowshare *was* bettered as man's cunning grew, and precisely because a barbarous new land had demanded it. A lean, light, graceful tool "as bereft of ornament as the peasant's speech," it met and mastered the need. With time, even the great clumsy cast-iron breaking plows with their long lines of toiling oxen were largely replaced by light steel plows, drawn by only one yoke of oxen or a three-horse hitch.

And the breaking of the prairie proceeded apace.

David Costello has said that the plow cut through tough rootlets and plant spurs with a sound like fusillades of tiny pistol fire, all amplified by the tempered steel moldboard in a steady ringing hum that might last fourteen hours a day. It sliced easily through the prairie sod, turning up long ribbons of black loam that were polished by the bright moldboard and lay shining black in the sunlight, each ribbon tucking itself into the furrow of the one before. In the wake of the plow was the confusion of the prairie's dispossessed: meadow mice, shrews, small snakes, insects, ground-dwelling bees, a whole multitude of minor citizens that dwelt in the grassroots, attended by clouds of wheeling Franklin's gulls that followed the plowman.

The steady work was almost never hindered by stumps or rocks. Although the prairie plowman might occasionally strike a glacial boulder the size of one of his oxen, he could usually break a quarter-section of new ground without ever seeing a stone larger than a walnut.

It was best to break sod between early May and mid-July. June was the favored month, although a passable crop could be raised the second season on sod turned over any time between the first starting of grass and midsummer.

The first plow cut was as shallow as possible; the thinner the sod was cut, the better it would rot. During the summer, fall, and winter the broken sod mellowed, its native plant parts weakening and slowly disintegrating. It would be several years before the grassroots became rich, smooth loam — but if the ground-breaking was done in spring, there was a good chance that a crop of sod corn could be planted for harvest in the first autumn. A man simply broke the prairie and struck his axe into the upturned sod, dropping seed corn into the hole. Or he could drop corn into every fourth row while plowing, and cover this by the plowing of the fifth furrow. Neither yield nor quality of such corn was high that first year, but it was sufficient, and the settler might make fifteen to twenty-five bushels per acre and that was far more than he could expect in the first year of a forest-farm claim.

The original plowing could be easily turned in the second spring, and second-year fields would be put to wheat, barley, or oats, and enough corn to feed cattle and hogs. It would be many years before corn would be the premium crop of the tall prairie country. And always, before and after the new fields were planted, the sod-breaking went on. Whatever other labors demanded his time, this would be the settler's continuing priority.

Oxen were the important draft animals of the first sod-breaking. Their great strength was almost essential for the breaking, but once the native sod had been turned, subsequent plowing became much easier. Fields that had required oxen and large breaking plows one spring could be easily managed with three horses and a 16-inch steel plow the next, and tillage became progressively easier as the soil mellowed. Most pioneers converted from oxen to horses with alacrity. It was no fun to drive oxen; it could even be downright irritating. The affection and respect that men felt toward good horses apparently never extended to oxen. The stolid brutes simply didn't have the personality to stir men's souls, and the average settler couldn't get rid of them soon enough.

Prairie tillage was prodigious labor at best, but men of the time marveled at its ease. "Imagine a land where there are more birds' nests than stones!" one pioneer rhapsodized, and in 1846 a prairie farmer wrote: "It is cheaper to haul fencing 2–3 miles than to spend ten years clearing the heavy timbered lands of Ohio, Indiana, Kentucky, and Canada. Besides, who ever knew of anyone who left the prairies for the tim-

ber?" Still, the new problems of prairie farming were intensified by the overwhelming urgency to do several things at virtually the same time: break the sod, get seed into the new
plowing if possible, and build at least a semipermanent
dwelling for the family. If any one of those projects failed, the
whole endeavor might collapse.

Some land-hunting settlers left their families behind temporarily, going out into the new country with a couple of sons
or a neighbor after the crops at home had been put by. They
might spend the winter on the new homestead, living off the
land and building a crude shelter into which the family could
move when everyone came west early the following spring.
This first shelter was often half-cabin, half-dugout, built on a
south-facing hillside and meant to be temporary housing
until a permanent cabin could be built. With luck, that cabin
could be raised late in the first summer after a garden had
been established and some fields plowed and planted. If there
was help from neighbors, cabin-building wasn't a formidable
job. It could even be a welcome social event, with the women
sharing neighborhood gossip, the boys and girls lollygoggling
at each other, and the men covertly sharing a jug after the
day's work.

The first prairie settlers, with free choice of land, had no
lack of sound building materials. They certainly had no lack
of experience; they simply built as they always had, hewing,
shaping, and fitting with practiced ease. If there were eight
or ten good men on the job, a cabin could be raised and
roofed in only a few days. The fewer the builders, the longer
it would take and the more flimsy the finished result was
likely to be. But with plenty of help to "carry up the corners"
of heavy log walls, the cabin would be a solid and enduring
home. Some early log cabins along the prairie frontier were
continuously occupied for seventy-five years.

If there was time, the hardwood logs of the cabin walls
might be squared with broadaxes. Pine was seldom available,

of course, and the walls were often made of white oak — although some early cabins were made almost entirely of black walnut. There were rarely any nails or other hardware available; joints were cleverly mortised and tenoned, or secured with pegs of black locust driven into auger holes. A roof was made by laying very straight small logs from gable to gable, and overlaid by clapboard slabs nearly five feet long. Weight poles were then laid over the roof, again secured with wooden pins.

Fireplaces and chimneys presented a special problem in that land with more birds' nests than stones. Some flues were made of sod plastered inside with clay, but the most common type was the "cat and clay" chimney made of small split stakes about three feet long, thickly plastered with clay. In cold weather, such chimneys frequently burned. The fireplace itself had to be built of stone — or of stone and clay, or wood faced with stone. In any case, it was usually planked on the outside of the cabin with short butts of logs to contain the rock and mortar.

The finished cabin might have a puncheon floor made of split logs, with storage chests and boxes kept under high bunks. In real frontier society, the squared inner walls of the cabin would be whitewashed, and the actual cooking and eating might be done in a smaller cabin a short distance away from the main house. The typical cabin, however, combined all the family activities in one room and perhaps a loft. The walls were lined with pegs for spare clothing and utensils; from the rafters hung sides of bacon, smoked hams, venison saddles, and rings of dried pumpkin and squash. And always, just over the door, were hung rifle, powderhorn, and bullet pouch.

Building materials grew progressively poorer farther out on the open prairies. Settlers there were denied oak, hickory, and walnut and were forced to rely on cottonwood, ash, and even willow. They would build cabins of cottonwood logs

that were roofed with willow and sod, and in extreme cases
they might even build family cabins entirely of willow poles.
But in the outer reaches of the tall prairie even those poor
building materials weren't to be had, and the settlers were
forced to make homes from the prairie sod itself.

Sloughgrass sod was the best, with its dense matrix of
strong interlocked roots. Lowlands of sloughgrass and big
bluestem were scalped of their sod, which was usually cut
into slabs a foot wide and two feet long. The course of a wall
was laid two sods wide, and the next higher course would be
laid at right angles to the first. This sealed all joints and the
wall of a sod house was a weatherproof two feet thick — cool
in summer and warm in winter. The roofs, made of pole
framing, were covered with thin turfs and thatched with the
tough sloughgrass. An elderly Nebraska lady once told me
that the roof of her sod home "leaked two days before a rain
and for three days after."

A fortunate prairie woman might have a soddy with whitewashed inner walls, and perhaps, later on, even a couple of
wooden-sashed glass windows. But rarely, if ever, would
there be anything but a dirt floor. A question arises: How
were such floors kept clean?

Just outside the Badlands National Park in South Dakota is
a privately owned sod house that is open to the public. The
owner once told us that he'd puzzled over this floor-sweeping
problem, knowing that pioneer women were as likely to take
pride in housekeeping as their sisters back East. One day a
family of Nebraska tourists visited the soddy. They had
brought great-grandmother, who took keen interest in the
sod house and its furnishings. When asked about the floor-
cleaning problem, the old lady laughed: "Why, one of my
jobs as a young girl was sprinkling salt on the floor. It worked
into the dirt and made a tough crust that was almost like lino-
leum, and 'twarnt hard to keep clean at all!"

Many soddies were never much more than miserable, depressing hovels, but a few were grand, two-storied, shingle-roofed affairs that might even have trimmings of Victorian gingerbread — about as wild a concession to both function and fashion as the prairies ever saw. As a rule, however, early settlers rarely took any pride in their soddies. Old wet-plate photographs of farm families outside their sod houses often included a few prized possessions that had been hauled outside for the occasion: a new organ, a canopied perambulator, and perhaps a table and chairs that had been "brought out from home." It was their way of letting the world know that they were getting ahead, even though they might live in a cabin made of earth.

As building supplies began to be available in the 1870s, with railroads and freight lines bringing finished lumber, glass, and hardware to the remotest corners of the prairie, sod houses began to vanish. The frame houses that replaced them certainly had advantages; they were usually roomier, airier, and more easily kept, and were great advances in status. But for all that, the frame house was a poorly insulated structure that might be less comfortable than the well-built sod house that it replaced, and a few settlers were in no great hurry to make the change. I have a friend who was born in a South Dakota sod house in 1929.

There were early attempts to use sod walls for fences, but this never did work out well. Neither did ditches around the pastures. Open range on the outer prairies remained open because there was no choice, and it wasn't until the invention of barbed wire in the early 1870s that the problem of fencing fields and pastures was really solved. Some writers believe that the coming of barbed wire, not the coming of the rail-roads, was responsible for the final settlement of the open prairies. Barbed wire was ideal for its purpose — relatively cheap, easy to string, a good barrier to animals, and it couldn't be wrecked by wind and didn't form snowdrifts. Of course, there was the problem of fenceposts. This was solved in central and eastern Kansas with the opening of stone quarries in the Flint Hills and the production of stone posts. Holes were drilled into limestone strata about eight inches apart, and "feathers" and wedges driven into these until the rock split. The resulting fencepost was about nine inches square, maybe six feet long, and weighed up to 450 pounds. These posts might be set only eighteen inches into the ground, but there they stayed! I recently set a Kansas fencepost at the edge of the little prairie patch behind my house with no help but a wheelbarrow, pry bar, and dedicated ignorance. It's a heavy way to spend three hours. Back in the 1880s, such posts were delivered to the fenceline for 25¢ each, and six or eight posts was a big load for a team of horses. Lines of stone posts can still be seen out around Salina, and the posts are commonly used around roadside parks along Interstate 70.

Fuel was a critical problem in the treeless northern prairies, and settlers were often forced to make long trips to timbered river valleys for firewood. Poor, sappy firewood might be stored in a stove oven in order to dry it enough to cook the next meal, and settlers even grubbed out stumps for fuel. To conserve precious firewood, a pioneer family might use "cats" of twisted prairie grass in special hay-burning stoves. A tightly twisted faggot of tough-culmed sloughgrass would burn hotly for as long as ten minutes. Piles of these "cats" were kept in the houses in winter, and prairie hay was stacked in the dooryards as a standby for severe storms. In one hour a prairie boy or girl could twist a day's supply of this fuel; years later, their grandchildren would gather corncobs from the hog lot for the kitchen range. In one form or another, grass cooked and heated for three generations of prairie folk.

The problems of these remote, treeless prairies went beyond the simple lack of fuel and building materials.

Older, first-settled prairielands had extensive forests through their valleys partly because those lands lay farther

east in more humid regions, and also because such deep valleys and streamcourses were sheltered, well-watered refuges
for trees. If those regions had been planed by glaciers at all, it
had been so long ago that distinct, deeply cut drainage systems had developed — providing not only shelter for trees,
but efficiently draining the uplands and creating "dry" prairies that were easily traveled and farmed.

But above the terminal moraines of the most recent Wisconsin glaciation, it was another matter. There the land was
young with few distinct features. It was often a poorly
drained wilderness of sloughs, ponds, potholes, lakes walled
with glacial boulders, and swales filled with snowmelt ponds
that might linger into midsummer. Even the Indian and buffalo seemed to avoid such regions. This was the "wet prairie"
deplored by early dragoons and land-lookers who flatly pre-
dicted that it would never be fit for agriculture.

Seen in the late summer and fall, it was a tawny landscape
of ripening grass and flowered hillsides that was promising
enough — easily traveled and quite arable. But woe to the
settler who moved on the strength of that first promise; in
late winter, spring, and early summer the bottom dropped
out of the land, isolating settlers from their markets and
sources of supply. On older prairies, even in wet seasons, it
was usually possible to travel the high, drier ridges. But here,
strangely enough, even the crests of the prairie swells might
be swampy — and the swales below were bottomless mires or
standing lakes. As late as 1875 there were northern Iowa
townships in which no land had been claimed, and not all of
northern Iowa's best farmland had been occupied by 1890.

In the summer of 1858, several Iowa farmers succumbed to
the lure of soaring prices and tried to haul five wagonloads of
flour from Vinton to Fort Dodge — a distance of about
ninety miles. They soon learned why freighted goods were
bringing such high prices at the Fort. The way was a roadless
horror of impassable sloughs and creek heads, of deep bogs

and quaking, saturated earth that was difficult enough for a walking man to travel, much less heavy wagons and ox teams. The exhausted freighters and their animals never got beyond Webster City, only a few miles from their destination. Between there and Fort Dodge, they were told, were two final sloughs: "Little Hell," in which most of their horses and oxen would probably be drowned, and "Big Hell," where oxen, horses, and men were sure to be drowned. So they sold their five tons of flour on the streets of Webster City for $8.75 per hundredweight — which was much less than they'd have gotten in Fort Dodge, but by that time they didn't care. They had been through hell enough, just getting that far.

This was the sort of country awaiting the last waves of prairie settlers — those Norwegians, Swedes, and Irish who arrived too late to claim well-drained prairielands that were dry above and timbered below. But they had the last laugh, at that. Draglines, bull ditches, and cheap clay tiles began to appear in the early 1880s, and the wet prairie changed almost overnight. Its very newness and lack of feature meant that it was unleached prairie soil of the highest quality, and today it is sold for $3000 per acre or more, if it's for sale at all.

❧

Most of this came after the time of homespun, buckskin, and linsey-woolsey. The first ripples of the Industrial Revolution were lapping along the prairie frontier, bringing calico, some mill-made woolens, cotton drills and flannels, and the first of the heavy denims. It was no longer necessary for the pioneer to make his own cloth; he might have been better off had he been able to do so, but the far grasslands offered little in the way of linen, wool, or raw cotton. The prairie settlers were dependent on eastern textiles — which must have worn pretty thin between shipments.

Pioneer boys had no distinctive dress; they usually looked like miniatures of their fathers, with similar jeans, shirts, coats, hats, and leather galluses, although on Sundays the boys were likely to wear knee-length trousers and "round-about" jackets. Girls wore shorter dresses than their mothers, with stout shoes and heavy cotton stockings for winter. In cold weather everyone wore homemade, ill-fitting undergarments of cotton flannel. Over these, boys and men wore old trousers and a pair of denim or heavy drill overalls to break the wind. In winter, they wore woolen visored caps of the style still sometimes seen on the northern plains, and boys and girls alike wore long mufflers of bright wool wound around their necks and ears. There were undoubtedly men and boys along the Middle Border who wore fur caps in winter; in the north these were probably of muskrat, for raccoons were unknown on the northern prairies during the early period of settlement.

For Sundays, weddings, and "buryin's," men and women wore suits of somber broadcloth and full dresses of heavy taffeta with a dearth of fancy trimming, and although a woman might wear a prized brooch or locket, her husband often dispensed with collar and cravat and made do with a steel collar button. One pioneer woman — the first white child born west of the Des Moines River in Iowa — told of "going to meeting" in the late 1830s when her father would wear a fawnskin vest, tanned with hair on, the soft tones and dappled patterning intact.

In summer, men and boys wore oat-straw hats, hickory or calico shirts, and jeans of some sort — although the boys usually got along without the shirts. Younger girls, wearing shapeless cotton shifts that reached below their knees, were usually bare-armed, bare-legged, and bare-footed. Their mothers, in even the hottest weather, wore full-sleeved cotton dresses that buttoned to the throat and reached to their ankles, but while putting up preserves in late summer they surely rolled up those sleeves and undid the top buttons of the bodice.

One of the hallmarks of the prairie frontier was "turkey red" calico that provided dresses for women and girls and shirts for men and boys — a cheap, dark red, small-patterned cotton. Work clothing was invariably patched and well-worn, with patches rarely matching the original material. Since the cheap dyes of that time were seldom fast, and because laundry was boiled in kettles with yellow homemade lye soap, those everyday clothes must have been bleached almost white before they were relegated to the patch basket.

Hair styles were simple and functional; adult women wore their hair up, combed tightly back into buns, and only small girls wore their hair loose or in long braids. The women usually wore sunbonnets when they could, often clinging desperately to the small vanity of trying to remain pale and ladylike. In the fields where they sometimes joined their husbands, however, sunbonnets might not be practical and the women often wore straw hats like their menfolk. Neither hat nor sunbonnet was very effective; what the sun didn't do, the never-ceasing wind did, and a prairie woman's face in middle age might be almost as leathery as her husband's. If any of those women wore trousers or overalls into the fields they never made a point of going on historical record. More often, they probably just pinned up their skirts above bullhide boots.

There were no overshoes nor "gum boots" on the prairie frontier. Footwear was of heavy leather that had to be incessantly greased and tallowed during the winter with waterproofings that ran the gamut from bear grease and mink oil to hog lard and catfish oil. Boots were generally bought a size or two larger than needed to accommodate for shrinkage and for several pairs of heavy socks. They were often made from the thick back leather of buffalo, with soles affixed by wooden pegs. The boots of a pair might be identical so that they could be changed from foot to foot and afford as much wear as possible, and the long "mule-ear" straps were essential:

Without them, it would have been impossible to pull on a pair of boots that had dried by the hearth. Children usually wore copper-toed boots that were ardently loathed as symbols of babyhood; in a shrewd effort to assuage young customers, some bootmakers offered fancy boots with red tops and colored cutouts on the legs — often flags or stars during the Civil War period.

In summer, of course, children never wore shoes except when going to meeting or to a settlement. Like that eminent son of Missouri, Huck Finn, the boys usually went unshod from spring thaw almost to the first snowfall — often walking barefoot over frost-whitened barnyards to do the morning milking. There was a trick to that: If there was no stanchion to confine Old Bossy, you roused her carefully so that as you milked her you could put your cold feet on the patch of warm earth where she had slept.

It was a world where children grew up quickly; yet their childhood was not denied them.

They had few store toys. There might be a clay-headed doll for sister, and her brother might have some cheap clay marbles (and rarely, a prized "aggie" or two) and maybe an India rubber ball. As they grew older she might be allowed to play with the china-headed French doll that mother had "brought out from home," and he would own a genuine Barlow jackknife. But most dolls, sleds, skates, and simple toys and games were homemade, and they sufficed.

With the exception of the family Bible, a *McGuffey's Reader*, and perhaps copies of *Aesop's Fables* and *Pilgrim's Progress*, books were almost nonexistent in the prairie homestead, and good storytellers and yarn-spinners never lacked attention. There were shivery "jump stories" told at the fireside by grandmother — scary tales that lost no savor after a hundred tellings, never failing to send children off to the bed-loft deliciously frightened. Or, father and grandfather might tell about the fall and winter when they had come west to prove up the claim, living off the land and hunting with a few wandering Osages or Mesquakies, learning the old sign talk and feasting on wild honey and fat puppy.

Winter brought the children blizzards, snow tunnels through drifts in the lee of barn and house, skating parties on frozen sloughs, games of fox-and-geese, and candlelit taffy pulls. Fall meant husking bees, and hunting trips for the older boys and men. Summer was a time of mudpies and swimming holes, pom-pom-pullaway and hunting bee trees in the creek timber. And always horseback riding, of course — herding cattle in the great fenceless pastures, or pounding down the dim little road that was bordered with tall sunflowers and that wandered along the ridgetops like a gilt ribbon, and then reining in on a rise to let Old Nimble blow and looking back toward home where father's new fields melted almost without a trace into the endless, sweeping vistas of grassland that swelled in long folds toward a far and open skyline.

Few toys, indeed.

※

The pioneer years were years of primitive abundance, and of strange and primitive dangers.

The most dreaded danger, and the most ingrained in the fiber of early prairie life, was surely Indians. For whether the settlers had come from the Mohawk Valley or the Dark and Bloody Ground — or from almost anywhere between — there were likely to be victims of Indians somewhere in their own families or among their neighbors. And even if there weren't, they had taken in stories of the red terror with their mothers' milk and had brought the old stories and old fears into the new land. They were not timid men and women; if anything, they were probably braver than most. But they weren't frontiersmen, either, and had no relish for high adventure and Indian fighting. They were just pioneer farmers with families, wanting only good land and peace enough to work it.

As it turned out, their fears were generally unfounded.

Most tribes in the tallgrass prairies had never been especially ill-disposed toward the whites. They had not been inflamed by white military factions as had the war nations of the eastern forests, and had not yet been driven to the fierce desperation that would be shown by the plains Indians a little later. Along much of the prairie frontier, the federal government followed a policy of not opening new lands until the title of the Indians had been "quieted." The Sauk and Fox had been moved out of much of Iowa before it was really settled, and the eastern Sioux had relinquished most of their lands in northern Iowa and southern Minnesota in 1851. In more southerly regions of the tall prairie the Osages, Kaws, Poncas, and others gave little real trouble to the first settlers, and such fierce peoples as the Kiowa, Pawnee, and Comanche were more active in the mixed prairies and plains a little farther west.

With some exceptions, troublesome Indians along the prairie frontier were more likely to be dangerous nuisances than deadly foes, and the real massacres in the tall prairie country came relatively late. It was in 1857 that Inkpadutah and his band of warriors wiped out the settlement of Lake Okoboji and Spirit Lake in northwestern Iowa, and it wasn't until 1862 that the Sioux erupted in southern Minnesota — by then a well-established farming region. That Minnesota Outbreak had been somewhat eclipsed by the early years of the Civil War, but it was the worst single massacre in western America. In one bloody week, the Sioux massacred over 450 settlers and drove thousands of others into refugee camps in New Ulm and other frontier villages.

But the Indian was not the only red terror on the early prairies; there was one far more common, and no less deadly.

As the tops of annual grasses die each autumn, their chlorophyll fading and their life retreating into roots, rhizomes, and seeds, the dead materials left above may return to the earth. Or, in a sense, to the sun. Tall prairie grasses, especially in dry autumns, are tinder of almost explosive quality. They always burned sooner or later, kindled by lightning strikes, careless settlers, or Indians. But whatever the cause, one thing was certain: Each autumn and spring the prairie fires would come.

By day there might be a strange haze in the air, and a smokiness flowing down the watersheds. By night, a reddish-orange glow was reflected from behind the horizons. If there was no wind, the haze and glow might last for days before the settler actually saw flames, and he had time to plow firelanes around his buildings and stackyards, and burn the grass within the plowing. The windless prairie fire would advance deliberately, marching across the grassland while tufts of bluestem vanished in lambent puffs of flame, with white smoke drifting into the blue sky. Coyotes and foxes exploited this, hunting before the flames to catch dispossessed rodents.

But if there was wind, there was fire blizzard — one of the greatest horrors of prairie life.

It came with walls of flame thirty feet high and a deep devouring roar, and black smoke instead of white, and the sun darkened and animals went mad. The glow of these great prairie fires could be seen for forty miles, and showers of ash and flake would be carried that far ahead by the wind. Single prairie fires were known to have burned more than two hundred square miles, and one fire traveled over twenty-two miles "as fast as a horse could run."

Within five miles of where I was born, a family of five Ohio emigrants died on a lovely October day in 1860 when they were trapped in a ravine by prairie fire.

In 1873, in Saline County, Nebraska, a fire blizzard roared across the grasslands toward a prairie schoolhouse. A mother who lived in a nearby soddy ran over to the school for her own children and some young relatives. The teacher begged her not to take them, but the hysterical mother wouldn't listen. The ten children and the woman tried to outrun the fire, but lost their race. All eleven died in the flames. The teacher and the other pupils were safe on a nearby plowed field, and the schoolhouse never did burn.

Old Sitting Bull himself, in the dry, flaming autumn of 1885, warned some Dakota schoolchildren that they could never run away from a prairie fire. "Go to bare ground," he counseled them, "or onto sand, gravel, or plowing. Or set a backfire. Go to a place with no grass. But do not run!"

Entire towns were destroyed by some of those prairie fires; in Leola, South Dakota, all but twelve of the town's hundred buildings were burned in 1889 by prairie fire that traveled forty miles in four hours.

Sensible pioneers took every precaution to prevent such holocausts, and there was a code of conduct governing use of fire on open prairie. For example, a man was never to burn his firebreaks alone with no help to control the flames.

Shortly after the turn of the century, a lone settler moved into the south edge of the Nebraska Sand Hills. When neighbors paid him a friendly visit to caution him about burning firebreaks unaided, the man simply snarled at them and told them to mind their own business. Later that summer, after harvesting his last hay crop of the year, he plowed the usual firebreak furrows around his buildings — two concentric rings a few yards apart. The strip of grass within those rings could then be burned to provide a firebreak. But the man tried to burn the grassy strip without help; the flames leaped over the outside plowing and ignited the prairie.

The fire was a bad one, with dozens of homes and outbuildings destroyed and a ten-year-old boy burned to death. The neighbors paid a second — less friendly — visit to the settler and found him forted up with rifle ready. They left without gunplay, but the incident was not forgotten.

On the following Fourth of July there was a neighborhood celebration at the nearby Diamond Bar Ranch. Late that evening, the Diamond Bar ramrod and a couple of his cowboys unaccountably vanished in the middle of a waltz, and a little later someone noticed a glow on the horizon in the direction of the settler's cabin. A group left at once to fight the fire, and arrived to find that the settler had burned to death in his bed when the flaming roof had caved in. The cause of the fire was never determined. There was said to have been a strong odor of kerosene around the place, but no one bothered to investigate.

Artist George Catlin once described a sloughgrass fire near Fort Leavenworth in eastern Kansas:

> There are many of these meadows on the Missouri, the Platte, and the Arkansas, of many miles in breadth, which are perfectly level, with a waving grass so high that we are obliged to stand in our stirrups in order to look over its waving tops, as we are riding through it. The fire in these . . . travels at an immense and frightful rate, and often destroys, on their fleetest horses, parties of Indians who are so unlucky as to be overtaken by it: not that it travels as fast as a horse at full speed, but that the high grass is filled with wild peavines and other impediments, which render it necessary for the rider to guide his horse in the zigzag paths of the deers and buffalos, retarding his progress, until he is overtaken by the dense column of smoke that is swept before the fire — alarming the horse, which stops and stands terrified and immutable, till the burning grass that is wafted in the wind falls about him, kindling up in a moment a thousand new fires, which are instantly wrapped in the swelling flood of smoke that is moving like a black thundercloud, rolling on the earth, with its lightning's glare, and its thunder rumbling as it goes.

Last Saturday, as I write this, I burned the "prairie" in my backyard. I do so every April, in defiance of several open-burning laws, in an effort to destroy cool-weather invading grasses that have gotten a head start in my patch of big bluestem, switch grass, and Indian grass. It's a ridiculous little dab of prairie, only a few hundred square feet, but its annual burning is something to see. There was a brisk westerly breeze when I put the match to it last week, and the little plot of cured grass exploded. Instantly there was a wall of flame twice as high as my head, and a gusty roar. My neighbor Roy Trudell, standing forty yards downwind, felt the heat and turned in surprise. Dycie was tilling our garden (good wife!) and paused to watch. She later said: "You know, when I've painted pictures of prairie fires, I've always made the flames only half as high as they should be . . ."

Prairie fires were dreaded by settlers, and even the small boys who found them exciting had to admit that there were drawbacks. Herbert Quick, the Iowa writer, told of the sharp, fire-hardened grass stubs on burned prairie that pricked a schoolboy's bare feet and caused festering sores. Of course, that could have been avoided by simply wearing shoes to school, but that's a dull alternative (the kind a mother would think of) when it's spring and you're ten years old and the prairies are greening up.

Those prairie boys found a friend in need in the pocket gopher. The big prairie gophers threw up mounds of soft, fine, cool earth, often in long lines, and prairie kids lived in the hope of walking all the way to school without stepping off a soft gopher mound. It never worked that way, of course. The gopher mounds usually wandered off in the wrong direction and so did the boy, and he ended up walking farther to school through burned grass stubble than if he'd taken a direct route in the first place. But sore as a prairie boy's feet might be, they were never sore from stone bruises.

❧

For the most part it was a rather healthy life, although probably never so healthy as some of the early gazetteers described it. In Rufus Blanchard's *Hand-Book of Iowa,* published in 1867, the author pointed out that the annual mortality rate in Iowa was one death to every 94 people, while in Massachusetts at that time the ratio was one death to 56.23 people. However, this surely relates to the postpioneer period after the Civil War in prairie regions that had been settled for some time. It's difficult to accept such a low death rate for the early pioneer period on the Iowa frontier or anywhere else.

Frontier Illinois had a particularly bad reputation for "fever and ague" although it was probably no worse there than in other frontier regions. One early settler reflected: "However, we do have our disadvantages — ague, fevers, and earthquakes [a reference to the New Madrid earthquake in southern Missouri]. You would deem it surprising to see a person shaking with cold on a hot summer's day, and see them looking like gloomy ghosts."

A sure sign of the greenhorn in many parts of the prairie country was not just his new clothing, but his appearance of health and his "animated expression." In writing of the heavily forested lowlands along the Illinois River, one observer said that the traveler "wonders not at the sallow complexion, the withered features, and the fleshless, ague-wracked limbs which, as he passes, peer forth upon him from the luxuriant foliage of this region of sepulchres; his only astonishment is, that in such an atmosphere the human constitution can maintain vitality at all."

An early Iowa settler, heading up the Mississippi with his family to Burlington, recalled seeing a riverbank hut from which two small children had crept, hollow-eyed and with teeth chattering, to sit in the warm sun and watch the riverboat pass. When the settler's wife asked about these obviously ill children, the captain of the boat replied:

"If you've never seen that kind of sickness I reckon you must be a Yankee; that's the ague. I'm feared you'll see plenty of it if you stay long in these parts. They call it the swamp devil, and it will take the roses out of the cheeks of those plump little ones of yours mighty quick. Cure it? No, ma'am. No cure for it; have to wear it out."

Settlers along the malarial flood plains of the Ohio and other major streams often believed that the real epicenter of "agues and chills" was out on the broad, open prairie, and at least one physician thought that forests were healthier because the trees tended to arrest "that gaseous agent, whatever it might be, which is said to be the true cause of the fever." This was not true, of course; malaria did occur as far north as Iowa, but only in the southern third of the state. It was virtually unknown in the more northerly prairies, and one of the reasons that some early settlers preferred high, drier prairie was that they believed it to be healthier than even the eastern states.

One of the most dreaded scourges of the prairie frontier was diphtheria, which my grandmother believed could be caused by eating snow. The disease was intensely contagious, and in the laryngeal form of diphtheria the trachea would fill with thick mucus, rendering the patient unable to breathe. If there was a doctor available, a tracheotomy might be performed — with a scalpel that the doctor may have wiped free of trail dust with his sleeve. And if the tracheotomy failed to restore adequate breathing, the courageous doctor might cover the incision with a handkerchief and attempt to suck out the mucus. Contagious as the disease was, this could be suicidal. One Nebraska physician, thinking it over on his return home and realizing the risk he had run, begged a plug of tobacco and chewed it. When he reached town, he "indulged most freely in alcohol as an antidote."

Epidemics of diphtheria, smallpox, typhoid, and yellow fever swept military posts and some prairie settlements. Emigrants in wagon trains were stalked by cholera and carried it with them across the prairies.

On much of the prairie frontier, food was often poor and diets badly unbalanced. Most families managed vegetable gardens, preserving the produce for winter use, but meat and dairy products were often less than fresh and such iron rations as beans and bacon were frequently the staples of the pioneer diet. Early military posts on the prairie frontier were sometimes ravaged by scurvy; in 1867 at Fort Stevenson in what is now central North Dakota, one fourth of the garrison had scurvy. Some early settlers used native plants — not as much as the Indians, perhaps, but learning enough about wild fruits, berries, tubers, and wild game to help round out their diets. However, many Scandinavian immigrants were appalled by such food, which they called "troll food," and ate it reluctantly if at all. Once an attempt was made to establish a utopian Swedish colony in northern Illinois on the Edwards River, and during the winter of 1846–47 when most of the emigrants lived in dark, damp dugouts in the slopes of a ravine, nearly 150 died. Their food, served in a large communal hall, was a skimpy ration of soup, corn, turnips, and cheese.

And in the grass itself there was dry, scaly death. Some of the tall prairies teemed with massasauga rattlesnakes — small gray reptiles that might be less deadly than the great timber rattlers that haunted the limestone bluffs, but what these prairie rattlers lacked in size they made up for in numbers. One northern Iowa settler claimed to have killed 300 rattlesnakes on his homestead. It was said that in some regions every herd of cattle had one or more cows with their lower jaws greatly swollen from snakebite. Oddly enough, there seem to be few early reports of pioneers being struck by these abundant little vipers. Those high bullhide boots must have done the job — but we've often wondered about the barefoot children.

Prairie pioneers debilitated by poor diet, overwork, inadequate clothing, and makeshift housing were susceptible to such respiratory diseases as influenza and pneumonia, in addition to diphtheria. Hamlin Garland, writing of pioneer schoolchildren in northern Iowa in the 1860s, said:

> They were all as hardy as Indians, and cared nothing for the cold as they ran about at recess, chasing each other like wolves. When they came indoors they barked like husky dogs, and puffed and wheezed so loudly that all study was for a time suspended. They

caught their colds in the house, and not in the open air; many a girl caught her death-cold in the miserable school-shack, and went to her grave a gentle martyr to shiftless management.

It was the women who suffered most from the privations and hardships of those early prairie years, exhausted by endless labor and almost annual childbearing. I have seen old cemeteries where a patriarch's headstone was flanked by those of several wives whom he had outlived, and several children who had died in infancy.

But the women who survived into old age were often marked by a special quality, a most difficult thing to assess. Courage was probably as much of it as anything; that, and

strength melded with a salty, quiet humor and unswerving, enduring faith. I remember our lovely Grandma Wilcox, prairie heroine epitomized, who at eighty-nine could still charm us children with the graceful, shuffling steps of the Corn Dance that she had learned as a girl. Granted, she might drop a stitch while knitting a woolen muffler and suddenly growl "Oh, shit!" but she would always look up over her spectacles at a listening child and explain: "Now, that's a nasty word but it ain't swearing and it ain't un-Christian!"

There's been a great deal of pap written about the stalwart virtues of pioneer life, but one note has a rather consistent ring of truth: the role of the real prairie woman. Some of the women, of course, were slatternly, whining drabs of little use to themselves or their families. But there is a valid image of the Prairie Mother, gallant repository of good things past and of all things kind and gentle, urging her children to work and laughter, an enduring catalyst for better things to come — teacher, cook, nurse, field hand, seamstress, inventor, gardener, dairymaid, food-preserver, hope-preserver, spiritual guide, and chief factotum. Such women, as much as any women anywhere, gave their families cohesion and strength of purpose. If the prairie pioneer survived and prospered, it was surely due as much to a good woman and the children she bore him as to the dogged labors with which he tamed the wildlands.

❧

If there were stalwart virtues on the prairie frontier, there were also stalwart defects. But although the settler's greatest strengths might also contain his cultural weaknesses, he was just too busy to care.

The new land demanded new ways, and learning the stark, simple lessons of survival was the first order of the time. A hard and pragmatic knowledge was needed, and needed early on. With almost no margin for failure, there was little time or concern for anything that could not be applied directly to the land and to survival of the family. Gentle custom and effete courtesies were scarcely thought of, and there was little use for amenities beyond the basic human decencies and the vital bond between neighbors. It was a culture reduced to functional essentials.

The prevailing tenor of the prairie frontier was anti-intellectual. Although the early settler could usually read, write, and do simple ciphering, he was likely to dismiss further learning as irrelevant. One of the stock figures of fun on the early prairies was the "educated fool" who might be able to construe Xenophon and Cicero, but who didn't know a whiffletree from an ox goad. To be sure, there were educated men on the frontier, but their learning was likely to be respected only if it could be directly applied to the problems at hand: knowledge of law, religion, medicine, and land mensuration. There was little regard for syntax or the well-turned phrase; even if a man were able to express himself well, he might deliberately distort his speech and claw it into the vulgate to avoid being accused of "putting on airs." It was a far greater reproach to be a poor shot with a rifle, or a poor horseman, or unable to plow a straight furrow, than to be a stammering semiliterate. It was an even greater reproach to be lazy, or to fail in one's bounden duties as a neighbor.

All in all, the prairie pioneers were typically self-educated, uncultured, pragmatic people who were as independent as hogs on ice and genuinely scornful of philosophy or esoteric theory that could not be applied to the problems of survival. They might seek knowledge, but only that of practical use, and they largely developed their own special areas of knowledge in their own ways. The struggle for survival in a strange and lonely land had developed a preoccupation with physical aspects, leaving little time or concern for philosophy, idealism, beauty, or grace. It was an emphasis on the tangible and pragmatic — and although this lent great strength to the economic advances of the opening land, it curtailed certain spiritual and cultural development.

In the real pioneer era of the western prairies there were few, if any, schools. And if there was one, it was likely to be presided over by a semiliterate teacher who "boarded around" and was scarcely more advanced than the older pupils. A poor system that could scarcely be termed education by even the rawest standards — and yet, something vital was often there. Those inept, ill-equipped teachers sometimes managed to inspire a special idealism and yearning for letters, and in later years were praised with deep affection and gratitude by men and women whose educations had begun with rote recitation in frontier school shacks with dirt floors and oiled-paper windows.

But however the early settlers may have scorned things philosophical, the most earthbound pragmatist among them would have admitted that he had come in search of an even fuller freedom. This quest amounted almost to a cultural constant that was bred into the fiber of those people. The first of the prairie pioneers were of American stock that had been tempered by a century or more of being free; each step in their social evolution had brought them new measures of freedom, and still they went on searching. They were their own people as much as any people can be, brooking no interference with personal rights and tolerating no social or political obstacles to their main chance of getting and keeping good land.

This vein of independence had flourished with the diversity of land use on eastern farms where most needs could be met by the timber, orchard, grainfield, pasture, and perhaps even water power on the farm family's own property. It was somewhat modified on the tall prairies where people were far removed from manufacturing centers and sources of supply, with agriculture less diversified and more concerned with small grain production. This resulted in a curious blend of dependence and independence, and from the earliest times of prairie settlement the capacity to cooperate has been a dominant character trait. But although a man had the right to expect certain things of a neighbor, he was always expected to be his own man and hoe his own row. Shiftlessness and laziness were unforgivable.

A special bond formed between settlers. It was partly need and partly loneliness and a yearning for people — that special value that uncrowded men and women accord the rare companionship of others. Neighbors might live twenty miles apart, but in a sense they were closer than they had ever been. Good fences had made good neighbors back in New England; on the early prairies, a twenty-mile fence of grassy wilderness made better neighbors still.

The people also shared that Main Chance, with all its privation and promise, sharing fears and sympathies and hopes that were *never* expressed in words, but clearly expressed in custom and deed. The fact that men and women were there at all spoke volumes for their characters. It was not necessary for them to prove themselves; on the contrary, they were accepted on faith until they had disproved themselves. Their word was their bond until it was broken, and it might then never be repaired. Men and women rallied to a troubled neighbor's aid without question — if he was a neighbor who had done his own share of helping, and if his troubles had not stemmed from sloth, dishonesty, cruelty, or intemperance. In my own time, I remember the bank sales of western Iowa farms during the Great Depression when neighbors banded together at foreclosure auctions and bought horses for five dollars and plows for two dollars, reselling them at cost to the original owners — and God help the sheriff or banker who interfered.

The original prairie homesteader always held an honored place in his community — and any defects of pragmatism

and single-minded preoccupation with the physical were
eclipsed by the fact that he had been among the first and had
survived, and in this lay all the honor that he required.
He felt no need for any apologies. In an old graveyard at
Prairie Ronde in southern Michigan there is a tombstone
that reads:

> D–Sept 10, 1872 aged 76 yrs 6 mo 8 da He plowed the 1st furrow
> & raised the 1st wheat on this Prairie or in this county Do not say
> what I have said, or done, to much or to little, for the absent can
> not reply

Today, looking backward at the lost wild world of the prairie, it's hard for some of us to accept "he plowed the 1st furrow" as an unqualified commendation. But it meant much to
those who did it, signifying a final victory over themselves
and the wild lands that they must have feared and loved at
once.

They changed that country, but even as they did so, it
changed them. It has been contended by some scholars and
historians that those wild prairies did not actually shape a
special character in the men and women who settled there,
but simply ripened traits that were implanted in the people
long before they had arrived. Yet, John L. McConnell states
in his *Western Characters* that: "Whatever the pioneers may
have been before their migration, they soon became more
meditative, abstracted, and taciturn."

It would have been remarkable if they had not become so.
The open land was calculated to turn a man in on himself. A
land without echoes or shadow except the one cast by him.
Wherever he stood, he was the compass point from which the
encircling horizons were drawn. A man may be hushed and
meditative when he is in such a place, with the whole lofty
vault of sky and sun resting on his shoulders alone, but he is
not likely to be humbled by it.

In the 1920s, Sherwood Anderson wrote of North Dakota in a letter to Waldo Frank:

> Is it not likely that when the country was new and men were often alone in the fields they got a sense of bigness outside themselves that has now in some way been lost? . . . Mystery whispered in the grass, was caught and blown across the American Line in clouds of dust at evening on the prairies . . . I am old enough to remember tales that strengthen my belief in a deep semi-religious influence that was formerly at work among our people . . . I can remember old fellows in my home town speaking feelingly of an evening spent on the big empty plains. It had taken the shrillness out of them. They had learned the trick of quiet.

9

After the Plow

WHEN JOHNNY CAME MARCHING HOME to his tall prairies after Shiloh and Chattanooga and all those other places, it was a different world.

Ma and Pa had been pioneers when he'd gone away, still living in the home soddy with the nearest folks five miles off, and Pa trying to work his new land with that sorry roan ox and the spavined mare that he'd traded half a crop of sod corn for. They'd got the land with Pa's army warrant and had broken half the quarter in spite of Pa's bad leg from Chapultepec, and for three long years Johnny had fretted about things back home. Ma had written that things weren't too bad, even after that Injun outbreak up in Minnesota, but Cap'n Henry had told them that six thousand troops had been sent out there under old Sibley and Sulley, and that gave a soldier something to think on.

But here he was back again, no longer a soldier and no more a boy, neither, and everything was just fine. Here he was, setting in a regular kitchen in Ma's new frame house with a glass window looking off to the south where the old soddy had been. Ma had a couple of young box-elders planted by that window, and a new range to bake in. Damnedest things he'd ever seen, and he'd said as much to Pa, but he didn't use army lingo around Ma for all that he'd come up the home lane wearing sergeant's chevrons on his tunic. That was another thing: the lane. It led down to a good road that went all the way to Fort Dodge past new fields planted by neighbors he'd never met, living in places where there was just raw prairie when he'd left.

Pa had three work horses now, and another quarter-section bought and broken. Oxen were gone from all over, mainly. Pa had a new patent reaper that had to be horse-drawn to work right, and he said that he hadn't put hand to an ox yoke or a cradle scythe since '62. Hard work and trust in the Almighty had done it all, Ma said — but Pa allowed that the new railroad was part of it. The railhead was only twelve miles away now, and that's where the grain-buyers and hardware stores were. Pa could trade anything he raised, getting hard money or new tools or both, and you could look around the house and see that Ma and the girls had some say, too.

People were coming into the country. When he'd walked that last eighteen miles home from Dodge, he had seen twenty wagons with pilgrims in them, and most couldn't even talk American. Swedes or Norskies or something, as near as he could make out, towheaded and jabbering at him, with a friendly way about them. Well, if they were anything like old Flogstad, they'd be damned good neighbors and welcome.

New houses, new neighbors, new tools, new animals, new ways. It made your head whirl. But the old folks had done just fine, for all of his fretting. And maybe Ma was right and it was God, and maybe Pa was right and it was mostly the railroad, and maybe it was all the same thing — but whatever it was, he hadn't come home crippled and things were turning out better than anything he and the boys used to yarn about. The times they were a-changing, and sure for the better, though he oftimes thought about the Rebs going back to those burned-over, shot-up places that he'd seen. Poor rag-

gedy cusses, with their wild yell. Pa's old roan ox would look
pretty good to some farmer down there, allowing that he still
had a plow. But no use studying on that.

He'd help Pa all this year, and with the planting next
spring. Had to get some money put by; he was old enough to
be having a place of his own. He'd ask Ma if there were any
new neighbor girls down the road. He'd ask Pa about the Dakota Territory.

❧

Out there on the far grasslands beyond the Mississippi, the
prairie pioneers of the 1840s and 1850s were practicing an
agriculture that had been virtually unchanged for centuries.
They were scarcely aware of the Industrial Revolution that
was transforming western Europe and the Northeast, and
even if they had been aware of it they couldn't have bought
the new machinery and tools that the revolution was producing. They were not counter-progress. They had simply outrun
progress, their westerly emigration proceeding faster than
new ideas and new trade routes. Crude as it was, the prairie
frontier was not a backwater of civilization — if anything
it was a forewater, and the people were waiting and
ready when the newfangled ways began to catch up with
them.

The Industrial Revolution was applied with awful efficiency by the factories of New England during the Civil
War — beating an agrarian South to its knees with overwhelming production and the help of coastal blockades. It
had revolutionized warfare, and even before Appomattox it
was revolutionizing prairie agriculture.

Almost overnight, a dynamic intercourse had been developed.

Out of the eastern milltowns and population centers new
rail routes were being extended to the banks of the Mississippi and beyond, with new transriver lines reaching into the

prairie country from cities along the western shore. The first bridge across the Mississippi was a stone and wood trestle built by the Rock Island Railroad in 1856 in northern Illinois. It was bitterly opposed by shipping interests as a menace to navigation, but the long legal fight was eventually won by the railroad (which, incidentally, had been represented by lawyer Abe Lincoln). Similar bridges soon spanned other parts of the Upper Mississippi, and downriver rail systems were closed in 1874 when Thomas Eads completed the world's first steel bridge at St. Louis.

New implements and goods were pouring out of the eastern mills and factories into the wild grasslands, where they were applied to the land to produce more meat and grain, which flowed in turn to the eastern centers in exchange for more supplies and machinery and people. From the East came riding plows, patent mowers and reapers designed to be horse-drawn, barbed wire, drain tiles, hardware, books, sawn lumber, trade goods. Along the Government Road and the old river routes came a floodtide of new immigration, and there would soon be a blizzard of new land warrants.

The postbellum South was suffering a vast and negative change in its agrarian traditions — but that change was no greater than the positive change that was at work in the postbellum prairies of the nation's midlands. It was a godsent balance that surely helped preserve the nation's sanity and economic systems. With one agrarian institution crushed and almost helpless in the toils of Reconstruction, another was beginning to pour milk and honey. Despair and ruin had crested in the south, but the old Jeffersonian dream of land reform was now cresting in the trans-Mississippi prairies — that age-old agrarian vision of small farms on which free men worked their own rich soils, supporting not only freedom and family but their government as well.

The old tallgrass prairie began to fade swiftly now. Only a few years before, the cultivated fields had been hardly a scratch on the vast wild meadows, and the timid little fields of wheat and corn were overwhelmed by the ancient grasslands. There were no fences, and the rare cabin was so insignificant that it seemed to intensify the lonely wildness rather than relieve it. The few roads were literally "traces," often laid out with log drags and used so seldom that they left scarcely a mark in the deep and limitless grasses.

Then, almost between one planting time and the following year's harvest, the settled lands began to be distinct checkerboards of small fields. The old regime was being overthrown by the Industrial Revolution at last — the natural order being swiftly replaced by a human order. The prairieland shrank with each spring, summer, and autumn day — retreating into wild hayfields and communal pastures that lay between the croplands, imprisoned behind barbed wire to be relished by patent mowers and growing herds. Frame houses began to appear, and the first of the windmills, and spur-lines sprouted from the main trunks of the railroads.

Even the sky was shrinking, for settlers were eager to close it out and have shade trees as quickly as possible. They avoided the slow-growing oaks and hard maples of the Old States, but were delighted to find that the elm of New England flourished in the deep prairie soils and might add a half-inch growth ring in only one year. Silver maple was another fast-growing shade-giver, and in the farthest reaches of the open prairie box-elder was a popular choice — not the best of all trees, maybe, but better than none.

A shade tree in the dooryard of a prairie homestead was a delicious luxury, especially if the house was on a prairie swell so that a man could sit in a pool of shade and look out over his growing fields. But the windbreaks along the western and northern sides of the farmstead were more than luxury — they were shields against the iron winds of winter, producing a sheltering effect that could be felt for a hundred yards to leeward. These are still called "shelterbelts" in the Dakotas, and in the old days they were considered to be virtually part of the main house.

For best service, the shelterbelt around a prairie homestead was at least partly conifers — and was sometimes entirely evergreens. Norway spruce probably ranked first on the north-central prairies, followed by blue spruce and white spruce. The native red cedar was out of the question if there were any apple trees in the area, for it was an intermediate host for apple rust that can spread for as far as two miles.

In the early days pines were often used in prairie shelterbelts, but they tended to self-prune and lose their lower branches and much of their sheltering effect. After a time, the settlers hit upon the best designs for windbreaks; one of the best formulas was at least three rows of conifers with the rows about twenty feet apart and the trees spaced a like distance within their rows, with pines in the middle and spruces at the sides. There might even be a belt of deciduous trees such as ash or box-elder planted adjacent to the main strip of evergreens, with rows and trees six feet apart.

Although the first prairie settlers quickly cut many of the original wild groves, these were often replaced by later plantings. Trees were wealth and comfort; a link with the old home states and a balm that gave a man and woman something to rest their eyes upon. And wonderfully, even though some of the new groves were miles out in the open prairie, woodland flowers and shrubs and birds always seemed to find them. Settlers were encouraged to plant trees; they were given tax incentives to do so, and out in Nebraska they even started a thing called "Arbor Day."

There could be no doubt about where an established farmstead existed; you looked for a distant clump or line of trees and there would be a house and barn behind them. Strange, how those old windbreaks had individual shapes and were landmarks for individual families. A native of the area could identify the farmsteads of various neighbors by the special notches and clumps in the treelines of distant windbreaks and groves. They were indices of ownership in the featureless croplands, coded and notched.

Carrying the farmstead shelterbelt a bit further, some progressive landsmen advocated the planting of long windbreaks around every quarter-section of prairie — not only to check the bitter winter winds and catch as much blown snow as possible, but also to break the power of the desiccating southwest winds of summer. The idea never got very far on the northern prairies, although some of the older prairie regions in Illinois and Missouri had fencerows of Osage orange — not so much for shelterbelts as for tough living fences.

I remember a certain farmer in northwestern Iowa who tried multiflora rose. At the time, it was believed that *Rosa multiflora* could not survive that far north — but this did. He planted nearly a mile of the tough shrub along the northern and western borders of his flat fields, and it thrived. It proved a superb windbreak, and after a winter storm the lee sides of the rose hedge had deep drifts that extended well out into the fields. Long into summer, the hay harvest along those lee borders exceeded that in the more exposed, windswept fields. On an early June afternoon the scent of the flowering hedges could be caught for a half-mile downwind, and the dense wall of fragrant flowers (horse-high, bull-strong, and hog-tight) was alive with a multitude of nesting, feeding songbirds.

The farmer's neighbors feared that the rose might spread into their fields, as indeed it can, although this was near the rose's northern range limit where it doesn't pose a great problem. The greater reason for objections was simply that the lovely hedge was "different." A court order was granted and the banks of multiflora rose were bulldozed and destroyed. *Sic transit multiflorus.*

Alas, the old windbreaks of our youth are also being

"cleaned up." They were often composed of rather short-lived trees to begin with — and even if they weren't, the prairie climate sometimes made for swift growth and premature demise by eastern standards. As they matured and died, many of the windbreaks were not replaced. They were no longer needed by farmers; they were no longer a part of the economic pattern. In times past, the gaunt frame houses needed any sheltering effect they could get. If they had any insulation at all, it was likely to be bales of straw stacked around the foundations, or perhaps a bed of manure that actually generated warmth and heated the foundation during winter — with a tingling ammoniac reek that was part and parcel of early farm life. But most of those old frame houses have been replaced with snug, well-insulated, one-story homes with gas heat and Thermopane windows that look out on bluegrass lawns and a few tastefully arranged trees — the ubiquitous face of Suburbia that frowns on the shaggy, unkempt shelterbelts of yesterday.

❧

What came after the plow? The plow. And again and always, the plow.

The little quarter-section flecks on the face of the wild prairie expanded and coalesced, the intervening grasslands shrinking apace. The wet prairies were among the last to go, wrung out by long lines of clay tiles and bull ditches that hastened runoff and dropped the water table, drying the land for the plow. Prairie pastures that had once been reserved for grazing and wild haying also passed — succeeded by the more durable bluegrass or perhaps even more plowing, for their value as grainlands exceeded that of pasture. Permanent sloughs and prairie lakes were ditched into the prairie streams, which, in turn, were plowed to their banks and straightened and canalized to hasten the demise of the native waters. The wealth of the tall prairie was its undoing.

Those of us who deal with prairie wildlife have been able
to note each successive stage of farm technology and eco-
nomics by its particular impact on wildlife, which can be an
infallible biological indicator of land use and misuse.

The loss of the original shelterbelts, and then of those that
replaced them in the Dust Bowl years of the 1930s, has been
a cruel blow to the ring-necked pheasants of the eastern Da-

kotas, northern Iowa, and southern Minnesota — regions in which the pheasants of my boyhood found winter shelter in thick slough edges and the snug windbreaks upwind of the farmhouses. I have seen two hundred pheasants in a shelter-belt only a hundred yards long — and nearly a thousand ringnecks in an old prairie slough that was thickly edged with cord grass and scattered plum thickets. All gone today, or nearly so. Clay tiles killed the slough, and the farmer says that the extra cornland now pays his taxes. A chain saw killed the old shelterbelt — that, and the incentive to add another ten rows of corn to the north field. Some of the pheasants lingered for a time in weedy fencelines and corners and a few grassed waterways, but when fall plowing became the mode and much of the northern cornbelt became black desert in fall and winter, many pheasants simply gave up in disgust and followed the prairie chicken.

Last November, on my way home from a ramble in central South Dakota, I stopped in northwestern Iowa at the Caylor Prairie — a quarter-section of rolling prairie that's too rough to plow. There was a sharp wind out of the north, and I had the place to myself. I skirted the southern edge, walking through sere uplands of little bluestem and low swales of dense cord grass, and returned along the northern fenceline. As I passed upwind of a cord-grass swale, a white-tailed buck caught my scent and started from his bed.

I've seen many walloping whitetails in the Midwest, which is notable for big deer, but never one like this. He floated up out of his sloughgrass bed with a lightness and grace that belied his 300-odd pounds. His neck was swollen and muscular from the rut, seeming as thick as a Holstein bull's, and his back and shoulders were broad and heavy from good living. At their burrs his antlers appeared to be as thick as a man's wrists, with the prodigious main beams sweeping back and outward in broad smooth curves that gave rise to the polished vertical tines. It was a crown of authority that reflected superb nutrition and rich soils, yet I was struck with pity as the magnificent buck floated off over a prairie swell a few hundred yards away. In every direction was black desert — a bleak panorama of fall plowing in which fences, fence cover, windbreaks, sloughs, and even the thin fringes of ash and willow along the prairie creeks had been stripped away. "You poor, landless, disinherited sonofabitch," I thought. "You're running as if you had someplace to go. But there's no other place; come back to bed, you'll not be disturbed again." And whitetails being what they are, that's surely what he did. He almost certainly cut back along the far fenceline and crept home through the swales, head down and furtive, to resume his hidden rest.

To be fair, there are prairie plowmen who have had second thoughts. My good friend Don Carper, a corn-and-hog raiser near Mount Pleasant, Iowa, is probably the only man in his township who refuses to fall plow. Don is a farmer apart; a man who cherishes the beavers in his little creek, and the pheasants and quail and deer of his field edges. He wrote us just the other day, lamenting: "Why, oh why, does that ninth or tenth pheasant hen fail to fly when the flushing bar of my mower goes over her?" Be at peace, Don. There isn't another prairie farmer in a hundred who's ever heard of a flushing bar on a hay mower, or who cares to.

And I remember the wistful old farmer who told me about the five-acre prairie slough of his boyhood where he trapped muskrats and mink and took a few drake mallards when the flight came through. As a boy he had recapitulated part of the Old Time; as a young man, he had yielded to the New Time and drained the slough. Then, as an old man, he was thinking about landless grandchildren and the lost wild slough-days that they would never know, and of how he might close a certain bull ditch and recapture part of the past, and would I advise him about wild blue flag and marsh orchids and the wild rice that would bring in the ducks? He died before it could be done, and his grandchildren inherited only a farm.

Nor is it unusual to hear of a farm wife who has persuaded her husband to preserve a little block of native prairie that lies along a hillside or in a swale that defies complete drainage. I sometimes receive tilted snapshots from them, with the plaintive query: "Is this *really* old-time buffalo grass?" Al-

though the photos are usually out of focus as well as tilted, I give them the benefit of the doubt and confirm their hopes. It makes us both happy.

But for the few prairie people who think like that, there are countless others who never think of it at all. The old currents of pragmatism and cupidity run strong and deep, and I often feel that the average prairie farmer could have a grove of sequoias growing on his back forty and show no interest in them at all — unless they could be sold at the local elevator.

The farmer's personal incentive to stamp out the last wild corners of the prairie country is lively enough, and it is inflamed by government bureaus that are less interested in pork than in pork barrel. Cynical and arrogant, withholding information and plans, minimizing environmental impact estimates and maximizing cost-benefit ratios, the great bureaus march across the prairies proselytizing landowners and kindling false dreams — ditching, wrecking, draining, scraping, damming, and pouring concrete and public funds into a dismal perpetuation of make-work programs. To those who love and understand the land base, and the people and wildlife that draw strength from it, such projects as the Starkweather Watershed Project and the Garrison Diversion in North Dakota are criminal infractions of biological law.

Twenty years from now, someone may pull this book from the back shelf of a library and see mention of the Starkweather and Garrison boondoggles and draw a total blank. No matter. Analogous boondoggles will doubtless be going on then, and fifty years from then, or until the people perceive that their birthright to good land is being stripped with the land itself. Yet, as we've noted before, it is of little real consequence in the long run. The prairie and its soils will prevail, and the only factor that can really check the prairie continuum is climate itself. We fancy ourselves as grand destructors, omnipotent and awful, but we are only mischievous imps pulling at a loose thread on a tapestry. Man may exhaust the prairie soils and send them to the sea, but the age-long geologic processes will renew them. The only tragedy is not a lasting destruction of the land, but the destruction of our capacity to use and enjoy it.

❦

It has been said that each of the great cultural systems of the past was developed on a particular group of soils. The truth of this is demonstrated in North America as well, where a complex social system has been formed on a correspondingly varied and complex group of soils.

Each American subculture has sprung from distinct soil groups and the climatic factors that helped shape them; our varied cultural patterns are due less to nationalistic origins

than to the wildly varied soil types and subclimates in which
the various nationalities took root. It was inevitable that the
Great Plains would produce the cowboy, that the northern
pineries would produce lumberjacks, and that the rocky New
England coastline formed the lobsterman. It is inconceivable
that such locales would produce anything else so typical. Our
crazy-quilt culture and mongrel strength can be attributed in
part to political structure and nationalistic amalgamation —
but their real basis lies in our incredible diversity of soils,
minerals, timber, and water.

It follows, then, that the strongest and most enduring subcultures be associated with the strongest and most enduring
resource systems. And of these, none possesses a greater
strength and endurance than the deep soils of the tallgrass
prairie region. It is not a spectacular resource and has not
produced spectacular subcultures — but in terms of enduring
worth of either soils or human values, it is significant.

Every now and then, travelers and sojourners rediscover
the prairie Midwest and its people to the pleased surprise of
everyone concerned. Writer Bil Gilbert, who hails from
Pennsylvania, was part of the Second Annual Great Bicycle
Ride Across Iowa (SAGBRAI), which drew curious cyclists
from many states. You'd be hard put to find a more bland adventure, but it was apparently a revealing one, and Gilbert
wrote in *Sports Illustrated:*

> Visitors have been struck by the inordinate number of friendly,
> sensible, out-going, just plain good people in Iowa. It may be
> that the state has some mean-spirited rascals but if so they are
> hustled into the backroom or tool shed when guests come to
> call — maybe Iowans have lived so long in a gentle, bounti-
> ful land that it has made them self-confident rather than self-
> righteous, openhanded rather than tightfisted. If so, Iowa is one
> place where a fundamental theory of modern social science has
> proved true. The theory is that a good environment has a good
> influence on the character of the people.

Such rediscovery of confidence and warmth always comes, in turn, as something of a surprise to midwesterners who may regard themselves as worldly and cynical as anyone. But we're apparently fooling only ourselves. I often sense this among eastern friends who seem to regard me as a cultural rustic wandering lost and alone in a predatory world. They hail cabs for me, and intercede with headwaiters. Stuff like that. At a recent meeting in Pittsburgh, when someone expressed concern about having lost his house key, I precipitated a puzzled silence by commenting that I'd lost my own house key several years ago and hadn't missed it very much.

If Cornbelters generally lack the cool suspicion of strangers that characterizes some other rural subcultures, it's largely because they have a brimming confidence in the rich soils in which they are rooted. But in a characteristic ambivalence, there is also that nagging concern that they reflect a sort of cultural anonymity, and they seek approval and acceptance in the tail-wagging, ingenuous manner that so many foreigners find naïve and amusing.

It's a valid concern because the prairie midlands, like their people, aren't likely to draw much attention. The region is a fertile interlude between Action East and Action West. In the American consciousness it has the same solid mediocrity as a U.S. Savings Bond — good to have but nothing to gloat over. As one of our Jawhawk friends said: "Kansas is a fine place to live, but you wouldn't want to visit here." And Eric Severaid has commented:

> In distant cities when someone would ask: "Where are you from?" and I would answer: "North Dakota," they would merely nod politely and change the subject, having no point of common reference. They knew no one else from there. It was a large, rectangular blank spot in the nation's mind.

But now and then, to my enduring surprise, urbane friends have expressed mild interest in the rural Midwest and its doings. I was once inclined to be wary of this, wondering if it were a "what-do-the-common-folk-do?" syndrome, but I've begun to sense a tinge of wistfulness in some of these queries, as if their authors were seeking reassurance that the ice cream social is alive and well somewhere in the heartland.

A while back, at dinner in New York, I responded to such a question and tried to describe the Fourth of July that we had just celebrated in Slater, Iowa — which is right there on the map, if you look close.

Our clan had gathered again, as it does about every third Fourth of July when Slater hosts the great day for its corner of Story County, coming to Cousin Marvin Ross's old Victorian house on the edge of town (in Slater, most houses are on the edge of town). Cousin Joy had added every leaf to her vast oak dining table — the kitchen crammed and the sideboards groaning with potato salads, roast pork just carved from the crackling pig, crusty fried chicken of a half-dozen styles, Aunt Gladys's famous Parker House rolls, baked ham, scalloped oysters, sweet corn, bowls of crisp radishes and sweet onions, creamed lettuce, pickled crabapples, more fresh strawberry shortcake than a regiment could manage, cakes beyond counting, and two ice cream freezers in action on the back stoop. The laughter and good talk everywhere, with the old family jokes and stories being retold for the kids, and Uncle Cliff telling small boys about "shooting the anvil" on long-ago Fourths.

And in and out through the long golden afternoon, with its summer sound of slamming screen doors, youngsters reporting back from the carnival in the park, sticky with cotton candy and needing more quarters. (And me irritated with our small daughter, who returned broke for the second time and cadged a whole dollar from Marvin — and him saying in his wise way: "Aw, John, where else can you buy so much happiness for only a dollar?")

Off and on — with lemonade breaks between sets — the

high school band playing patriotic airs with a tympany of firecrackers, the martial music overlaid with the merry-go-round's calliope and cymbals, small boys running, and farm women in lawn chairs cooling themselves with pasteboard fans swiped over the years from various church suppers and funeral parlors. Their men, wearing wash pants and standing apart in small groups, white foreheads contrasting strongly with sun-darkened faces, talking about soybean futures and tractor prices. And later on, the Slater Volunteer Fire Brigade having its annual hose battle with the Sheldahl Volunteer Fire Brigade, and neither side being very careful about where they point the hoses, and the front ranks of the crowd yelling in mock protest. "First time today they've been cool," says Cousin Marvin.

Finally the great event itself, the fireworks painting the sultry night with colored fire, their aerial salutes waking tired babies. The band playing "Home, Sweet Home" and friends parting, saying: "Well, we didn't want rain today but we could stand some tomorrow." Then Ford headlights are streaming down the gravel roads, shining through rolling clouds of dust that whiten young corn leaves in the darkness, driving down through creek hollows where the night air is pooled in delicious coolness, and a flicker of heat lightning glows briefly in the west. Looks like the little ones are finally wore out, mother, and wasn't it good to see all the folks again?

There was more than that and I guess I laid it on pretty heavy, but it's not easy to bring an Iowa Fourth into a New York restaurant. Across the table, a lady of Manhattan looked into her wine glass and said quietly: "I really can't remember what we did on the Fourth of July."

❧

The differences between American and European cultures — as well as regional variations within America itself — were inevitable. Such differences invariably occur as basic clashes when a heritage is carried from an older culture's birth-soils into new landscapes that present strikingly different possibilities and requirements. These conflicts often ramify broadly and deeply, extending from the personal life of the individual to the political institutions that he supports.

Even though English common law and custom were readily transferred from the light, leached soils of western Europe to the similar soils of our eastern seaboard, certain clashes appeared early. But these were nothing to the deep conflicts that occurred when the old heritage began moving into the great black lands of the mid-American prairies and the arid plains that lay beyond them. This surely constituted one of the deepest wrenches of all, demanding adaptations from which there was no return.

To many Europeans, and even to some Americans, the failure to preserve a transferred heritage was a net loss to traditional political and cultural institutions. No matter. They might as well have frowned on the winds for all it meant, for the strange new soils and landscapes themselves demanded change. New lands invariably do — and failure in those lands is invariably the result of failure to adapt. And although a culture may persist strongly even on weakening birth-soils, it rarely survives the transfer to significantly stronger soils and markedly different landscapes. It soon shows a different flower, evolving into a new species even though there may be conscious effort to perpetuate the old forms.

This began to occur with the first English colonies of the New World and gathered impetus as the colonists diffused into the interior lands. Each successive shift to different landscapes and soil types affected the American personality by producing a new facet of culture and economy. It was a process that resulted in regional differences that varied as widely as the soils and landscapes themselves.

Yet, as a native midwesterner, I have a notion that I'm part of a common national denominator. For if there's a middle ground in all this, it may literally exist in the middle ground of the continent where the deep black soils nourish a cultural root system that permeates so much American thought and attitude. It is not a region likely to produce revolutionary change. It is, rather, a repository of traditional attitudes that are metered out through the root system in subtle but powerful ways. It is a region whose soil base has lent the freedom and stability that men need to reach free and stable conclusions. Those are seldom revolutionary, for what purpose is served by rebelling against a full stomach and strong land? And just as there is no point in reckless revolt, there is none in recklessly embracing every social and political whim what wafts in from more reactionary climes. Regional character is a reflection of land, and the prairie region mirrors a solid, level-to-slightly-rolling conservatism that may rarely produce change but usually fuels it.

Vincent Canby, film critic for the *New York Times,* has commented:

> Middle America is not exactly the fastest moving target in the world. You don't have to be a sharpshooter to hit it. It just sits there like someone on a giant billboard, wearing an ear-to-ear grin, waiting to be defaced by anyone who has the price of a can of spray paint.

It's doubtful, however, that any amount of critical spray paint will efface the ear-to-ear grin of a region that banks on such soils, and knows that the check won't bounce.

10

People Pastures

THIS CHAPTER TITLE belongs to Jim Wilson, a seed grower out in Polk, Nebraska, who specialized in native grasses and preached a gospel of grasslands for livestock and people, extolling tallgrass prairie as prime pasturage for the human spirit.

Being a good salesman, Jim was all for planting as much prairie grass as possible — and there's no denying that big is beautiful where prairie is concerned. Still, he advocated prairies of any size, whether original stuff that had never known plow or cow, old pasture being returned to bluestem by thoughtful farmers, or just a clump of native ornamentals in the backyard. Jim's retired now and we don't know if he quit rich or not, but we hope he did. He deserved to.

A prairie-seed salesman ought to make out pretty well these days.

Interest in tallgrass prairie is keen, part of the general environmental concern for all original American landscapes. Tall prairie is of historical and cultural interest and of high biological worth — but above all, it is tragically rare. As an endangered species of American biome, it has a certain underdog appeal as well as curiosity value. For any or all of these reasons, a surprising number of prairie restorations are being made by park boards, arboretums, colleges, universities, and backyard naturalists. Some are simply people pastures; others are pragmatic prairies that exist for basic and advanced research and as outdoor classrooms.

A patch of genuine prairie — an unshorn, unbroken, uncurried piece of the original — has special significance to the soil physicist, agronomist, plant geneticist, and taxonomist. Such workers see native prairie as a unique and valuable baseline for a whole array of esoteric studies that are more than just exercises in pure science; they have some highly significant applications. There is considerable risk in our blithe dependence on a few crops that are adapted to broad regions. All crops are vulnerable to constantly evolving diseases with devastating potential, and plant breeders have often returned to the wild ancestors of our modern crops in the search for disease-resistant genes. Such wild plants are germ-plasm pools that are stocked against emergencies.

However, the destruction of original biomes and the discarding of primitive crops have seriously depleted the diverse and irreplaceable genetic resources found in nature. Native prairie is one of those biomes; it constitutes a germ-plasm pool of wild grasses that can be vital to agronomists and botanists — and it is a pool being drained by biological impoverishment.

The Smithsonian Institution, in early 1978, listed almost 10 percent of the 22,000 plant species native to the continental United States as being endangered or threatened. An alarming number of these are characteristic tallgrass-prairie species. We scarcely understand their individual importance, much less the domino effect of their disappearance. Peter Raven, director of the Missouri Botanical Garden, has said that a vanishing plant species can take with it 10 to 30 dependent species of insects, higher animals, and even other plants.

No scientist appreciates native prairie more than the wildlife biologist who views it as an oasis in the desert of corn and soybeans — harboring not only common game species, but many unique prairie species as well.

In Iowa, study plots of native grasses showed high nesting use by pheasants, bobwhite quail, and songbirds. For example, switch grass study plots produced 12.4 successful pheasant nests per hundred acres. Not that switch grass stands are all that much greater for nesting than fields of alfalfa and orchard grass — but switch grass is one of the native "warm-season" grasses that are not mowed or grazed as early as pastures of "cool-season" forage, and pheasants have time to bring off their broods. In meadows of such cool-season forage crops as alfalfa and orchard grass, mowing operations in early June wrecked all of the pheasant nests and killed 73 percent of the pheasant hens.

Then, too, native prairie grasses stand up well through all kinds of weather while most introduced grasses tend to "go down." A substantial clump of native prairie grass can be a good roost in winter and a good nesting site the following spring, enduring heavy rain, snow, and ice with equanimity. Don Christisen of the Missouri Department of Conservation tells of a little three-acre patch of switch grass in seventy acres of corn and soybeans that provided a hunter-harvest of over 200 cottontail rabbits in one season. That patch was also home to a large covey of quail, and such a place is ideal for white-tailed deer. Small birds and mammals flourish in a native grass stand, which tends to have a rather closed canopy overhead but is surprisingly open at ground level.

In every patch of Iowa prairie of over 100 acres I've visited during late May or early June, I have found active pheasant nests. This really doesn't involve many nests over several years' time, but it may be significant that I always found the nests quite by accident. I was never actively searching for them, nor were they always revealed by flushing hens. I simply happened on them by chance — and the odds against doing that are rather high unless there is a substantial number of nests on an area.

But you needn't look at prairie as a germ-plasm pool or a pheasantry to find values worth considering. Christisen knows a Missouri farmer whose steers gained about 1.5 pounds per day on switch grass pasture during midsummer — a time when cattle usually lose weight on pastures of introduced cool-season grasses like bluegrass or brome. Another Missouri farmer told Don that he advocates native prairie hay heavily laced with bluestem and Indian grass for beef production. He found that two tons of lime per acre on those hay meadows was a good investment, resulting in 200 to 234 tons of high quality hay each year. This was enough to feed his own cattle with some hay left for sale. And in addition to putting fast gains on beef cattle, native forage fed with legumes is said to prevent scours in dairy stock and keep the animals in better health.

Yet, some farmers still speak of native grass as "horse hay" with the inference that it's not respectable cattle feed. They forget that their grandfathers who fed cattle a simple fattening ration of clean water, salt, yellow corn, and prairie hay found that individual gains were seldom less than three pounds per day. We've come a long way since then. Now, with protein supplements, chopped clovers and bromes, mixed commercial feeds and expensive minerals and supplements, gains often range from 1½ to 2½ pounds per day. Maybe, as dad used to say, we've been educated beyond our intelligence.

There are stockmen, of course, who have growing appreciation of the unique qualities of tall native grasses — their hardiness, forage value, dependability, long growing season, efficient use of moisture, and maximum pasturage with minimum attention. Yet, it's the esthetics of tallgrass prairie that seem to be drawing the most intense interest. Prairie not as livestock forage, but as people pasture.

So where does one find it? Again, classic tallgrass prairie country is heartland that's about as far from an ocean as you can get. It coincides with the best of our midwestern cornlands. Although certain palouse grasslands of the Northwest and some savannahs of the Southeast and Gulf Coast could qualify, the tallgrass prairie we're concerned with lies east of the 100th meridian and north of the 35th parallel — within that great sprawl of country generally north of Tulsa, south of Winnipeg, west of Indianapolis, and east of Bismarck.

At the risk of offending some Texans or Kentuckians, let's consider the prime tallgrass prairie region as the eastern Dakotas, western and southern Minnesota, southern Wisconsin, northern and western Indiana, parts of Ohio, northern Illinois, most of Iowa, eastern Nebraska, eastern Kansas, and northern and western Missouri.

There are still prairie relicts in all these states. Those in private ownership grow fewer each year, and the largest and best are administered by state and federal natural resource agencies, The Nature Conservancy, county park boards, and colleges and universities. The roster to be found in the Appendix is far from complete. Certain wildlife refuges, parks, and state game management lands contain prairie remnants that are not included in the official descriptions, and a few small prairies have been omitted from this general list at the request of the administering agency because those sites have been getting too much public traffic as it is.

New prairie preserves are being acquired as funds and sites become available, and at this writing several states are negotiating for prairie areas. See the Appendix for a list of some prairielands that exist for public use.

The great majority of prairie sites linger as small relicts along country roads and at old lane-ends, in little abandoned cemeteries and along railroad rights-of-way, and in the ownership of a few farmers who happen to cherish their scraps of original landscape. Such fragments are rarely on public record, but are often known to tireless prairie-hunters who scout the back forties in search of neglected parcels of land with that unmistakable prairie look. They may be teachers, botanists, photographers, hunters, or amateur ecologists who just happen to love wild prairie for what it is — and they grow amazingly adept at finding its remnants.

An absorbing breed, these prairie-hunters, often swapping information with other prairie fans and sometimes compiling surprising rosters of good sites. Here in Illinois, for example, a small company of prairie buffs recently conducted a county-by-county survey of old cemeteries to determine their value as prairie remnants. Most of the places didn't amount to much — but a surprising number were quality sites with a broad selection of native plant species.

A typical prairie-hunter, I suppose, is Dr. Robert Betz, a botanist and ecologist at Northeastern Illinois University in Chicago. He has found about twenty small prairies in his area and hopes to see them preserved. Surprisingly, these fragments of native grassland are within the Chicago city limits in the Cook County Forest Preserve.

Two of my favorite prairie-hunters are a pair of Iowa boondockers named Roger Landers and Carl Kurtz. Dr. Landers is a former plant ecologist and professor of botany at Iowa State University — a gifted researcher and teacher and long-gone prairie buff. Carl was a hard-working young farmer until he went astray, majored in wildlife biology at Iowa State, fell in with Landers, and became a superb photographer and naturalist. If there's an Iowa prairie those two don't know about, it's probably not worth knowing — and if there are better men to walk those prairies with, I haven't met them.

Many prairie enthusiasts are academic types like Drs. Clair Kucera of the University of Missouri, Peter Schramm of Knox College in Illinois, Paul Christiansen of Cornell College in Iowa, Grant Cottam of the University of Wisconsin, and Lloyd Hulbert of Kansas State University — to name only a few. Such people are usually highly accredited plant ecologists and fine field naturalists. Their field naturalist side enables them to ferret out scraps of native prairie, while the ecologist side challenges them to either restore badly abused prairies or start from scratch and create "prairies" where none have existed for decades.

The re-creation of native prairie can be as simple as planting a small area to a few tallgrasses, or as complex as restoring a long roster of original native plant species more or less complete with appropriate soil organisms and insects. Of course, prairie restorations or re-creations are not the real thing. For a long time they can be only reasonable facsimiles, at best. If we knew everything we needed to know, and had exactly the right equipment and sources of seeds, we might be able to re-create a fairly authentic prairie in as little as a century — although Peter Schramm's best estimate is from 300 to 500 years.

It may never be possible to completely restore native prairie where it has been wholly destroyed and its base soils drastically altered — but again, we can't even be sure of that. We do know that the process of total restoration is infinitely complex, extremely slow, and involves factors of which we have only slight understanding. For example, certain highly specialized insects necessary to the effective pollination of some native forbs may be lacking. Furthermore, the disturbed soils on which prairie restorations are usually made may lack the complex associations of fungi and other soil micro-organisms necessary to a healthy, balanced prairie. At the Morton Arboretum in northern Illinois this was found to be true of hoary puccoon, a lovely orange prairie flower that could be reared in greenhouses but gradually declined and died. However, when some puccoons were transplanted from a relict prairie, the flowers thrived — the soil in their roots apparently contained the key micro-organisms vital to survival of the plants.

Dr. Grant Cottam is guardian angel of the 65-acre Curtis

Prairie that was developed on the outskirts of Madison by the University of Wisconsin. It was begun by the old Civilian Conservation Corps in the late 1930s and sowed and planted to prairie species by a dedicated band of students and professors who combed old cemeteries, railroads, and fallow pastures for prairie grasses and forbs. Today, about forty years later, it's a fairly authentic example of wild prairie. Dr. Cottam believes this was possible only because the area had never been plowed and had always been in pasture. But for that, it might have taken a century or more for a reasonable degree of restoration.

Dozens of midwestern colleges and universities have pet prairie projects. Most are restorations, and the re-creation of tall prairie is a congenial and highly instructive labor. But luckiest of all is the teacher with his own personal plot of original, easily accessible tallgrass prairie. In that category is Dick Trump, a high school biology teacher in my old home town of Ames, Iowa.

A few years ago, Ames High School went with the current of change and moved out to the suburbs. The new school was built at the edge of open countryside on uplands above the flood plain of Squaw Creek. Just west of the school, and part of the school's property, is an open prairie ridge with all the essentials. It didn't take Dick long to size up the possibilities. A few steps down the hall from the biology classroom, out the back door, across a service drive, and the student is in a patch of original Iowa — a biology teacher's dream come true. And, as it turned out, a dream endangered. The Board of Education was hunting for a new warehouse site and it didn't take them long to draw a bead on that patch of empty ground behind the high school. It didn't take much longer than that for a militia of nature lovers and ecologists to draw another bead on the city fathers, and things started getting pretty lively. The hassle was finally resolved when The Nature Conservancy, that doughty defender of little prairies, arrived

with money — surely the most effective ammunition in skir-
mishes like that. The Ames High School Prairie was saved,
and as a warehouse of educational materials it beats anything
that could have been built there.

Incidentally, if there's a spearhead of national prairie preservation it's surely The Nature Conservancy — a nonprofit
group dedicated to preserving original landscapes of unique
ecological value. They have helped save many prairie areas
that wouldn't have survived otherwise. At this writing, The
Nature Conservancy has acquired at least 59 tallgrass prairie
areas in the Midwest and has assisted in the acquisition of 13
others. Withal, a most worthy outfit.

A prairie restoration can take several forms. It may simply
consist of letting what is essentially prairie go fallow and take
its own course to recovery. Or, it can be a painstaking seeding and transplanting program on ground that has been disturbed. It can be hundreds of acres or a few square yards.

Down near the bottom of the scale is my backyard "prairie" — a tiny patch a few hundred feet square. Yet, this prai-
rielet has a fair roster of the basics: native switch grass, big
bluestem, Indian grass, compass-plant, wild indigo, butterfly
milkweed, dotted gayfeather, Turk's-cap lily, and rattlesnake-master. Partridge pea and a couple of kinds of goldenrod have volunteered. I leave it alone, nursing a futile hope
that it will take off and somehow spread into adjacent bluegrass sod. Certain friends regard that benign neglect as a
scheme to convert lawnmowing time into fishing time — a
cynical attitude not without basis. Still, I find the tiny patch
of artificial prairie novel and interesting, and a distinct relief
from bluegrass lawns and iris beds.

A point of ethics here: It is tempting, while establishing a
prairie garden, to simply transplant grasses and forbs found
in prairie remnants. But the practice is roundly deplored by
those who truly prize prairie, and this makes sense if
you've ever seen a little prairie relict that's been badly

wounded by do-it-yourself landscapers or even commercial florists and decorators, to say nothing of the fact that many prairie species may not survive the stress of transplanting. And even if they can, the relict prairie from which they came will be impoverished and degraded.

Still, one learns more about prairie plants and their growth processes if they are established with seed. Seeds of both prairie grasses and forbs are available commercially and may be obtained from local sources. Some prairie experts advise us to go with local plants as much as possible. They not only have the greatest chance of success, but reduce the danger of weakening native plant strains with the infusion of importations.

If you plan a small area you can always gather the seeds yourself. It sort of rounds out the project — finding small prairie relicts, identifying their plants, and obtaining seeds for your own prairie facsimile. It'll never replace weekend football as a national pastime, but there are worse ways to spend a fall afternoon.

Not long ago I was driving an Illinois highway that runs beside an abandoned railroad. While in use the right-of-way had been burned regularly; now it is deteriorating prairie that is succeeding rapidly to woody growth. I stopped and walked through it, finding nothing spectacular, and then went up over the old roadbed and down the other side, out of sight of the highway. I found myself at the edge of a long patch of rattlesnake-master, the largest I have ever seen and a prime source of seed and rootstocks. A few weeks later, on a little hillside between a country graveyard and a soybean field, I came across an unexpected stand of wild indigo. I filled the pocket of my old hunting coat with seed pods, knowing that weevils probably got to them first but hoping there were enough seeds to make it worthwhile. There were.

Times of seed harvest for prairie plants vary greatly since there is a progressive wave of ripening from spring into autumn. The seed pods or ripened floral heads of forbs may be collected by hand through summer and early fall — although in the case of very small seeds such as the prairie clovers, it's easier to place a small plastic bag or fine nylon mesh over the developing seed heads.

The seed heads of ripened grasses can be stripped by hand into paper bags, preferably by bands of semiorganized kids who don't get any sandwiches until the job is done. Expect to get more chaff than seed. A characteristic of most wild prairie grasses is the astounding amount of chaffy junk that comes with the seeds and adds to the difficulty of planting by machine.

For a typical tallgrass prairie restoration, whether twenty square yards or twenty acres, the basic grasses must include big bluestem and Indian grass. Depending on the drainage and elevation of your site, sloughgrass may be planted in low areas and little bluestem seeded where it's higher and drier. There are dozens of other possibilities, of course, but the staples are almost always big bluestem and Indian grass.

Of the original prairie forbs, those especially quick to become established include such rugged composites as prairie coneflower, false sunflower, downy sunflower, and purple coneflower. In the second rank of ease of establishment are rattlesnake-master, compass-plant, and prairie dock. The showy prairie legumes usually take more doing, and more special care.

If you're starting your prairie plot with seed, the best germination of both native grasses and forbs will be obtained with "stratified" seed that has been given a cold-damp conditioning.

Dr. Peter Schramm of Knox College mixes his seed with about half its volume of damp vermiculite and stores it in plastic garbage cans. It should be held in cold storage at about 34° F for two or three months. Freezing won't hurt the seeds, but warmer temperatures may cause seed to mildew.

For my small-scale operation I've had good results with an old refrigerator out in the garage. With some shelves removed, it was plenty large for the little quantities of seed I was handling. I've used damp vermiculite but have done about as well with damp sand.

It's best to plant in late spring and early summer. Schramm says no earlier than late May and no later than late June. He's in northwestern Illinois, of course, and those dates may be adjusted slightly for more southern and northern locations. But wherever you are, planting on the late side enables you to harrow germinating weeds through late spring before seeding the prairie site.

Most authorities recommend that fertilizer not be applied to the prairie seedbed, since this would only increase the vigor of competing weeds and grasses. A big problem in planting prairie is keeping annual weeds at a minimum until the prairie is able to take care of itself. Once the prairie plants are established, there is no longer a problem — they can handle almost any weedy invasion from then on. But in the beginning, it's tough.

Fall plowing may help, for this allows frost to kill the roots of perennial weeds. Prairie planting is possible the following spring although it may be best to leave the field fallow for at least a year, harrowing and discing it regularly to keep it weed-free. Jim Wilson says that prairie grasses can be planted in the spring after April 1 on weed-free sites, but sites infested with grassy weed seeds should be planted toward mid-June after the first weed-growth season is over. On such sites, Jim works the ground shallowly two or three times through the spring to sprout and kill weeds. If the site is a fall-plowed area and relatively free of other plants, plowing may be unnecessary for grass-planting. Wilson has said: "The harder the seedbed, the better for the tall prairie grasses. Clay soil as hard as pavement may produce a fine stand." He simply broadcasts the seed evenly and rakes it in, covering it with up to a half-inch of soil. He never fertilizes such prairie plantings, and puts in warm-season grasses in spring or early summer — or after November 1 so they don't sprout until the following spring. Seed planted in late summer may sprout and winterkill.

It's been said that exotic weeds and grasses are often better adapted to survive in disturbed ground than our native plants simply because the home soils of the immigrants *have* been disturbed for thousands of years. Whether or not there's anything to that, the fact remains that most exotic plants are cool-season types that get the annual jump on our native warm-season grasses and forbs. Native grasses are also slower in germination and seedling growth than most cultivated annual and perennial crops. The time for succession from annual weeds to perennial prairie grasses will require at least two or three years, since eons of evolution in our xeric and mesic climates have developed prairie plants that grow down, not up, during their first summer of life. A big bluestem seedling only an inch high may have roots 12 inches long. As a result, annual weeds and forbs invariably dominate the first season of a newly planted "prairie" and the desirable species are inconspicuous.

Stratified seeds can be planted as they come out of cold storage, vermiculite and all. Prairie grass seed, however, may demand some special handling. It tends to be extremely light, fine, and chaffy, and is often difficult to plant with ordinary grain drills — the machines used for planting such small grains as wheat, oats, and barley. Unlike corn planters that drop several seeds at intervals of ten inches or so, a grain drill trickles a steady flow of tiny seeds into a furrow opened by shallow-running disks. Unless it is carefully adjusted, a grain drill can't cope with masses of chaffy native seeds. One solution to this is the Nesbet Drill, which is said to be able to handle anything from pepper to feathers, although planting with the Nesbet Drill is something of an art and takes some practice. The Truax Native Grass Drill, which appeared on the market early in 1978, is said to give excellent results. It is almost axiomatic that prairie grass seed can't be used with conventional equipment — yet Carl Kurtz tells us that he's had good luck planting big bluestem seed with an ordinary oat drill. It may not work as well as a Nesbet or Truax — but Carl feels it works well enough if the special drills aren't available.

A reasonably dense grass planting should have a couple of dozen seeds per square foot, a density that's not hard to achieve by hand broadcasting over a fairly sizable area. Peter Schramm recommends that the seed bed be lightly harrowed or raked, and thoroughly rolled after being seeded. A little plot the size of mine, of course, can be seeded by hand and then set with a tamper or just tromped by foot. If it is unusually dry in late June and early July during the time that the prairie grasses should be germinating and making early growth, some sort of overhead watering may be useful. However, this is seldom necessary in the main tallgrass region — and by mid-August the root systems of the seedlings should be well enough developed to carry them through fall.

Seeds of forbs, stratified or not, can be mixed in with the grass seed — especially if it is being broadcast by hand. It may be better, however, to give these flowering forbs a head start. A good method is to plant a dozen of the seeds in two-inch peat pots in May. If they've been stratified, most will germinate within a week or so and the pots can be placed in desired locations in early June.

Weed control in a new prairie site can range all the way from meticulous hand work to total neglect. In my little patch, I simply pull most weeds by hand if they are coming on too strongly. On a larger area, fast-growing annual weeds can be mowed when they grow higher than prairie seedlings. Some prairie culturists use tractor-drawn rotary mowers, taking care to mow above the prairie plants and clip only the weeds. However, others feel that a mower puts clippings in a solid swath that may smother seedlings, and prefer to use rotary shredders.

Mowing at least once, and preferably twice, in the first season can help control weedy plants that compete so strongly with prairie species for moisture, nutrients, and light. One mowing in the second year can reduce growth of annual weedy forbs, but from then on the native grasses should take off in good shape. Until then, it can be mighty discouraging. The weedy stuff towers and spreads while the native grasses are hardly begun. In a small plot, you can set your lawnmower to cut three to four inches high and clip off the weedy stuff when it shades 70 percent of the ground. But even though you may do this a couple of times in that first year, you can expect a dismal weed patch. The real miracle is still a year or two away.

Here's a rather typical failure-success story:

As executive director of the Boone County Conservation District in northern Illinois, Roger Gustafson undertook an experiment in the District's 53-acre Spencer Park. He and some friends thoroughly rototilled a strip of ground to reduce weed competition as much as possible, and visited a nearby railroad right-of-way to hand-strip blazing-star, prairie dock, big bluestem, Indian grass, yellow coneflower, purple coneflower, aster, butterfly milkweed, and little bluestem. They mixed it all up with damp sand and divided it into two parts; half was put in a refrigerator for the winter, and the rest was taken to the site and broadcast by hand and lightly raked.

In the spring, the stratified seed was spread over the remaining half of the site and lightly raked. Apparent disaster. The first summer produced only a dense stand of daisy fleabane. There was some insignificant greenery beneath the waist-high mass of exotic fleabane, but nothing impressive. The site was summarily ignored for the rest of that first growing season. It didn't look any better early in the second season, either. But late in the second year someone happened to notice the planting site was thick with yellow coneflowers in spite of the heavy growth of fleabane. Closer inspection revealed a number of other forbs and grasses coming on.

By the third growing season it was apparent that the project was taking hold and well on its way to becoming a very acceptable prairie facsimile. The whole thing was rather slapdash, and probably quite unscientific, but it demonstrates that some prairie species can thrive with no care at all. Incidentally, that part of the site planted to stratified seeds had a definite head start on the other half, and produced healthier and larger plants.

In Iowa, Roger Landers and Paul Christiansen found that test plots planted to the stratified seeds of 65 prairie species, and kept weed-free for the first year, resulted in a high level of establishment with over half of the species flowering in the second year. By the end of the fourth growing season, all species had flowered in plots that were kept weed-free the first year, and all had flowered in wheat-and-weed competition plots except the compass-plants. The transplanting of prairie species by means of sods 25 centimeters in diameter and 10–20 centimeters in depth was successful for 42 species during early spring. However, the team felt that a fall transplanting would have worked as well.

Landers and Christiansen believe that most prairie species can be transplanted or seeded directly into suitable soil if weedy species are controlled during the first year. "Many species are able to compete with the annual weeds outright," they wrote, "replacing or restricting them after several growing seasons, but few are able to do well against established perennials such as bluegrass or smooth brome."

Bluegrass, in particular, is an archenemy of newly planted prairie grasses. It is remarkable in its persistence in pastures, and its dense sod-forming habit and vigorous growth in early spring makes replacement by native grasses very difficult.

My little backyard prairie was created by transplanting sods of native grass in old bluegrass ground that had first been thoroughly turned. The prairie grasses made it, but after ten years it's still a Mexican stand-off. There is no way the big bluestem and Indian grass can invade the bluegrass sod, which is not only solidly established but closely mowed for six months each year. On the other hand, the bluegrass hasn't a chance to invade the tiny patch of prairie. Those towering grasses and their ground-layer of mulch would blot out any adventurous bluegrass. And whenever I burn that mass of dried plant materials it is well into spring before the prairie grasses have begun growing, but at a time when any cool-season bluegrass is well along in its spring growth.

Once a prairie restoration is on its way and producing a lush annual growth, frequent spring burning is an effective suppressant of any non-native "cool-season" species that may somehow establish a beachhead on the prairie site. Clair Kucera has found on Missouri prairies that a three-year interval between burnings will maintain grass dominance and the species diversity that are typical of native prairies. Even native grass densities tend to decline where heavy litter is not occasionally destroyed by fire. There's the question, of course, of how often to burn. Clair found that on plots burned annually, production and densities of native grasses were in some cases 100 percent greater than plots that were not burned at all. On plots burned once every five years, results were about the same as on fire-free plots, and the total root-rhizome mass in the upper inch of soil was as much as 39 percent less than on prairie burned annually.

Although fire tends to kill out many weedy annuals, it actually stimulates most prairie plants. When I burn my little prairie patch in late April, it never retards the native grasses or forbs but it sure raises hob with those fast-growing, cool-season grasses and weeds. By the way, don't burn prairie in the fall — it's just too valuable as winter wildlife cover. And although burning later in the spring, such as late April and May, may not harm the prairie grasses and larger forbs, it can be tough on some spring-nesting prairie birds.

The famed Morton Arboretum at Lisle, Illinois, has ten acres seeded to prairie plants, and a plot may be hand-weeded as often as three times during the first growing season and at least once in the second spring. By the third spring, accumulation of plant material is usually dense enough to sustain fire — and from then on, the only real maintenance is with spring fire. Such fires are set with matches, not torches, between March 30 and April 10. Firing the prairie plantings at such a late time achieves good weed control. Incidentally, those six acres at the Morton Arboretum now support about 120 established prairie species. The most conspicuous failures have been with such spring-blooming types as lousewort, Indian paintbrush, puccoon, and yellow star-grass.

Obviously, the more complete the prairie restoration, the more time and effort involved. Peter Schramm was able to establish a pretty good prairie facsimile of a half-dozen grasses and about thirty wildflowers in five years. At the Morton Arboretum, hand-seeding, greenhouse culture, setting seedlings by hand, and hand-weeding have cost thousands of man-hours to establish about 120 prairie species on what was weedy farmland. The University of Wisconsin's Arboretum staff has worked since 1936 to establish 26 kinds of grass and 300 species of prairie flowers on its hundred acres of prairie.

Transplanting prairie grasses and forbs is possible and practical, and far easier with some species than others. I've transplanted tallgrass sods in both spring and fall with little discernible difference and a high rate of success. Blazing-star and prairie button snakeroot are quite easy to transplant, as is butterfly milkweed, but care must be taken to include as much rootstock as possible.

The first compass-plant I ever transplanted was higher than my head at the time, with a typically massive taproot. It was somewhat like transplanting a tree sapling, for I included about 18 inches of taproot that was nearly as thick as my wrist near the surface. When this was transplanted into my prairie patch, it "died" almost at once. But within three weeks we noticed small new leaves appearing at the base of the cluster of dried stems, and by Labor Day there were several large, oak-like leaves. That compass-plant flourishes apace; in late July it towers over the limestone Kansas fence-post leaning beside it.

A restored prairie is not the real thing, of course. But it is a start, and can only improve with age. Mine has been an enduring source of satisfaction. Not only has it kept me out of poolhalls, but it's an island of constantly varying form and color that becomes richer through spring and summer. It is extremely rugged; several years ago, during an unusually hot and dry summer, my bluegrass lawn was as brown and crisp as excelsior, with inch-wide cracks in the soil. Small trees died nearby, and even large trees suffered. Yet, the tall-grasses of my little prairie were lush and green. By late summer their culms stood nine feet tall, slowly turning wine and bronze. The prairie flowers bloomed as they always had, their deep root systems easily enduring the drought.

❧

Not long ago, in the Milwaukee suburb of New Berlin, the Donald Hagars moved into a house on two and a half acres in the Sun Shadows West subdivision. Struck with the possibilities of a return to nature, they planted some wild Wisconsin prairie grasses and let nature take its course. Neighbors more attuned to riding mowers than bobolinks had the Hagars hailed into court for violating a local "noxious weed" law. The judge, however, was sympathetic to the Hagars and their reverting acreage, and returned them to the arms of their

prairiescape with the blessings of the bench. It may be a sign of the times. It may even be significant that the news story quoted Goethe: "No one feels himself easy in a garden which does not look like the open country." So much for keeping up with the Joneses.

Jim Wilson knows a Madison Avenue advertising man who planted his personal field of prairie grasses about twenty miles up the Hudson River from New York. When he comes home after a particularly hectic day in the clamor of Madhattan, he takes to his prairie instead of a jugful of martinis. Nothing, this executive claims, soothes him quite so much as simply going out and sitting in his grass for a while.

Wilson has seen such things before, and holds a theory that it reflects a hunger for stability and authenticity: "People seem to long for something that will give them a sense of security and continuity and permanence, and somehow these prairie grasses and flowers seem to do it. The darn things seem to reassure people somehow. They represent permanence and persistence in the face of danger — *persisting* things, you know."

In Peoria, the Caterpillar Company has planted some of its roadsides to native grasses and forbs. The Fermi National Accelerator Lab near Batavia, Illinois, turned over 600 acres of its land for a prairie restoration that was begun in 1974 — a project under the guidance of Northeastern Illinois University.

The new Kansas City airport has planted grounds to prairie grasses and flowers. Certain state highway departments, as in Nebraska, are planting some roadsides to native grasses and flowers that not only are highly appropriate, but cheap to maintain. Landers and Christiansen point out that many roadside sites could be planted to native prairie mixtures without expensive maintenance, although this is sometimes resisted with the traditional viewpoint that roadsides should look like mowed lawns. Still, one of the finest little prairie restorations in Iowa is at a rest stop on west-bound Interstate 80 about twenty miles west of Davenport. Only one tenth of an acre, it contains a large number of prairie species.

Attitudes toward tallgrass prairie preserves range from keen enthusiasm through a broad band of indifference to overt hostility. I've seen both extremes demonstrated at Kalsow Prairie in northwest Iowa.

One early July day photographer Patricia Caulfield and I were working at Kalsow, completing a magazine assignment. We came out of the prairie in midafternoon and were at the car pouring coffee when a pickup truck pulled up and stopped. It was a farmer who owned land adjacent to the prairie. He had a profound lack of interest in what we were doing, and couldn't understand what there was to photograph out there. (Pat had shot over a hundred color pictures that day.) He asked me if I knew anyone in the conservation department in Des Moines, "the outfit that owns this place." Yes, I did. At that, he unburdened himself.

For one thing, he was tired of having weeds get over into his soybeans; those sunflowers and other stuff on this state ground spread badly and he couldn't see why the state didn't keep a wide buffer strip plowed, or burned, or something. What's more, the whole place was a damned silly waste of good land.

That's about when Pat broke in. She told him that she had been photographing tallgrass prairie from the Cross Timbers of Texas to the Manitoba line, and in all that great reach of land this little quarter-section of native prairie was the only one of its kind. There were some other native prairies, in original form, to be sure, but few as large and none like this one. He grunted and returned to his truck, as stolid and tame as the soils he farmed.

Four years later, almost to the day and hour, I was again at Kalsow having a tailgate lunch when a car drove up. Several adults and children got out, walked over into the prairie, read the big sign, wandered fifty yards down the path in a what-shall-we-do-now sort of way, and returned to the road. A young man came over to me and asked if I could tell him anything about the place. He explained his interest.

"I'm originally from southern Minnesota," he said, "and for several years I have been teaching in Germany. Our geography text includes material on original American landforms and there is a section on North American prairie that mentions Kalsow Prairie by name.

"When we came home on leave and drove down to Iowa to visit friends, I learned that the famous Kalsow Prairie was only forty miles away. So here we are. But now what? I want to take some pictures, but I don't know what I'd be photographing. Can you help?"

The prairie was in midsummer bloom, dressed fit to kill, and I probably told him more than he really wanted to know. I usually do. But we talked flowers, grasses, the deep soils, birds and animals, and the men and women who settled this country and how they broke it — and how it sometimes broke them. He filled a small notebook and used all his film and some of mine, departing in late afternoon beaming and excited as only a genuine teacher can be when he has first-hand, illustrated grist for his mill. It's good to think on that, knowing that a classroom in some gray German factory town is being brightened by the gaudy, sundrenched July prairie that we shared that day.

A display of extremes: a farmer who saw only weedy wasteland invading his cash grainfield, and a foreign teacher who found a wild garden. A telling irony, as well — that the children of the farmer, who may also be the great-grandchildren of pioneers who settled that part of Iowa, would know less about their Kalsow Prairie than some schoolchildren in Germany.

All surviving tallgrass prairie preserves, as we've said, are relatively small. In Iowa or Illinois, as much as a square mile of virgin tallgrass prairie would be a huge and immensely valuable tract. Yet, in spite of the high intrinsic value of tallgrass prairie, there are proposals for large tallgrass prairie parks.

One of the most extravagant of these surfaced awhile back in northwestern Iowa, where a prominent physician tried to promote a prairie national park as the nation's 200th birthday present to itself. He envisioned a park that would "combine the best features of Yellowstone Park, Disneyland, Williamsburg, the St. Louis Zoo, and the McCormick Convention Center in Chicago."

The good doctor's park would be about six miles square, with native trees and shrubs around the perimeter and a creek or small river dammed to form a lake. There would be a "pioneer village" and steamboats to carry visitors on the

river, as well as a railroad line so that the parkgoers could see
herds of buffalo, elk, deer, prairie chickens, foxes, antelope,
coyotes, wild turkey, and prairie dog villages. One corner of
the park would have a sort of cornbelt Disneyland, with another corner featuring "a model city of the future." The center of the park would be a large tract of restored prairie.

He felt the cost of such a national park "should not exceed
$20 million" — and at the time of the proposal, it might not
have. But today, land acquisition alone could top $81 million.
And the cost of re-establishing native prairie on, say, thirty
square miles of farmland? Name any figure. Anyway, despite
the doctor's best efforts, his brainchild died *en utero.*

The dream of a Prairie National Park, however, has been
fanned in Kansas by a coterie of prairie enthusiasts who have
held fast against great political and economic odds. Unlike
the Iowa proposal, a Prairie National Park in Kansas would
have no amusement park overtones and would be tallgrass
prairie restored on a grand scale with representative wildlife.

The only major surviving tract of tall prairie in the United
States lies in the Flint Hills of eastern Kansas, where cultivation has been largely discouraged by chert formations lying
close to the surface. Although the soil is of prairie origin and
quite fertile, much of it is simply too shallow to plow. As a
result, it is some of the finest grazing land available and the
"bluestem hills" of eastern Kansas are famous among southwestern cattlemen.

Some Flint Hills ranches have been in the same ownerships
for generations, and the thought of uprooting those old ranch
families in favor of a public park isn't a happy one. Flint Hills
ranchers have bitterly opposed the concept of a Prairie National Park. One can't much blame them. Their resistance to
the idea is rooted in long-standing kinship to that land, although their position is somewhat weakened by their ratio-
nale that 1) it's not necessary to create a Prairie National
Park since the native prairie is already there for every-

one to see, and 2) there's no reason to feel that the Flint Hills will ever be anything but prairie.

Those Flint Hills, of course, are not really "prairie" but bluestem pastures — and there's a difference. They are grazing lands in which broad vistas of native grasses and forbs never achieve full growth or form. The Hills are native prairie that's been subjected to considerable grazing pressure for a long time — and in some cases, overgrazing.

Nor is it true that the Flint Hills will never be anything but what they are. They're as endangered by change as any other original landscape. Small lakes, ponds, and overland electrical transmission lines are altering the face of the Kansas prairielands, and they are no longer safe from the plow. Some ranchers have begun to plant tall fescue and smooth brome in an attempt to increase the carrying capacity of their ranges — in spite of the fact that it can cost three times as much to fertilize such grasses as a landowner can charge in rent. If grassland rents at $8 per acre for grazing, with a cost of $25 per acre to fertilize the brome or fescue, it could require three years just to regain the money spent on fertilizer — and brome and fescue require hefty slugs of nitrogen.

Still, those cool-season grasses may stay green much of the winter and support early spring grazing. Some ranchers argue that fescue can graze as much as three times as many cattle per acre as can the "poorer" native grasses on their ranches. True, perhaps, but it tends to overlook the facts that those native grasses have often been badly overgrazed, and that the fescue that replaces them would require considerable nitrogen fertilizer to support trebled grazing pressure.

For better or worse, range use appears to be shifting from summer grazing of steers to year-long grazing of cows and calves in the Flint Hills. As a result, winter pasturage has become more important. Since native grasses tend to decline in nutritive value when they cure in place and are not cut as hay, and since food supplements are essential for half the year in order to maintain a cow-calf operation, it may be desirable to have at least part of the range in cool-season forage for fall, winter, and early spring feeding. And so, starting in about 1974, thousands of acres of the Kansas Flint Hills have been seeded to brome and fescue. Both will grow in spring and fall when native grasses are dormant — and the native grassland shrinks and is more restricted to steep, rocky areas.

Kansans are like anyone else, of course, in being often blind to the wonders they walk among. There have always been Kansans who believed their native grasses could be improved upon. A hundred years ago, Senator John Ingalls made his famous declaration that "grass is the forgiveness of nature — her constant benediction." However, the Kansas senator was speaking of bluegrass, not bluestem. He scorned his native Kansas prairie grasses, saying they would nourish mustangs, antelope, and Texas cattle, but never thoroughbreds.

"But bluegrass!" he effused. "Bluegrass does more than nourish splendid horses. It supports a whole society of muscular men and voluptuous women; upon its foundations rest palaces, temples, peaceful institutions, social order. " If Kansas could be seeded to bluegrass, Ingalls believed, it could become another Kentucky. And while Kentucky is assuredly a very fine place, I'd reckon that Kansas has at least as many muscular men and voluptuous women. Maybe more. After all, my old friend Frank Phipps used to say that his native Kentucky was famous for three things and any one of them could kill you: horses, bourbon, and women. Not so in Kansas. Along the highway leading into Pratt is a series of signs instructing the traveler: "KANSAS SUNFLOWERS, KANSAS WHEAT, KANSAS WOMEN CAN'T BE BEAT." And I'm not about to go into a west Kansas saloon and say otherwise.

Back to the park proposal.

It's being spearheaded by the group called "Save the Tallgrass Prairie, Inc." They are pressing for a national park of at least 60,000 acres — an area about ten miles square but only one third of one percent of all Kansas grasslands. With such a national park, 98 percent of the Flint Hills would still be in private hands. Yet, that two percent is apparently too much.

On the other side are ranchers and others of the "Kansas Grassroots Association, Inc.," who contend that there is prairie in the Flint Hills today because of ranchers, and not in spite of them. Not surprisingly, the Kansas legislature and congressional delegation side with them, and the legislature has passed at least one resolution asking the federal government not to create a national park on privately owned grasslands.

There's a sad quality to all this, as there usually is in such things, with the park advocates often labeled feather-witted idealists and the landowners branded as thick-skinned spoilers bent on environmental rapine. Both generalizations are inaccurate and cruelly unfair.

But one thing is certain: There are holes in our national park system, and an urgent need for quality examples of all major American landscapes. This goes beyond mere scenery. Each park or national monument should entail characteristic landforms, of course, but should also seek to preserve major vegetative types typical of the region. This is underway in Alaska, where fjord systems, mountains, tundra, and rain forest biomes are being placed in the national park system.

In the lower forty-eight states it is important that we include national parks or monuments that represent major examples of our three basic grasslands: tallgrass prairie, mixed prairie, and shortgrass plains. Of the three, tall prairie will be the most difficult to establish because it is the rarest of all major American biomes, and because even relict prairies are now among our most valuable agricultural lands. Yet, those very arguments against creating a prairie national park or monument are the most compelling reasons for doing so.

The Flint Hills of eastern Kansas have all the elements for such a park — a fine lift and roll to the land, almost all the original plant species, and enough physical dimension so this great people pasture would look the way such a place ought to look, with far and open horizons.

It would be a special place, with an essence not found in mountains, desert, or any other openlands. Jim Wilson said there is a mysterious something about the native grasses — a power, a spirit that both stirs the soul and quiets it. Whatever that mysterious essence, it lives only on true prairie under a broad vault of pure and intense light — where the young prairie-born winds comb tallgrasses, carrying larksong and scent of ancient gardens, running unchecked from pasque-flower ridges down to sloughgrass meadows where the blue flag and wild orchid grow.

APPENDIX
SELECTED REFERENCES
INDEX

———•———

Appendix

Some Representative Prairie Preserves (1979)

ILLINOIS

Name of area	Prairie (acres)	County	Location
Flora Prairie	10.	Boone	SW corner of county, E of Ill. Central RR tracks on N side of Poole Rd. Parking and trails.
Ayers Sand Prairie Nature Preserve	115.	Carroll	3 miles SE of Savanna, ½ mile E of Hwy. 84. Dry sand prairie. Parking, no trails.
Thomson-Fulton Sand Prairie	——	Carroll & Whiteside	Between Thomson and Fulton, W of Burlington-Northern RR right-of-way.
Crabtree Nature Center	——	Cook	Barrington Hills, entrance on Palatine Road 1 mile W of Barrington Road. Prairie restoration included in 1100 acres of preserved land. Exhibit bldg. and several miles of trails.
Gensburg-Markham Prairie	110.	Cook	In Markham, E of Kedzie Ave., W of I-294 & between 155th and 157th sts. Access by permission from NE Ill. Univ.

Name of area	*Prairie* (acres)	County	Location
Morton Grove Prairie	1.9	Cook	In Morton Grove at NE end of 16-acre Prairieview Park.
North Branch Prairie Project	——	Cook	Along bicycle path in Cook County Forest Preserve on N branch of Chicago River in Chicago & Morton Grove.
Sand Ridge Nature Preserve	70.	Cook	Near Calumet City, E of Torrence Ave., W of Penn Central RR tracks, N of Michigan City Rd. No parking or trails.
Somme Prairie	18.	Cook	Northbrook, ½ mile W of Waukegan Rd. N of Dundee Rd. in Somme Woods Forest Preserve. No parking or trails.
James Woodworth Prairie	5.	Cook	Glenview, on E side of Milwaukee Ave., ½ mile N of Golf Rd. Owned by U. of Ill. at Chicago Circle; center bldg. open and trail guides available daily 10–3, June–Sept.
Belmont Prairie	10.	Du Page	Downers Grove, S of Ogden Ave. (Rt. 34), W of Belmont Rd., at end of Prairie Ave. Trails exist.
Morton Arboretum Prairie Restoration Project	——	Du Page	At Lisle, ½ mile N of Hwy. 5 on Hwy. 53. Restored prairie. Self-guided trails; admission fee.
12-Mile Prairie	——	Effingham Fayette Marion	From Watson to Kilmundy, between Ill. Central Gulf RR tracks & Hwy. 37.
Prospect Cemetery Prairie Nature Preserve	5.	Ford	SE edge of Paxton on Vermilion St. Parking on street; no trails.
Goose Lake Prairie Nature Preserve	1,513.	Grundy	SE of Morris, N of Lorenzo Rd. on Jugtown Rd. Interpretive center and trails.

Name of area	Prairie (acres)	County	Location
Iroquois Country Conservation Area	1,240.	Iroquois	NE of Beaverville at eastern end of conservation area. Wet to dry prairie and marsh. No facilities.
Père Marquette State Park	15–20.	Jersey	W of Grafton on Hwy. 100. Loess hill prairie.
Heron Pond–Wildcat Bluff Nature Preserve	6.	Johnson	4 miles SW of Vienna. Limestone glade within 1939-acre nature preserve.
Knox County Field Station	several areas	Knox	4½ miles S of Victoria on county road 15.
Berkeley Prairie	18.	Lake	Highland Park, S side of Berkeley Ave., W of Ridge Rd.
Illinois Beach Nature Preserve	829.	Lake	S part of Ill. Beach State Park, Zion. Wet to dry sand prairie.
Green River Conservation Area	——	Lee	12 miles S of Dixon Co. 12. Sand prairie scattered through 2330-acre refuge.
Henry Allan Gleason Nature Preserve	110.	Mason	3 miles N of Topeka within Sand Ridge State Forest.
Reavis Spring Hill Nature Preserve	53.	Mason	5½ miles S of Easton, 8 miles E of Kilbourne, S of Co. 5. Loess hill prairie; no trails.
Sand Prairie–Scrub Oak Nature Preserve	1,460.	Mason	9 miles S of Havana and 3 miles E of Bath, S of Co. 17. Dry sand prairie; parking and trails on E side of area.
Queen Anne Prairie–Eckert Cemetery Conservation Area	1.	McHenry	On Queen Anne Rd. N of Charles Rd. NE of Woodstock. Interpretive trail.
Weston Cemetery Prairie Nature Preserve	5.	McLean	½ mile E of Weston, N of Rt. 24.
Fults Hill Prairie Nature Preserve	623.	Monroe	1 mile E of Fults on Miss. River bluffs, N side of Bluff Rd.

Name of area	Prairie (acres)	County	Location
Beach Cemetery Nature Preserve	2.25	Ogle	S of Davis Junction on N side of Big Mound Rd. Managed by Natural Land Institute, Rockford. Permission required.
Pine Rock Nature Preserve	35.	Ogle	4 miles E of Oregon on Rt. 64. Northern Ill. Univ. Permission required; Pine Rock Committee, Taft Field Campus, Oregon.
Freeport Prairie Nature Preserve	5.	Stephenson	S edge of Freeport on Walnut Rd. Parking and trail.
Grant Greek Prairie Nature Preserve	78.	Will	In Des Plaines River Conservation Area, E of I-66, ½ mile S of Blodgett Rd. No trails.
Bell Bowl Prairie	15.	Winnebago	SW edge of Greater Rockford Airport, N of Belt Line Rd. Dry gravel prairie owned by Greater Rockford Airport Authority; access by permission only.
Harlem Hills Nature Preserve	53.	Winnebago	E of Rt. 173 and S of Nimitz Rd., one mile SW of Rock Cut State Park. Parking and trails.
Searls Park Prairie	142.	Winnebago	NW edge of Rockford on Central Ave. Parking and trails.

INDIANA

Hoosier Prairie	304.	Lake	Section 33 & 34, Township 36N, Range 9W. Wet, mesic, and dry sand prairie, and dry-mesic sand savannah.
Beaver Lake Nature Preserve	64.	Newton	Section 2, Township 30N, Range 9W. Preserved as prairie chicken habitat, with some savannah and prairie plants.

Name of area	Prairie (acres)	County	Location
Willow Slough and Jasper-Pulaski Fish and Game Areas	——	Jasper Pulaski	Large portions of these fish and game areas contain prairie and savannah vegetation.

IOWA

Name of area	Prairie (acres)	County	Location
Martin Little Sioux Access	10.	Cherokee	4 miles east of Larrabee.
Ranney Knob Area	20.	Cherokee	1 mile SW of Washta.
Silver Sioux Recreation Area	30.	Cherokee	7 miles south of Cherokee.
Twin Ponds Park	31.	Chickasaw	7 miles SW of New Hampton.
Hartman Wildlife Area	10.	Hardin	1 mile N of Steamboat Rock.
Headquarters Area	1.	Hardin	8 miles NW of Steamboat Rock.
Cleppinger Area (private)	15.	Jasper	1 mile S of Reisnor (sand prairie).
Krum Nature Preserve	39.	Jasper	3 miles W of Grinnell (newly planted area).
Mariposa Recreation Area	5.	Jasper	6 miles NE of Newton.
Morris Prairie	20.	Jasper	5½ miles NE of Newton.
Turner Station Railroad Right-of-Way	14.	Jasper	1 mile of railroad right-of-way near town of Turner (wherever that is).
Matsell Bridge	20.	Linn	
Rock Island Preserve	15.	Linn	W side of city of Cedar Rapids.
Cedar Bluffs Recreation Area	11.	Muscatine	3½ miles SE of Conesville.
Saulsbury Bridge	33.	Muscatine	7 miles NW of Muscatine.
Hickory Grove Park	23.	Story	3 miles SW of Colo.
Cooper's Marsh	10.	Story	7 miles NE of Ames.
Rossow Prairie	40.	Webster	6 miles NE of Fort Dodge adjacent to County Road D14.

Name of area	Prairie (acres)	County	Location
Hayden Prairie	240.	Howard	5 miles N of Saratoga. Fine example of native prairie.
Mark Sand Prairie	36.	Black Hawk	NW of Cedar Falls. Owned by Wayne Mark family.
University of Northern Iowa Campus Prairie	8.	Black Hawk	Reconstructed prairie on campus in city of Cedar Falls.
Conrad Sand Prairie	15.	Marshall	2½ miles SW of Albion. Private, but entry will be granted on request.
McLaughlin Prairie	30.	Wright	1½ miles SW of Belmond. Ask permission of owner.
I-35 Overlook	—	Story	Approx. 6 miles N of Ames.
Liska-Stanek Prairie	20.	Webster	4 miles SE of Moorland.
Union Slough National Wildlife Refuge	—	Kossuth	5 miles E of Bancroft. Narrow upland slopes of native prairie, and some planted areas.
Kalsow Prairie	160.	Calhoun	Approx. 5 miles NE of Manson. State-owned native prairie.
Highway 7 Railroad Right-of-Way	—	Buena Vista	For 11 miles W of Storm Lake an old railroad right-of-way runs along Highway 7. Has a fine prairie plant community.
Cayler Prairie	160.	Dickinson	4 miles W of West Okoboji Lake. Probably Iowa's most scenic prairie. A State Preserve and National Natural Landmark.
Freda Haffner Preserve	110.	Dickinson	4 miles S and 1 mile E of Cayler Prairie on east side of Little Sioux River. A walk-in area; cannot be seen from road.

Name of area	Prairie (acres)	County	Location
Steel Prairie	200.	Cherokee	2 miles NW of Larrabee. Largest virgin Iowa prairie still in private ownership. Mowed annually for hay. Entry permission not required.
Sheeder Prairie	20.	Guthrie	4 miles W of Guthrie Center, 1 mile N of Highway 64.
Gitchie Manitou	91.	Lyon	Extreme NW corner of Iowa. Outcroppings of Sioux quartzite surrounded by virgin prairie.
Loess Hills Game Management Area	1200+.	Monona	5 miles N of Turin. Many open south-facing prairie slopes and ridges.
Waubonsie State Park	——	Fremont	5 miles SW of Sidney.
Loveland Overlook	12.	Pottawattamie	1½ miles E of Loveland on I-80. Well-established tallgrass planting.

KANSAS

Name of area	Prairie (acres)	County	Location
Konza Prairie	8,616.	Geary	6 miles S of Manhattan, bounding K-177 on the E and I-70 on the S. Termed "most significant" tallgrass prairie area in Kansas. Managed by Kansas State Univ.
Flint Hills	——	——	An immense tract of rolling prairie rangeland lying generally between Topeka and Manhattan and extending south for over a hundred miles.
Sand Prairie Natural History Reservation	80.	Harvey	W of Newton. Managed by Bethel College.
Ordway Prairie Preserve	2,200.	Greenwood Butler	Near Cassoway. Inquire locally. Area being grazed by cattle.

MICHIGAN

Name of area	Prairie (acres)	County	Location
Newaygo Dry Prairies	80.	Newaygo	Brooks Twp., Sect. 35, NE Qr. Inquire Ronald Rapp, Provost, Alma College, Alma MI 48801. Owned by U.S. Forest Serv.
Allegan Oak Plains	122.	Allegan	Site is on Allegan State Game Area, DNR, Allegan, MI 49010.
Algonac State Park Prairies	35.	St. Clair	Consists of 4 tracts, 3 of which are wet prairie. Contact Algonac State Park, Algonac MI (DNR).
Bowerman Prairie	45.	Barry	Barry State Game Area. Wet to mesic prairie and sand barren. DNR.
Minong Prairie	10.	Monroe	Petersburg State Game Area. Wet sand prairie. Inquire M. Cooley, DNR, Lansing MI 48908.
Ann Arbor Wet Prairie	5.	Washtenaw	Wet prairie and mesic RR strip prairie. Flood plain on S bank of Huron Rd., E of Geddes Bridge 5A. City of Ann Arbor Pks. & Rec. Dept.
Bakertown Fen	7.	Berrien	Fen and wet prairie. Owned by City of Buchanan.
Helmer Brook Fen	30.	Calhoun	Fen with adjacent mesic prairie. Owned by City of Battle Creek.
Middlebelt Prairie	20.	Wayne	N bank of Huron Slough S of Huron River Rd., ¼ mile W of Middlebelt Rd. Owned by Huron-Clinton Metro. Authority.
AMTRAK RR Strip Prairies	——	——	Six sites on the Michigan Central line between Kalamazoo and Michigan City, totaling ca. 4 miles of right-of-way. Varied

Name of area	Prairie (acres)	County	Location
AMTRAK RR Strip Prairies (cont.)			prairie communities. Lease pending to Nature Conservancy. Inquire Margaret Kohring, Fernwood, Inc., 1720 Range Line Rd., Niles MI 49120.
Earl's Prairie	10.	Lapeer	Reconstructed prairie; the largest in state. Wet-mesic prairie. Owned by Mich. Audubon Soc. Inquire Dan Farmer, Seven Ponds Nature Center, Dryden MI.

MINNESOTA

Name of area	Prairie (acres)	County	Location
Minneopa State Park	200.	Blue Earth	W of Mankato.
Lake Shetek State Park	20.	Murray	N of Currie.
Old Mill State Park	30.	Marshall	5 miles NW of Ellereth.
O. L. Kipp State Park	200.	Winona	
Rice Lake State Park	20.	Steele	6 miles E of Owatonna.
St. Croix Wild River State Park	50.	Chisago	
Sakatah Lake State Park	20.	LeSueur	1 mile N of Waterville on State 13.
Sibley State Park	100.	Kandiyohi	18 miles N of Willmar.
Split Rock Creek State Park	30.	Pipestone	6 miles SW of Pipestone.
Traverse des Sioux State Park	10.	Nicollet LeSueur	5 miles N of St. Peter.
Upper Sioux Agency State Park	100.	Yellow Medicine	3 miles SE of Granite Falls.
Whitewater State Park	20.	Winona	25 miles E of Rochester.
Maplewood State Park	50.	Ottertail	5 miles E of Pelican Rapids.
Afton State Park	60.	Washington	10 miles E of St. Paul.

Name of area	Prairie (acres)	County	Location
Big Stone Lake State Park	60.	Big Stone	5 miles N of Ortonville.
Blue Mounds State Park	1,200.	Rock	8 miles N of Luverne.
Buffalo River State Park	400.	Clay	15 miles E of Moorhead.
Camden State Park	150.	Lyon	10 miles SW of Marshall.
Crow Wing State Park	100.	Crow Wing Cass Morrison	4 miles SW of Brainerd.
Flandreau State Park	20.	Brown	3 miles S of new Ulm.
Fort Snelling State Park	100.	Dakota Hennepin Ramsey	3 miles S of New Ulm.
Frontenac State Park	100.	Goodhue	8 miles E of Red Wing.
Glacial Lakes State Park	1,000.	Pope	4 miles S of Starbuck.
Helmer Myre State Park	300.	Freeborn	2 miles E of Albert Lea.
Western Prairie Scientific and Natural Area	600.	Wilkin	North unit 8 miles NW of Rothsay. South unit 6 miles W-NW of Rothsay.

Note: There is no exact inventory of prairie vegetation on all Department of Natural Resources Lands, and the foregoing is only a partial summary of prairie lands protected by the DNR. For more complete information, contact the Minnesota Department of Natural Resources, 300 Centennial Bldg., 658 Cedar St., St. Paul 55155. The Nature Conservancy has 55 preserves in Minnesota totaling over 12,000 acres. About 7000 acres are prairie. Their sites in northwest Minnesota are helping to preserve the prairie chicken. Queen's Bluff in Winona County, Schaefer Prairie in McLeod County, and Roscoe Prairie in Stearns County are good examples of the prairies they have preserved. Visitors to Nature Conservancy lands are asked to obtain permission from The Nature Conservancy, 328 East Hennepin Avenue, Minneapolis MN 55414. Phone: (612) 379-2134.

MISSOURI

Lichen Glade	——	St. Clair	6 miles W of Osceola on N side of Hwy. B. Mostly oak, but some prairie glade.

Name of area	Prairie (acres)	County	Location
Taberville Prairie	1,360.	St. Clair	2½ miles N of Taberville on Hwy. H. Some 376 plant species recorded.
Schell-Osage Prairie Relicts (Schell-Osage Wildlife Area)	5 tracts from 3.5 to 15 acres	St. Clair	6 miles SW of Taberville Prairie.
Wah-Kon-Tah Prairie	640.	St. Clair	2½ miles NE of El Dorado Springs. Has resident flock of prairie chickens.
Mo-Ko Prairie	416.	Cedar	1 mile E of El Dorado Springs.
Monegaw Prairie	270.	Cedar	2½ miles E of El Dorado Springs on S side of Hwy. 54.
Little Osage Prairie	80.	Vernon	6 miles S of Nevada on Hwy. 71.
Osage Prairie	1,115.	Vernon	6 miles S of Nevada on Hwy. 71. Prairie chickens on area.
Tzi-Sho Prairie	240.	Barton	4 miles S and W of Liberal.
Hunkah Prairie	160.	Barton	5½ miles S and W of Liberal.
Wah-Sha-She Prairie	160.	Jasper	2 miles N of Asbury. Resident flock of prairie chickens.
Mount Vernon Prairie	40.	Lawrence	4 miles NE of Mt. Vernon.
Golden Prairie	320.	Barton	3½ miles S and W of Golden City. Resident flock of prairie chickens.
Pawhuska Prairie	77.	Barton	9 miles E and N of Lamar.
Penn-Sylvania Prairie	160.	Dade	2¼ miles E and S of Sylvania.
Niawathe Prairie	240.	Dade	10 miles N of Lockwood; 4 miles E of Sylvania.
La Petite Gemme Prairie	37.	Polk	3 miles S and W of Bolivar off Hwy. 13.
Friendly Prairie	40.	Pettis	10¼ miles SW of Sedalia off Hwy. 65.
Rider Tract	76.	Pettis	1 mile E of Friendly Prairie.

Name of area	Prairie (acres)	County	Location
Tucker Prairie	146.	Callaway	Beside I-70, 2½ miles W of junction of I-70 and Hwy. 54. U. of Mo. research prairie.
Gayfeather Prairie	76.	Vernon	4 miles W of Montevallo on road E.
McNary Tract	160.	Barton	1½ miles E of Hwy. 71 at Sheldon on county road B, 1½ miles S on gravel road.

Note: All Missouri prairie preserves are located in the southwest quadrant of the state. Most are northwest of Springfield. This remarkable state prairie system totals over 12,000 acres and is the result of cooperative acquisition by the Missouri Department of Conservation, The Nature Conservancy, the Missouri Prairie Foundation, and the University of Missouri.

NEBRASKA

Willa Cather Prairie	600.	Webster	5 miles S of Red Cloud on Highway 281.
Pawnee Prairie	1,100.	Pawnee	7 miles S, 1 mile E of Birchard.
Cuming City Cemetery	11.	Washington	Near Ft. Calhoun

Note: These areas are typical tallgrass sites in the eastern part of the state. The Sand Hills rangelands of northwestern Nebraska are mixed prairie, with pure stands of tallgrass prairie on lower elevations that have not been put into domestic grain or hay crops. A combination tract of about 54,000 acres comprising sandhills grassland, eastern ponderosa pine woodland, and eastern deciduous woodland has been acquired by The Nature Conservancy. Headquarters area is about 15 miles north of Johnstown in Brown County.

NORTH DAKOTA

Not named	640.	Benson	Section 36, Township 155 N, Range 69W. Native, rolling prairie.
Forbes Prairie	12,800.	Dickey	5 miles W and 3 miles N of Forbes. Mixed-grass prairie and wooded ravines on edge of Coteau du Missouri.

Name of area	Prairie (acres)	County	Location
Colvin Prairie	13,000.	Eddy	8 miles N, 3 miles W of McHenry. Mixed-grass prairie on stagnation and end moraine with numerous wetlands.
Dahlen Esker	105.	Grand Forks	3 miles NE of Dahlen. Esker 4½ miles long containing many prairie species.
Oakville Prairie Biology Station	800.	Grand Forks	2 miles E of Emerado. Lowland and upland prairie. Univ. of N. Dak.
Grand Forks County Prairie Chicken Range	2,808.	Grand Forks	2½ miles N of Mekinock. Low prairie grassland in saline soil.
Logan County Prairie	5,760.	Logan	13 miles N, 3 miles E of Lehr. Large prairie tract on end moraine at 2100 feet elevation.
Tallgrass Prairie	40–60.	Ransom	SW qtr. and NE qtr. of Section 20, Township 136N, Range 38W.
Piper Sandhills	100.	Richland	3 miles S, 1 mile W of Leonard.
La Mars Prairie	40.	Richland	3 miles N of La Mars. Moist tallgrass prairie, fen and aspen grove. White lady's slipper.
Havana Prairie	2,097.	Sargent	7 miles E of Havana. Largest remaining tract of prairie in Coteau des Prairies in North Dakota.
Stutsman Prairie	8,000.	Stutsman	3 miles N, 2 miles W of Vashti. Largest tract of unbroken prairie in county.
natural prairie	80.	Traill	South 80 acres of SW qtr. of Section 9, Township 146N, Range 53W.

Note: Some mixed-grass prairies are included here because they contain extensive low areas and tallgrass stands.

OHIO

Name of area	Prairie (acres)	County	Location
Irwin Prairie Nature Preserve	147.	Lucas	13 miles W of Toledo at intersection of Irwin Road and Dorr Street near Berkey Quadrangle. Finest wet prairie in state. One of last vestiges of the ancient Black Swamp, which covered most of NW Ohio and part of SE Michigan in postglacial times.
Adams Lake Prairie Nature Preserve	22.37.	Adams	2 miles N of West Union, W of S.R. 41 at southern boundary of Adams Lake State Park. Small xeric prairie surrounded by dry oak forest.

SOUTH DAKOTA

Name of area	Prairie (acres)	County	Location
Aurora Prairie	30.	Brookings	2.7 miles. E of Brookings on Highway 14, then S 3.5 miles.
Clovis Prairie	157.	Brown	8 miles N of Columbia, 3 miles W.
Vermillion Prairie	22.	Clay	15 miles NW of Vermillion.
Altamont Prairie	62.	Devel	From intersection of US 77 and the road from Altamont, go 3 miles N on Highway 77. Turn right on gravel road and go 7.5 miles E.
Sioux Prairie	200.	Moody	Take I29 N from Sioux Falls to State 34, go W 1.5 miles to old Highway 77, go N 3.5 miles.
Samuel H. Ordway Memorial Prairie	7,600.(?)	McPherson	9 miles W of Leola on state highway 10.

WISCONSIN

Name of area	Prairie (acres)	County	Location
Faville Prairie	60.	Jefferson	4 miles N of Lake Mills at end of Lang Road off CTH "G." Univ. of Wisconsin Arboretum.
Scuppernong Prairie	25.	Waukesha	1½ miles NW of Eagle at SE corner of junctions of CTHs "GN" and "N." Dept. of Natural Resources.
Brady's Bluff Prairie	10.	Trempealeau	Within Perrot State Park; access by foot via Brady's Bluff Trail. Dept. of Natural Resources.
Dewey Heights Prairie	7.	Grant	2 miles NW of Cassville, within Nelson Dewey State Park. Dept. of Natural Resources.
Midway Prairie	3.	La Crosse	2 miles N of Onalaska, on slope between CTH "OT" and railroad track. La Crosse County Park Commission.
Crex Meadows Prairie	79.	Burnett	7 miles NE of Grantsburg along North Refuge Road. Dept. of Natural Resources.
Ripon Prairie	1.	Fond du Lac	2 miles NE of Ripon on Hwy. 44 to Locust Road, W to railroad tracks. Ripon College, Biology Dept.
Oliver Prairie	4.	Green	2 miles SW of Albany, ¾ mile W of Hwy. 59 on S side of Oliver Road. Univ. of Wisconsin.
Swenson Prairie and Oak Opening	40.	Rock	5 miles S of Brodhead, ¼ mile E of CTH "T" on S side of Smith Road. Dept. of Natural Resources.

Name of area	Prairie (acres)	County	Location
Avoca River Bottom Prairie	320.	Iowa	1½ miles E of Village of Avoca, ½ mile N of Hwy. 133 via Hay Lane Road. Dept. of Natural Resources.
Five-Mile Bluff Prairie	10.	Pepin	4 miles NE of Village of Pepin along edge of Chippewa River Valley. Dept. of Natural Resources.
Buena Vista Prairie and Meadow	120.	Portage	From junction of CTH "F" and Hwy. 54 W of Plover, go 6 miles S on "F" then E ¾ mile to area N of road; to other tract go 8 miles S on "F" from 54, then E on town road ¾ mile to area N of road. Dept. of Natural Resources (leased).
Kettle Moraine and Low Prairie	50.	Waukesha	2 miles N of Eagle on Hwy. 67, then W on dead-end road to parking lot. Walk W ¼ mile to areas on N and S of lane. Dept. of Natural Resources.
Newark Road Prairie	23.	Rock	About 5 miles NW of downtown Beloit, 2½ miles W of Hwy. 213 and ½ mile E of Smythe School Road on Newark Road. Nature Conservancy.
Young Prairie	52.6	Walworth	5 miles E of Whitewater, off Bluff Road ½ mile S of County Line Road. Dept. of Natural Resources.
Muralt Bluff Prairie	62.	Green	3 miles W of Albany on S side of Hwy. 39, 1½ miles W of junction with Hwy. 59. Custodian: Green County. Contact: County Clerk, Courthouse, Monroe.

Selected References

Aikman, J. M. "Burning in the Management of Prairie in Iowa," *Iowa Academy of Science*, Vol. 62 (Dec. 15, 1955).

Aldrich, Charles. "The Old Prairie Slough," *Annals of Iowa*, 3rd Series, Vol. 5.

Alexander, J. D., J. B. Fehrenbacher, and B. W. Ray. "Characteristics of Dark Colored Soils Developed Under Prairie in a Toposequence in Northwestern Illinois," *Proceedings of Symposium on Prairie and Prairie Restoration*. Galesburg, Ill.: Knox College, Sept. 14–15, 1968.

Allen, Durward L. *The Life of Prairies and Plains*. New York: McGraw-Hill Book Company, 1967.

Allen, William G. *A History of Story County, Iowa*. Des Moines: Iowa Printing Company, 1887.

American Heritage Publishing Company. "A Prairie Dream Recaptured," *American Heritage*, Vol. 20 (Oct. 1969).

Anderson, Kling. "Burning Flint Hills Bluestem Ranges," *Proceedings, Third Annual Tall Timbers Fire Ecology Conference*. Tallahassee: Tall Timbers Research Station, 1964.

————. "Fire Ecology — Some Kansas Prairie Forbs," *Proceedings, Fourth Tall Timbers Conference*, 1965.

Anderson, R. C. "Prairies in the Prairie State," *Transactions, Illinois Academy of Science*, Vol. 63, No. 2 (1970).

Anderson, Roger. "The Prairies," *Outdoor Illinois*, February 1972.

Andrews, Clarence A., ed. *Growing Up in Iowa — Reminiscences of 14 Iowa Authors*. Ames: Iowa State University Press, 1978.

Angle, Paul M. *Prairie State — Impressions of Illinois, 1673–1967, By Travelers and Other Observers*. Chicago: University of Chicago Press, 1968.

Barnes, William B. *Indiana Nature Preserves.* Indianapolis: Indiana Department of Natural Resources, undated.

Beard, Daniel B. "Plants and Animals in Natural Communities," *The Meaning of Wilderness to Science.* San Francisco: The Sierra Club, 1960.

Benson, Lyman. *Plant Classification.* Boston: D. C. Heath & Company, 1957.

Blanchard, Rufus. *Hand-Book of Iowa.* Chicago: Blanchard and Cram, 1867.

Bland, Marilyn K. "Elsah Bluff Prairies: Ecological Antiques," *Historic Elsah Foundation Leaflet No. 3,* The Historic Elsah Foundation, 1972.

————. "Prairie Establishment at the Michigan Botanical Gardens," *Proceedings of Symposium on Prairie and Prairie Restoration,* 1968.

Boardman, Walter S. "Wildlife and Natural Area Preservation," *Proceedings, Sixth Tall Timbers Conference,* 1967.

Bohart, G. E. "Management of Habitats for Wild Bees," *Proceedings, Tall Timbers Conference on Ecological Animal Control by Habitat Management.* Tallahassee: Tall Timbers Research Station, Feb. 25–27, 1971.

Branch, E. Douglas. *The Hunting of the Buffalo.* Lincoln: University of Nebraska Press, 1962.

Brewer, Richard. "Death by the Plow," *Natural History Magazine,* Aug.–Sept. 1970.

Brotherson, Jack DeVon. "Species Composition, Distribution, and Phytosociology of Kalsow Prairie, A Mesic Tall-Grass Prairie in Iowa," Ph.D. dissertation, Iowa State University, Ames, 1969.

Cahalane, Victor H. *Mammals of North America.* New York: The MacMillan Company, 1954.

Cather, Willa. *My Ántonia.* Boston: Houghton Mifflin Company, 1954.

Christisen, Donald M. "The Dispossessed," *Missouri Conservationist,* March 1972.

————. "Prairie Fire," *Missouri Conservationist,* March 1967.

————. "A Vignette of Missouri's Native Prairie," *Missouri Historical Review,* Vol. 61 (January 1967).

Clements, Frederic E., and Victor E. Shelford. *Bio-Ecology.* New York: John Wiley & Sons, 1939.

Comstock, John Henry. *Introduction to Entomology,* 9th edition. Ithaca: Comstock Publishing Co., Inc., 1949.

Conard, Henry S. "The Vegetation of Iowa — An Approach Toward a Phytosociologic Account," *Studies in Natural History,* Vol. XIX, No. 4 (1952), State University of Iowa.

Costello, David F. *The Prairie World.* New York: Thomas Y. Crowell Company, 1969.

Curtis, John T. *The Vegetation of Wisconsin: An Ordination of Plant Communities.* Madison: University of Wisconsin Press, 1959.

Dary, David. "The Flint Hills — Where Grass Burning Is Winning Favor," *Kansas City Star Magazine* (April 23, 1972).

Davids, Richard C. *How to Talk to Birds*. New York: Alfred Knopf, 1972.

Dondore, Dorothy Anne. *The Prairie and the Making of Middle America — Four Centuries of Description*. Elmira College, New York: Antiquarian Press, Ltd., 1961.

Duffield, George C. "Memories of Frontier Iowa," related for *Annals of Iowa*, 1906.

Evers, Robert A. "Hill Prairies of Illinois," *Illinois Natural History Survey Bulletin*, Vol. 26 (August 1955).

Farb, Peter. *Face of North America*. New York: Harper & Row, 1963.

Flower, George. "History of the English Settlement," Edwards County, Ill., 1817.

Garland, Hamlin. *Boy Life on the Prairie*. Lincoln: University of Nebraska Press, 1961.

Gleason, Henry A., and Arthur Cronquist. *The Natural Geography of Plants*. New York: Columbia University Press, 1964.

Glenn-Lewin, David C., and Roger O. Landers, Jr., Editors. *Fifth Midwest Prairie Conference Proceedings*. Ames: Iowa State University, 1976.

Gregg, Josiah. *The Commerce of the Prairies*. Lincoln: University of Nebraska Press, 1967.

Gue, B. F. *The Homestead Manual*. Des Moines: Homestead Company, 1881.

Haddock, William J. *The Prairies of Iowa*. Privately printed, 1901.

Hall, E. Raymond. "Tallgrass Prairie National Park," *American Forests*, December 1971.

Harmon, Keith W. "Prairie Potholes," *National Parks & Conservation Magazine*, Vol. 45 (March 1970).

Hayden, Ada. "Report on State Parks and Preserves." Conservation Committee. *Journal of the Iowa Academy of Science*, Vol. 51 (1944).

Hess, John. "Where Have All the Writers Gone?" *Holiday Magazine*, June 1970.

Hitchcock, A. S. *Manual of the Grasses of the United States*. Washington: U.S. Government Printing Office, 1935.

Hole, Francis D., and Gerald A. Nielson. "Soil Genesis Under Prairie," *Proceedings of Symposium on Prairie and Prairie Restoration*, 1968.

Houlette, William. *Iowa, The Pioneer Heritage*. Des Moines: Wallace-Homestead Book Company, 1970.

Huff, Elizabeth. "Gospel of Trees," *Nebraskaland*, March 1972.

Hulbert, Lloyd C. "Gates' Phenological Records of 132 Plants at Manhattan, Kansas, 1926–1955," *Transactions, Kansas Academy of Science*, Vol. 66, No. 1 (1963).

Illinois Nature Preserves Commission. *Preserving Illinois' Natural Heritage*, 1975–76 Biennial Report of the Commission. Rockford, Ill.

Ingam, William H. *Ten Years on the Iowa Frontier.* Privately printed. Undated. Algona, Ia.

Iowa, State of. *A Guide to the Hawkeye State,* American Guide Series. Compiled and written by the Federal Writers' Project of the WPA. New York: Viking Press, 1938.

Iowa State Historical Society. "Pioneering Doctors and Druggists," *The Palimpsest,* Vol. 50 (June 1969), Iowa City.

Iowa State Preserves Board. *A Directory of State Preserves.* Des Moines, 1978.

Irving, Washington. *A Tour on the Prairies,* new edition (copyright 1956). Norman: University of Oklahoma Press.

John Deere Company, The. "The Story of John Deere," from a pamphlet printed by the John Deere Company, 1970.

Kansas State University. "A Proposed Prairie Research Area," Division of Biology, Kansas State University, Manhattan (July 1968).

Kilburn, Paul D. "Hill Prairie Restoration," *Proceedings of Symposium on Prairie and Prairie Restoration,* 1968.

Knauth, Otto. "Launch Drive for Native Prairie Site," *Des Moines Register* (April 12, 1971).

Komarek, E. V. "Fire Ecology — Grasslands and Man," *Proceedings, Fourth Tall Timbers Conference,* 1965.

Kraenzel, Carl Frederick. *The Great Plains in Transition.* Norman: University of Oklahoma Press, 1955.

Kucera, Clair L. "Ecological Effects of Fire on Tallgrass Prairie," *Proceedings of Symposium on Prairie and Prairie Restoration,* 1968.

Landers, R. Q., Paul Christiansen, and Terry Heiner. "Establishment of Prairie Species in Iowa," *Proceedings of Symposium on Prairie and Prairie Restoration,* 1968.

Landers, Roger Q., and Robert E. Kowalski. "Using Iowa's Prairie Species to Fight Roadside Weeds," *Iowa Farm Science,* Vol. 22 (June 1968).

Lemon, Paul C. "Prairie Ecosystem Boundaries in North America," *Proceedings of Symposium on Prairie and Prairie Restoration,* 1968.

Leopold, Aldo. "Report on a Game Survey of the North Central States," Sporting Arms and Ammunition Manufacturers' Institute. Madison, Wis., 1931.

Lock, Ross. "Meadowlark," notes on Nebraska fauna, *Nebraskaland,* March 1972.

Lommasson, Robert C. *Nebraska Wild Flowers.* Lincoln: University of Nebraska Press, 1973.

Lyon, Bessie L. "The Menace of the Bluestem," *The Palimpsest,* Iowa Historical Society. Vol. 21 (1940).

MacBride, Thomas. "Landscapes of Early Iowa," *The Palimpsest,* Iowa Historical Society. (1926).

Malin, James C. *The Grassland of North America Prolegomena to Its History*, with Addenda. Gloucester, Mass.: Peter Smith, 1967.

Marcy, Randolph B. *The Prairie Traveler*. A Hand-Book for Overland Expeditions. New York: Harper Brothers, 1859.

McFarland, Julian E. *A History of the Pioneer Era on the Iowa Prairies*. Lake Mills, Ia.: Graphic Publishing Company, 1969

McManis, Douglas R. "The Initial Evaluation and Utilization of the Illinois Prairie, 1815–1840," Dept. of Geography Research Paper No. 94, University of Chicago, 1964.

Milton, John R. "The Dakota Image," *South Dakota Review*, Vol. 8, No. 3 (1970).

Missouri Prairie News. Missouri Prairie Foundation, Vol. 1 (August 1967).

Musil, Faye. "Red Buffalo," *Nebraskaland*, June 1970.

Naden, Corinne J. *Grasslands Around the World*. New York: Franklin Watts, Inc., 1970.

Napoleon Homestead, The. Napoleon, N.D. (March 1887).

Nature Conservancy Preserve Directory. The Nature Conservancy, Arlington, Va., 1974.

Nebraska — A Pictorial History. Lincoln: University of Nebraska Press, 1967.

Nebraskaland Magazine. "Butterfly Weed," Vol. 49 (June 1971).

———. "Prairie Doctors," Vol. 49 (July 1971).

Newhall, J. B. *A Glimpse of Iowa in 1846* or *The Emigrant's Guide*. Burlington, Ia.,: W. D. Skillman, 1846.

Nichols, Stan, and Lynn Entine. *Prairie Primer*. Extension Service, University of Wisconsin (January 1976).

O'Connor, Gaylord (Mrs.). "Legends from up Salt River," talk to Pike County Historical Society, *Louisiana* (Mo.) *Press-Journal*, undated.

Ode, Arthur H. "Some Aspects of Establishing Prairie Species by Direct Seeding," *Proceedings of Symposium on Prairie and Prairie Restoration*, 1968.

Ohio Department of Natural Resources. *Directory of State Nature Preserves*. Columbus: Ohio Department of Natural Resources, 1978.

Oosting, Henry J. *The Study of Plant Communities*. San Francisco: W. H. Freeman and Company, 1956.

Parker, N. Howe. *Iowa As It Is in 1856*, a gazetteer for citizens and a hand-book for immigrants. Chicago: Keen and Lee, 1856.

Pearson, James E. "Grand Detour: John Deere Historic Site, A Touch of Vermont," *Outdoor Illinois*, Aug.–Sept. 1972.

———. "That Cussed Barbed Wire," *Outdoor Illinois*, October 1971.

Petersen, William J. "Across the Prairies of Iowa," *The Palimpsest*, Iowa Historical Society, Vol. 12 (1931).

———. "Weather—A Comment by the Editor," *The Palimpsest*, Iowa Historical Society, Vol. 52 (January 1971).

Phillips Petroleum Company. *Pasture and Range Plants.* Phillips Petroleum Company, Bartlesville, Okla., 1963.

Poggi, Edith M. "The Prairie Province of Illinois — A Study of Human Adjustment to the Natural Environment," *Illinois Studies in the Social Sciences,* Vol. 19, No. 3. Urbana: University of Illinois, 1934.

Quick, Herbert. *One Man's Life.* Indianapolis: Bobbs-Merrill, 1925.

Rickett, Harold Williams. *Wild Flowers of the United States.* 2 vols. The New York Botanical Garden. New York: McGraw-Hill, 1965.

Riley, Denis, and Anthony Young. *World Vegetation.* London: Cambridge University Press, 1966.

Rölvaag, O. E. *Giants in the Earth.* New York: Harper & Brothers, 1927.

Ross, Earle D. *Iowa Agriculture — An Historical Survey.* State Historical Society of Iowa, Iowa City, 1951.

Rydberg, Per Axel. *Flora of the Prairies and Plains of Central North America.* The New York Botanical Garden, 1932. Reprint. New York: Dover Publications, Inc., 1971.

Sandoz, Mari. "Dakota Country," *American Heritage,* June 1961.

Schmidt, John L., and Douglas L. Gilbert, Editors. *Big Game of North America.* Harrisburg: Stackpole Books, 1978.

Schramm, Peter. "A Practical Restoration Method for Tall-Grass Prairie," *Proceedings of Symposium on Prairie and Prairie Restoration,* 1968.

Schulenberg, Ray. "Summary of Morton Arboretum Prairie Restoration Work, 1963 to 1968," *Proceedings of Symposium on Prairie and Prairie Restoration,* 1968.

Sears, Paul B. *Land Beyond the Forest.* New York: Prentice-Hall, 1969.

Sharp, Mildred J. "Early Cabins in Iowa," *The Palimpsest,* Iowa Historical Society. Vol. 52 (January 1971).

Sheviak, Charles J. "An Introduction to the Ecology of the Illinois Orchidacae," Scientific Paper XIV. Illinois State Museum, Springfield, 1974.

Shimek, Bohumil. "The Persistence of the Prairie," University of Iowa Studies in Natural History, Iowa City, 1925.

———. "The Prairies," *Bulletin* of the Laboratory of Natural History, University of Iowa, Iowa City, 1911.

South Dakota Department of Game, Fish, and Parks. *Annual Report, 1958–59.*

Stanford, John L. *Tornado — Accounts of Tornadoes in Iowa.* Ames: Iowa State University Press, 1977.

Stewart, Omer C. "Barriers to Understanding the Influence of Use of Fire by Aborigines on Vegetation," *Proceedings, Second Tall Timbers Conference,* 1963.

Telford, Clarence J. "Third Report on a Forest Survey of Illinois," *Illinois Natural History Survey Bulletin,* Vol. 16 (March 1926).

Tessendorf, K. C. "How the Midwest Was Won," *Natural History Magazine*, February 1972.

This Fabulous Century: 1870, Prelude 1900. New York: Time-Life Books, 1970.

Tomanek, G. W., and F. W. Albertson. "An Analysis of Some Grasslands in the True Prairie," paper: criteria for a national park or monument.

Toney, Thomas E. *Public Prairies of Missouri*. Jefferson City: Missouri Department of Conservation, undated.

Transeau, Edgar Nelson, "The Prairie Peninsula," *Ecology*, Vol. 16, No. 3 (1935).

U.S. Department of Agriculture. *Climate and Man*. Yearbook of Agriculture. Washington: U.S. Government Printing Office, 1941.

———. *Grass*. Yearbook of Agriculture. Washington: U.S. Government Printing Office, 1948.

———. "Grasshoppers: The Biblical Plague," Agricultural Research Service (June 1971).

———. "Hunger Fighters" editorial, Agricultural Research Service, Vol. 20 (May 1972).

———. *Insects*. Yearbook of Agriculture. Washington: U.S. Government Printing Office, 1952.

———. "Soil Classification: A Comprehensive System" (The 7th Approximation.) Soil Conservation Service (August 1960).

———. *Soils & Men*. Yearbook of Agriculture. Washington: U.S. Government Printing Office, 1938.

———. "Wildlife Today and Tomorrow on Northern Prairie Farmlands," Soil Conservation Service. SCS-CI-10. December 1959.

U.S. Department of Interior. "A Proposed Prairie National Park," National Park Service (July 1961).

Vierling, Philip E. "Grassland Parks of Northeastern Illinois," *Illinois Country Outdoor Guide No. 5*, Chicago, 1976.

Voigt, John W. "The Vast Natural Meadows of Illinois," *Illinois Magazine* (October 1978).

———, and Robert H. Mohlenbrock. *Prairie Plants of Illinois*. Springfield: Illinois Department of Conservation, Division of Forestry, 1979.

Weaver, J. E. *North American Prairie*. Lincoln, Neb.: Johnsen Publishing Company, 1954.

———. *Prairie Plants and Their Environment: A Fifty-Year Study in the Midwest*. Lincoln: University of Nebraska Press, 1968.

———. "Who's Who Among the Prairie Grasses," *Ecology*, Vol. 12 (October 1931).

———, and Frederic E. Clements. *Plant Ecology*. New York: McGraw-Hill, 1938.

Whitford, Philip B. "Edaphic Factors in the Prairie-Forest Border in

Wisconsin," *Proceedings of Symposium on Prairie and Prairie Restoration,* 1968.

Wiggins, James Russell. From the Ellsworth (Maine) *American. St. Louis Post-Dispatch,* St. Louis, Mo., December 12, 1978.

Wilford, John Noble. "Prairie Partisans Move to Save Grasslands," *New York Times* (Oct. 18, 1970).

Williams, Ira A. "Lost in an Iowa Blizzard," *The Palimpsest,* Iowa Historical Society. Vol. 2 (Jan. 1921).

Wilson, Jim. "Tips on Planting Prairie Grasses," promotional literature from Wilson Seed Farms, Polk, Neb.

Wisconsin Department of Natural Resources. "Wisconsin Scientific Areas — Preserving Native Diversity," *Technical Bulletin No. 102,* Wisconsin Department of Natural Resources. Madison, 1977.

Zochert, Donald. "A Few Mountain Men." *Outdoor Illinois,* May 1972.

Index

Achilles, 104
Aesop's Fables, 219
Agriculture, prairie, 238
Ague, fever and, 226–27
Alfalfa, 259
Allen (naturalist), 16
Allouez, Claude Jean, 6
American germander, 87
American Journal of Science, 47
Ames High School Prairie (Iowa), 264–65
Amorpha canescens, 7
Anderson, Sherwood, 235
Andropogon, 97; *A. gerardi*, 62, 65; *A. scoparius*, 66–67
Animals, spreading of grass seeds by, 58–59. *See also* Mammals, prairie
Antelope, 129, 155; little goat-, 127, 158; pronghorn, 126–27, 157–58
Antennaria neglecta, 82–83
Arbor Day, 241
Armistice Day Blizzard of 1949, 169–75
Asclepias tuberosa, 88
Aster, 94; *A. turbinellus*, 94

Aster(s), 89, 94; many-flowered, 94; prairie, 94; sky-blue, 94; smooth, 94; willow, 94
Atwater, C., 16
Australopithecus, 125–26

Badger, 155, 156–57
Badger willow, *see* Snowberry
Badlands National Park (South Dakota), 212
Bamboos, 56
Baptisia, 84
Barleys, wild, 58–59
Baum, L. Frank, *The Wizard of Oz*, 185
Bear: black, 130, 157; grizzly, 157
Beaver, 132, 157, 158
Bed-straw, 73
Bees, 97, 99, 158, 159; honey, 160; species of, 160
Beetles, soldier, 99, 158
Bergamot, wild, 87
Betz, Robert 262
Big bluestem, 67, 71, 73, 75, 77, 79; dead roots of, 117–18; described, 62–66; foliage of, 74;

Big bluestem *(cont.)*
  location of, 68, 69; southeasterly origin of, 70; used for sod houses, 212
Bindweed, 73
Birds, prairie, 127–29, 130; migration of, 150–51; return of migrant, 152; species of, 146–47; winter, 151–52. *See also names of individual birds*
Bird's-foot violets, 83
Bison, 129, 132, 133–34, 135–36, 152, 155
Bitterns, 144
Bitter-weed, 73
Black-eyed Susan, 93–94
Black grass, *see* Sloughgrass
Black samson (purple coneflower), 79, 87, 89, 101, 104; described, 93
Blanchard, Rufus, *Hand-Book of Iowa,* 225
Blazing-star, 73, 79, 89, 105, 106; described, 96; resistance of, to drought, 100–101; used to increase speed and endurance of ponies, 103
Blizzards, 134, 135, 166–68, 176–78, 179–81, 191; Armistice Day (1940), 169–75; 1856–57 (Massacre Winter), 175–76, 178; 1880–81, 178; 1886, 178–79
Blue-eyed grass, 79, 84
Blue flag, 99, 158
Bluegrass, *see* Kentucky bluegrass
Bluejoint, bluejoint turkey foot, *see* Big bluestem
Blue milk-vetch, 71
Bluestems, 57, 97, 106. *See also* Big bluestem; Little bluestem
Bobcat, 157

Bobolink, 52, 151
Bombus, 160
Bonesets, 89
Boone, Daniel, 9
Boone County Conservation District (Illinois), 271
Bottle gentian, 79, 97, 99, 159
Bouteloua curtipendula, 69
Brady, Diamond Jim, 137
Brewer, Richard, 147
Bridger, Jim, 200
Bridges, building of, 239
Brome, 79
Brook lobelia, 97
Broomsedge, 71
Brunizems, 119, 121
Bryant, William Cullen, 19, 166
Buck, white-tailed, 246–47
Buffalo, 132–34
Buffalo wolf, 155
Bullsnake, 131
Bumblebee, 97, 99, 158, 159, 160
Bur oak tree, 43–44, 48, 51
Buttercups, 98; yellow upland, 84
Butterflies, 158; monarch, 52, 89, 99, 158, 159; painted lady, 99, 158
Butterfly milkweed, 88–89, 99, 102, 103, 158, 159
Button snakeroot, 96, 100–101. *See also* Blazing-star

Cabins: log, 210–12; sod, 212–13
Cactus, 42
Calcium carbonate, 109, 111, 121
Canada thistle, 79
Canada wild rye, 57, 66, 70, 71, 73; described, 62
Canby, Victor, 255
Canis latrans, 155; *C. lupus,* 155
Carper, Don, 247

Carrying capacity, defined, 130
Carson, Kit, 200
Caterpillar Company, 277
Cather, Willa, 56; *My Ántonia*, 192
Catlin, George, 224
Caulfield, Patricia, 277–78
Caylor Prairie (Iowa), 246
Ceanothin, 104
Cenchrus pauciflorus, 59
Character, of prairie settlers, 230–35
Chernozems, 119–21
Chicken, prairie, 129, 131, 136, 150; courting of, 142–43; disappearance of, 138–39; in Flint Hills, 139–41, 142; hunting of, 137–38; winter quarters of, 151
Chicory, 93
Chinch bugs, 160, 161
Christiansen, Paul, 262–63, 272, 277
Christisen, Don, 259, 260
Cinquefoil, prairie, 89
Civilian Conservation Corps, 264
Civil War, 221, 238
Clark, William, 10; *Journal* of, 47
Climate, prairie, 32–38, 40, 41, 42, 49; extremes vs. temperateness of, 190–94; seasons of, 111–12. *See also* Blizzards; Summers; Thunderstorms; Tornados; Winters
Clothing, pioneer, 216–18
Clovers, prairie, 96, 97, 101
Cole, John, 169–72
Columbine, red, 159
Commelinaceae, 85
Compass-plant, 79, 89, 106, 158; described, 92–93; taproot of, 100, 101

Compositae, 89
Conard, Henry, 39
Coneflowers, 89, 93, 158; purple, *see* Black samson; yellow, 79
Continental Divide, 33
Cook County Forest Preserve, 262
Cool-season grasses, 69–70
Cord grass, 62
Cornbelt, 119
Cornell College, 262
Corolla, 58
Costello, David, 208
Cottam Grant, 262–64
Coyote, 130, 155–56, 158
Cranes: giant, 152; sandhill, 144; whooping, 144
Cretaceous Period, 32–33
Crèvecoeur, Michel de, 200; *Letters from an American Farmer*, 199
Crockett, Davy, 200
Croghan (English traveler), 8
Culms, 57, 59
Cumberland Gap, 9, 20, 132
Cuming, Fortesque, 30
Curlews, 151, 152; Eskimo, 145, 149–50, 151, 158; long-billed, 145, 149, 150
Curtis Prairie (Wisconsin), 263–64
Cyclones, 184
Cypripedium, 88; *C. reginae*, 88

Daffodils, 84
Daisies, 87, 89–94, 98, 158; ox-eye, 89, 94
Dandelion, 79, 93, 94, 158; false, 84
Dayflowers, 85
Decreasers, 73, 74
Deer, 135, 158, 175–76; mule, 157; white-tailed, 130, 131, 157, 246–47

Deere, John, 207
Dickens, Charles, 19; *American Notes,* 17
Dickinson, Emily, poem by, vii
Diet, 227–28
Diphtheria, 227, 228
Diptera, 160
Disk flowers, 93
Dogs, prairie, 129, 153–54
Dough-birds, *see* Curlews, Eskimo
Doves, mourning, 152
Downy gentian, 97–98, 99
Dragonfly, 52
Drills: Nesbet, 269–70; Truax Native Grass, 270
Dropseed, prairie, 68, 70, 71, 79
Droughts, 44, 45, 193
Ducks, 143, 144, 145, 150, 152. *See also* Armistice Day Blizzard of 1940
Dust Bowl, 193, 244
Dwight, Timothy, 199

Eads, Thomas, 239
Earthquakes, 226
Echinacea, 104
Edge effect, defined, 130
Education, 231–32
Egrets, 144
Elk, 129, 131, 134–35, 175–76
Elymus canadensis, 62
Epidemics, 227
Euphorbiaceae, 89
Evaporation, degree of, and presence of prairie, 40–41

False dandelion, 84
False indigo, 84
Fencing, 213–14
Fermi National Accelerator Lab, 277

Fertilizer, 123, 268
Fever and ague, 226–27
Field goldenrod, 94
Fires, prairie, 44, 45–50, 222–25
Fleabanes, 89
Flies: bee, 160; biting, 160; green-headed, 161; robber, 160; stinging, 160; tabanid, 161
Flint Hills (Kansas), 63, 65, 67, 78, 214; prairie chickens in, 139–41, 142; proposed prairie national park in, 280–84
Flower, George, *History of the English Settlement,* 12–13
Flowers, prairie, 81–82, 104–6; autumn, 97–98; colorful pioneer uses of, 103–4; pollination of, 97, 98–99; prevernal, 82–83; resistance of, to fire, drought, and insects, 100–103; spring, 83–87; summer, 87–97. *See also names of individual flowers*
Footwear, pioneer, 218–19
Forbs, 48, 79, 98
Fox Prairie (Illinois), 147–48
Frank, Waldo, 235
Fringed gentians, 97
Fringe tree, 83

Garland, Hamlin, 26, 136, 228–29
Garrison Diversion, 249
Gayfeather, 103, 106; dotted, 96. *See also* Blazing-star
Geese, 143, 144, 145, 150, 152; blue, 145–46; Canada, 145; snow, 145–46
Gentian, 105; bottle, 79, 97, 99, 159; downy, 97–98, 99; fringed, 97
Gerhard, F., 50
Gibbon, Edward, 124

Gilbert, Bil, 250
Glacial till, 109–10
Glaciers, 31–32, 35, 143–44
Gnaphalium, 83
Goethe, Johann Wolfgang von, 276
Goldenrods, 89, 94–96, 99, 158; field, 94; Missouri, 94; showy, 94; stiff, 94
Goldstem, *see* Indian grass
Gophers, plains pocket, 130, 131, 153–54, 225
Government Road, 239
Grand Prairie (Illinois), 201
Grass(es): cool-season, 69–70; flowers, 58; fruits, 58; hydric, 61; leaves, 57–58; mesic, 61, 64; seeds, 58–59; stems, 56–57, 59; warm-season, 69–70; xeric, 61–62
Grasshoppers, 161–64
Great American Elk Hunt, 134–35
Great Depression, 233
Great Plains, 19, 20, 119, 162, 186, 250; antelope in, 155; badgers in, 155, 157; little bluestem in, 67; long-billed curlews in, 149; rainfall in, 40; semiarid conditions in, 193
Groundplum, 84
Grouse: pinnated, 142; ruffed, 130
Gustafson, Roger, 271

Habenaria leucophaea, 88, 158
Haddock, William, 166
Hagar, Mr. and Mrs. Donald, 275–76
Hall, James, 204; *Plumbe's Sketches,* 14, 15
Hawk, 151; red-tailed, 52, 53, 152
Hay, native prairie, 260

Haymows, 182
Headache root, *see* Pasqueflower
Heidelbauer, Frank, 172–74
Helianthus, 94
Hemiptera, 160
Henderson, Bob "He-Dog," 140, 142, 156
Hennepin, Père Louis, 7; *Description de la Louisiane,* 6, 8
Herons, 152
Horseflies, 161
Horse mint, *see* Wild bergamot
Horses, 126, 209
Houses, frame, 213, 236, 240, 243. *See also* Cabins
Hulbert, Lloyd, 262–63
Hummingbirds, 99, 159
Humus, in prairie soil, 112, 113, 114–17, 121–22
Hydric grasses, 61

Illinois River, 174
Illness, 226–29
Increasers, 73, 74
Indian grass, 57, 66, 70, 71, 79; dead roots of, 117–18; described, 65
Indian paintbrush, 84
Indians, 176, 220–21
Indigo, false, 84. *See also* Wild indigo
Industrial Revolution, 216, 238, 240
Influenza, 228
Ingalls, John, 282
Inkpadutah ("Red Tip"), 176, 221
Insects, prairie, 158; dependence of plants on, for pollination, 97, 98–99, 158–59; and Rocky Mountain locust, 161–65; spe-

Insects (*cont.*)
  cies of, 160. *See also names of
    individual insects*
Iowa State University, 184, 262
Iridaceae, 89
Irises, 84, 99, 158
Ironweeds, 89, 93
Irving, Washington, 17–18, 19,
  160

Jefferson, Thomas, 10, 30
Joliet, Louis, 5–6, 47
Joutel (French explorer), 6
Juchereau (French trader), 133
June grass, 68, 70–71

Kalsow Prairie (Iowa), 71, 151,
  277, 278–79
Kankakee River, 138
Kansas Grassroots Association,
  Inc., 283
Kansas State University, 262
Keller, Will, 188–89
Kentucky bluegrass, 72, 73, 74–75,
  79; described, 70; proposed
  seeding of, in Kansas, 282
Kites, 152; swallow-tailed, 147,
  148
Knox College, 262, 267
Kucera, Clair, 262–63, 273
Kurtz, Carl, 89, 103, 262, 270

Labiatae, 89
Labrador Tea, 35
Ladies'-tresses, 88
Lady's slipper orchid, 88; yellow,
  88, 104
Lahontan, Baron de (Louis Ar-
  mand de Lom d'Arce), 6
Lamb's quarters, 73
Landers, Roger, 262, 272, 277

Land warrants, 202, 239
Lane, John, Jr., 207
Lane, John, Sr., 206–7
Laramide Revolution, 33, 34
Larkspur, 87, 102, 104; prairie, 89
La Salle, Sieur de (Robert Cave-
  lier), 6–7, 8
Last of the Mohicans, 4
Leadplant, 73, 79, 89, 101; de-
  scribed, 96–97
Legumes, wild, 96–97
Leguminosae, 89
Lewis, Meriwether, 10; *Journal* of,
  47
Liatris, 96, 103; *L. punctata,* 96; *L.
  pycnostactya,* 96; *L. scariosa,*
  96; *L. spicata,* 96
Ligule, 57
Lilies, 98, 99; prairie, 87; tiger, 87;
  Turk's-cap, 87
Lincoln, Abe, 137, 200, 202, 239
Little bluestem, 69, 70, 71, 73, 79;
  described, 66–68
Lobelia, brook, 97
Lobelia kalmii, 97
Locust, Rocky Mountain, 161–65
Loess, 32, 109, 110
Louisiana Purchase, 10, 200
Lousewort, *see* Wood betony
Lynx, 157

McConnel, John L., *Western Char-
  acters,* 234
McGee, Jim, 137
McGee, Sam, 181
McGuffey's Reader, 30, 219
Madson, Chris, 140
Madson, Dycie, 146, 225
Malaria, 227
Mammals, prairie, 126–27; charac-
  teristics of, 127, 129; overlap of

eastern and western, 130–32; species of, 152–58. *See also names of individual mammals*
Many-flowered aster, 94
Many-flowered *psoralea*, 96
Marigold, marsh, 84
Marquette, Père Jacques, 6, 8
Marsh marigold, 84
Maximilian's sunflower, 94
Meadowlark, 148–49
Melanoplus spretus, 161, 164; *M. mexicanus*, 164
Membré, Zenobius, 6
Mesic grasses, 61, 64
Michigan, Lake, 175
Milkweed, butterfly, 88–89, 99, 103, 158, 159
Mima mounds, 71–73
Mima Prairie (Washington), 71
Minnesota Outbreak, 221
Mint family, 87, 98–99
Mississippi River, 107, 174–75, 238; first bridge across, 239
Missouri, University of, 262
Missouri Botanical Garden, 258
Missouri Department of Conservation, 259
Missouri goldenrod, 94
Missouri River, 50, 146
Moccasin-flower, *see* Lady's slipper
Mollisols, 119
Monroe, James, 10, 30
Morris, Thomas, 9–10
Mortality rate, pioneers, 225–26
Morton Arboretum (Illinois), 263, 274
Mosquitoes, 160–61
Moth, 158; crepuscular sphinx, 88, 99

Mouse: jumping, 153; prairie meadow, 154–55; prairie white-footed, 154

Napoleon (North Dakota) *Homestead*, 177
Nature Conservancy, The, 103, 261, 264–65
Nebraska, University of, 101
Needle-and-thread, 71
Needlegrass, 58–59, 70–71, 117; described, 68–69
Nesbet Drill, 269–70
New Jersey tea, 101–2; 104
New York Central Railroad, 132
New York Times, 255
Nielsen, Ole, 177
Nitrogen, 114–15, 117
Nodes, 57
Northeastern Illinois University, 262, 277
Northern and Western Railway, Duck Special of, 145

Oak grubs, 102
Oak tree, bur, 43–44, 48, 51
Ohio River, 107, 133, 204, 226
Okoboji, Lake, Iowa, Indian massacre at, 176, 221
Old-man's beard, 83
Old-man's whiskers, *see* Purple aven
Orchard grass, 259
Orchidaceae, 89
Orchids: lady's slipper, 88; white-fringed, 88, 99, 158; wild, 87–88; yellow lady's slipper, 88, 104
Orthoptera, 161
Otter, 132, 157, 158
Owen (geologist), 11

Owls, short-eared, 152
Oxen, 209
Ox-eye daisy, 89, 94

Pacific air mass, 33
Panicum virgatum, 62, 79
Paranthropus, 126
Parkman, Francis, 4
Parks, proposed prairie, 279–84
Parnassias, 97
Parsley family, 98
Pasqueflower, 83, 98, 100, 104, 159; described, 82
Pelicans, 144
Penstemon, 79
Phanerophytes, trees as, 44
Pheasants, 259; ring-necked, 110–11, 244–46
Phipps, Frank, 282
Phlox, prairie, 89, 102, 105
Picket-pins, 153, 158
Pike, Zebulon, 10
"Pikes," 199–200
Pilgrim's Progress, 219
Pinks, prairie, 84
Plants, original prairie, 73, 78–79; pollination of, by insects, 97, 98–99, 158–59
Pleurisy root, *see* Butterfly milkweed
Plovers, 144–45, 151, 152; golden, 151; upland, 145
Plows, prairie, 206–9, 243
Pneumonia, 228
Porcupine grass, 68, 71
Posegate, Eli, 136–37
Potholes, prairie, 144
Prairie anemones, 83
Prairie aster, 94
Prairie beardgrass, *see* Little bluestem

Prairie cat's-foot, 82–83
Prairie cinquefoil, 89
Prairie clovers, 96, 97, 101
Prairie cord grass, *see* Sloughgrass
Prairie dropseed, 68, 70, 71, 79
Prairie larkspur, 89
Prairie lilies, 87
Prairie National Park, proposed, 280–84
Prairie phlox, 89, 102, 105
Prairie pinks, 84
Prairie rose, half-shrub, 101
Prairie shoestring, *see* Leadplant
Prairiesmoke, *see* Pasqueflower; Purple avens
Prairie sunflower, 94
Prairyerths, 119–23
Preparation Canyon, 25
Preserves, prairie, 261–62
Promachus, 160
Psoralea: many-flowered, 96; silver-leaved, 96
Puccoons, 84, 85; hoary, 263
Puma, 157
Punic Wars, 124
Purple avens, 83
Purple coneflower, *see* Black samson
Purple prairie clover, 79
Purple vervain, 79

Quick, Herbert, 88, 225

Ragweed, 79, 96
Railroads, 238–39, 240
Rainfall, 192–93; ratios of, to evaporation, 40–41
Ratibida, 93
Rattlesnake-master, 73, 78, 79, 89, 100; described, 98

Rattlesnakes: massasauga, 228; timber, 130, 228

Raven, Peter, 258

Ray flowers, 93

Reconstruction, 239

Red cedar tree, 39

Red clover, 79

Red columbine, 159

Redroot, *see* New Jersey tea

Restorations or re-creations, prairie, 263–65, 271–73, 277, 279; seeding program for, 265–70; spring burning of, 273–74; transplanting of, 274–75; weed control for, 270–71

Rhizomes, 59 ·

Ridgeway, Robert, 147–48

Ripgut, *see* Sloughgrass

Rock Island Railroad, 239

Rocky Mountain locust, 161–65

Rocky Mountains, 20, 33, 34, 186

Rodents, 152, 154–55, 156; grassland, 127

Rölvaag, Ole E., *Giants in the Earth*, 162–63, 178, 197–98

Rosaceae, 89

Rosa multiflora, 242

Roses, 98; half-shrub prairie, 101; multiflora, 242; wild, 73, 87

Rosinweeds, 89

Ross, Marvin, 252, 253

Rudbeckia, 93

Rupture root, *see* New Jersey tea

Rynning, Ole, *True Account of America*, 202

Sackville-West, Victoria, "The Land," 207

Salle, Nicolas de la, 132

Sandbur, 59

Sand Hills (Nebraska), 67, 223

Save the Tallgrass Prairie, Inc., 282–83

Schramm, Peter, 262–63, 267, 268, 270

Scrophulariaceae, 89

Scurvy, 227–28

Second Annual Great Bicycle Ride Across Iowa (SAGBRAI), 250

Settlers, prairie, 197–205; breaking new ground by, 205–9; building cabins by, 210–13; character of, 230–35

Severaid, Eric, 251

Sheeder Prairie (Iowa), 77

Shelterbelts, 240–43, 244–46

Shimek, Bohumil, 41

"Shooting Star Hills" (Wisconsin), 103

Shorebirds, 143, 144, 149

Showy goldenrod, 94

Shriner, Herb, 107

Sickle-bills, *see* Curlews, long-billed

Sideoats grama, 69, 71, 79

Sierra Madre, 33

Sierra Nevada, 33

Silicon, 56

Silver-leaved *psoralea*, 96

Sioux Indians, 176, 221

Sitting Bull, 223

Skunk, 130

Sky-blue aster, 94

Sloughgrass, 62, 63, 65, 69, 71, 79; described, 60–61; and Mima mounds, 73; southeasterly origin of, 70; used for sod houses, 212

Smithsonian Institution, 258

Smooth aster, 94

Snapdragons, 85, 98–99

Snowberry, 157

Soil, prairie, 38–40, 51–52, 107–8, 124; age of, 118–19; bacteria in, 114; classification of, 119–21; humus in, 114–17, 121–22; materials comprising, 108–11; organic materials returned to, 117–18; richness of, 112–13; structure of, 121–23
Sorghastrum nutans, 65, 66
Spartina pectinata, 60
Spencer Park (Illinois), 271–72
Spermophile, thirteen-striped, 127, 153
Spiderwort, 85
Spiranthes, 88
Spirit Lake, Iowa, Indian massacre at, 176, 221
Sports Illustrated, 250
Squirrels: Franklin ground, 153, 158; ground, 127, 153
Stanford, John, 184–85
Starkweather Watershed Project, 249
Stegner, Wallace, 67
Stichel, 182
Stiff goldenrod, 94
Stiff sunflower, 94
Stipa spartea, 68
Stolon, 59
Storytelling, 219–20
Subculture, prairie, 249–55
Summers, prairie, 181–84, 192, 194. *See also* Tornados
Sunflower(s), 73, 89, 93, 94; Maximilian's, 94; prairie, 94; stiff, 94
Survival, lessons of, 230–31
Swans, 144, 145; trumpeter, 152
Switch grass, 66, 70, 71, 74, 117; described, 62; pheasant nests in, 259

Tabishir, 56
Taylor, Bayard, 199–200
Tertiary Period, 125
Tester, John, 72
Thistle, 93, 99, 158
Thunderstorms, 183–84, 185; heat, 192
Tiger lilies, 87
Tornados, 184–90, 191
Toys, pioneer, 219, 220
Transeau, Edgar, 40–41
Transpiration, of plants, 40, 41
Truax Native Grass Drill, 270
Trudell, Roy, 225
Trump, Dick, 264
Trumpet vine, 99, 158–59
Tufa, 97
Turkey, eastern wild, 130
Turkey foot, *see* Big bluestem
Turk's-cap lilies, 87
Twain, Mark, 179; *Huckleberry Finn,* 107

Umbelliferae, 89

Vaseyochloa multinervosa, 58
Vasseygrass, 58
Vetch, 84, 96
Violets, 96; bird's-foot, 83; heart-leaved, 84; meadow, 84; prairie, 84
Vole, prairie, *see* Mouse, prairie meadow

Walker, Thomas, 9
Warm-season grasses, 69–70
Waterfowl, 144, 145
Waubun Prairie (Minnesota), 72
Weather, *see* Climate, prairie
Weaver, John, 101
Weed species, 73

Weevils, black, 99
Wet prairie, 215–16, 243
Wheatgrasses, 68, 70, 71
White-fringed orchids, 88, 99, 158
Wilcox, Grandma, 230
Wild bergamot, 87
Wild indigo, 73, 78, 79, 89, 96, 99; described, 84; use of, as cathartic and emetic, 104
Wild legumes, 96–97
Wild roses, 73, 87
Wild strawberry flowers, 84–85
Williams brothers, 175
Willow aster, 94
Wilson, Jim, 257, 268–69, 276–77, 284
Wind: dependence of grasses on, 58, 59; effects of, on prairies, 41–42, 45, 56
Windflowers, *see* Prairie anemones
Winters, prairie, 166–69, 176–78, 179–81, 193–94; Armistice Day

Blizzard (1940), 169–75; of 1848, 178; of 1855–56, 178; of 1856–57 (Massacre Winter), 175–76, 178; of 1886, 178–79; of 1936, 179
Wisconsin, University of, 103, 262, 264, 274
Wolf: buffalo, 155; lobo, 155; prairie, 155
Woman, role of prairie, 229–30
Wood betony, 79, 85
Wood-sage, *see* American germander

Xeric grasses, 61–62

Yarrow, 104
Yellow coneflower, 79
Yellow lady's slipper orchid, 88, 104
Yellow star-grass, 79, 84
Yuccafolium, 98